Disabling America

DISABLING AMERICA

The "Rights Industry" in Our Time

RICHARD E. MORGAN

Basic Books, Inc., Publishers

NEW YORK

Copyright © 1984 by Basic Books, Inc.
Library of Congress Catalog Card Number: 83–46096
ISBN 0-465-01659-6
Printed in the United States of America
Designed by Vincent Torre
10 9 8 7 6 5 4 3 2 1

CONTENTS

PREFACE

THIS BOOK falls into the literary genre of "things-I-must-get-off-my-chest." I have not minced words in doing so, since mincing words is a besetting contemporary sin (and *that's* something I needed to get off my chest). It is, therefore, more than usually important to absolve all who have helped me from any responsibility for what follows.

My thanks to Barbara Kelly, Debra Rosenthal, and Ann O'Reilly who were my research assistants during the period in which the book was conceived and written. My colleague David McConnell read and helpfully commented at length on the manuscript (I already wish I had taken more of his advice). Martin Kessler of Basic Books grappled with every page and saved me from myself in numerous instances.

Suzanne Theberge performed small miracles in getting my scratchings typed, and Virginia Linkovich gave crucial help in the stretch. My wife Eva put up with more than the usual outrageous claims of composition—for complete silence, "no plans" for three months, "don't ask me to do that," that "I just forgot," and so on.

Finally my thanks to my students in constitutional law over the past decade—many of whom will probably be glad to remain anonymous after reading the book. You made me do it!

RICHARD E. MORGAN
North Harpswell, Maine

Disabling America

CHAPTER 1

The Rights Industry
Run Amok

WE MUST FACE the fact that beginning after World War II, and especially over the past twenty years, the American law of civil rights and liberties has been increasingly manipulated, redefined, and expanded at the urging of people with little understanding or sympathy for the traditions and ideas on which this body of law is properly based. A consequence of this, largely unintended by the rights-and-liberties militants, has been to marginally disable major American institutions, both governmental and private. It has also rendered more difficult the already daunting task of maintaining minimum standards of public manners and morals.

Many interest group advocates, law professors, activist lawyers, and publicists—what I call, collectively, the American rights industry—are no longer committed to the excruciating job of balancing individual claims against the claims of organized society. They are engaged in a different enterprise—creating new rights with unreflective enthusiasm. They have become separated from the frame of intellectual reference necessary to thoughtful decision making about liberty and fairness. They have liberated themselves from the text and historical understandings of the Constitution. They have increasingly ignored or distorted important aspects of the American tradition which bare on the adjustment of liberty and fairness claims. They have unashamedly embraced flimsy social and philosophical arguments to justify the results they desire, and in a variety of issue areas they have been successful.

I came to the study of civil rights and liberties after conventional academic training in three fields: political philosophy, constitutional law, and that stream of political science that deals with the interaction of organized groups in society. The concern that drew me into research and teaching was the delicate task of balancing the claims of organized society, acting through government, against the claims of individuals—claims to do as they pleased or claims that government was treating them unfairly. The most visible institution performing this task in America is the United States Supreme Court, and I followed a well worn path in combining interest in political and social thought with study of the Court. My political science training, however, made it clear that studying the Court in isolation was an inadequate way of understanding how civil liberties and civil rights were defined and judicially applied in American society. I came to see the Court as a part, albeit the most important part, of a subsystem of constitutional politics in which activist lawyers, academic partisans, interest groups, and media publicists play important roles.

I became, in short, a professional watcher of professional civil libertarians, studying behavior and interaction of persons and organizations who urge courts to adopt new interpretations of the Constitution and urge legislatures to create new rights. Some of these actors are influential and familiar, such as the American Civil Liberties Union and its many state affiliates. Some are relatively obscure (but not insignificant) formations such as the National Association of Advocates of Children and the New York University Civil Rights Clinic (this last of which recently persuaded a federal judge to rule that the New York City physical test for firefighters was sexually discriminatory because all the women who had taken it had failed).[1] Like most persons trained in political science during the 1960s my early writings were concerned with describing the process by which policy is shaped and with mapping the alignment of forces rather than with evaluating the substantive content of policy. Nonetheless, firmly seated in the back of my mind, was the substantive interest in reconciling the need for governmental authority with claims of liberty and fairness. As I grew older and grappled yearly with the task of explaining new laws and Supreme Court decisions to students, a conviction grew until it weighed on me like lead—that many civil libertarians had become unhinged.

This is a serious charge. I propose to support it by examining five areas of American law in which legal intellectuals and interest group advocates, wielding flawed arguments, have successfully urged innovation on judges and legislators in the name of enhancing civil rights or liberties (chapters 2 through 6). The chapter titles speak for themselves: "Isolating the Churches," "Destabilizing Public Schools," "Enfeebling Law Enforcement," "Undermining Order Maintenance," and "Preempting Private Choice." Other areas of rights activity could easily have been chosen or added. We might have looked with profit at the attempted rewriting of the history of the Eighth Amendment prohibition on "cruel and unusual punishments" in order to achieve judicially the abolition of the death penalty which could not be achieved legislatively.[2] Or we might have surveyed the work of professional civil libertarians in the mid-1970s in savaging the intelligence agencies.[3] Or we might have explored the unmanning of the military in response to the radical feminism of the past decade.[4] But the examples chosen will suffice.

These chapters are followed by one (chapter 7) analyzing certain illegitimate modes of constitutional interpretation that have been used to justify and to urge a considerable amount of bad constitutional law. Certainly not all the innovations examined in this book are matters of constitutional law; some involve statutory law and administrative regulations (bureaucratic law). But even in these latter cases, the statutory or administrative initiatives are often justified and defended as advancing some general constitutional purpose or further safeguarding some constitutional right. Whether rights activists are operating in a court, within the staff of a congressional committee, or within an administrative agency, constitutional arguments and rhetoric are deployed in depth. Because of this, chapter 7, which deals with fashions in constitutional interpretation (or noninterpretation), is necessary.

The civil libertarian enterprise was obviously important to America's development and will be to its future. It is no part of my intention to belittle or attempt to undermine our national preoccupation with rights and liberties. It is, I assume, a good part of the reason most of us are happy to be here. We need a set of specialized elites professionally concerned with these things. More the pity, therefore, that this set of elites has, in our time, withdrawn so far from the mainstream of American intellectual history. In an increasingly specialized language, the professionals of the rights industry are talking increasingly to themselves, while working on American society and institutions in various disabling ways, which many, if not most, of their their countrymen cannot understand and would disagree with if they did. These themes are developed in chapter 8.

A word about my choice of terms is in order here, particularly the key words "unhinged" and "disable." Perhaps using such language will invite a slanging match and make it easier for critics to avoid the substantive thrust of what follows. I can only say that I have not been able to come up with better words. Neither word is used loosely to convey some general, insulting message; each has a precise meaning which I shall develop. I certainly do not desire a slanging match; my goal is to stimulate wider ranging debate of the issues that divide people like me from the mainstream of the rights industry. But this cannot be done by pulling punches or resorting to circumlocution.

"Unhinged" has metaphorical reference to the hinge of a scales. If, as I argue, the essence of responsible thinking about rights and liberties involves balancing the claims of individuals and groups against the costs of those claims to society, and if, as I also argue, many in the rights industry are ignoring or severely discounting the social costs of rights creating, then the scales are *kaputt,* unhinged. This does not mean that the individuals involved are addled or dull witted; indeed, many are remarkably bright. It does mean that an essential piece of intellectual equipment for the job they undertake is not in working order.

Similarly, "disable" is not used with any overtones of wreaking or sabotage. But when costs are externally imposed on institutions —direct dollar costs, exclusion from public programs, cumbersome new procedures, substantial reductions in leadership authority, reduced discretion in recruitment and personnel decisions, and so on—the institutions will be less able to pursue excellence in performing their primary function, whether it be infantry combat, original work in medieval history, making widgets, or teaching children to read. They will be marginally disabled. In the same way, when popular majorities are forbidden to use the machinery of government in traditionally accepted ways to reinforce minimum standards of public behavior, these majorities are marginally disabled.

There is a familiar response to my general line of argument (dare I call it a reflex?) that is useful to anticipate here. This is the assertion that far from imposing disabling costs, the creation of new rights furthers institutional excellence and revivifies public mores by making people happier and less frustrated and thereby increasing the aggregate of talent and energy available to the society. This, as recent American history surely demonstrates, is largely bunkum.

While it may not be true that *every* new legal protection of individuals involves costs in institutional efficiency or degradation of our social environment, most can only be purchased by payment in this coin. Examples of rights innovations in which the cost to the achievement of institutional goals is outweighed by assuring individuals that they will be treated more fairly, thus improving morale and stimulating creativity, are painfully hard to find. When such examples are profferred, as in the case of court-ordered racial balance in public schools, the costs are usually understated and the benefits inflated. Costless innovations are often promised, seldom delivered.

Indeed, the notion of costless innovation in civil rights and liberties demeans and obscures the moral seriousness of the enterprise. We are often quite well advised to accept disabling costs in order to protect individuals or groups. Protecting people from genuinely harsh and arbitrary treatment is, after all, worth something. No one would suggest that we return to the brutal disciplines of Wellington's Peninsular army no matter how excellent an infantry force it would produce. By the same token, however, there is little doubt that the notoriously circumscribed disciplinary authority of today's American military leadership has been purchased at the cost of lowered fighting quality. The present danger is not, as it might have been in times past, that we reflexively refuse to accept the social costs involved in protecting individuals and groups; the danger is that we (or many of us) have developed precisely the opposite reflex.

One final point that is appropriate to this introduction has to do with assessing the costs of ill-considered innovation in rights and liberties. It should go without saying in serious discourse that none of the manifold ills that afflict our institutions and society can be attributed to a single cause. Thus when I argue that some new legal rule or procedure has imposed a cost, I am not suggesting that this cost, by itself, explains an unsatisfactory institutional performance or social situation. New, "person-regarding" disciplinary procedures only *contribute* to the low levels of discipline in today's American military. By the same token, new constitutional doctrines which inhibit policy in enforcing minimum standards of public behavior only *contribute* to the problem of disorder in the streets. In the case of the American criminal justice system, for instance, it suffers the institutional equivalent of the torments of Job; but because it is in trouble in so many ways is precisely why we should not lumber it with the added burden of sweeping exclusionary rules. To respond to an argument about a particular social cost with the defense of multivariant causality is puerile. In what follows I take for granted that however much the reader may disagree on particular points, we all accept that it is a complicated, highly interconnected world out there and that I am not "blaming civil libertarians" for all, or even most, of what is wrong with it. But they haven't been helping much lately either. Societies are sometimes disabled totally and suddenly as the result of some unambiguous and easily identifiable cause such as a war or natural disaster. More often, they are progressively disabled in a variety of subtle, interlocking, and marginal ways. It is to this latter sort of process that the rights industry is contributing.

Finally, it should be said that this is primarily an essay in the history of ideas—of arguments. While I am concerned (some will say morbidly preoccupied) with the negative impacts of these ideas on American institutions and society, it is the origins and validity of the arguments that are at issue here. Ideas matter—and bad ideas have consequences. Nowhere is this clearer than in American public law. In the chapters that follow we will see judges, legislators, and bureaucrats making constitutional and statutory law based on deeply flawed arguments. We may be familiar with the policies, but most of us are not so familiar with the provenance of the arguments. In beginning his Victorian romanticization of the northern Indians, Longfellow asked:

> Should you ask me, whence these stories?
> Whence these legends and traditions, . . .
> I should answer, I should tell you,
> "From the forests and prairies,
> From the Great Lakes of the North land,
> From the land of the Ogibways", . . .[5]

Similarly, if I were asked about the intellectual undergirding of much recent civil rights and liberties law:

> Whence these strained and fake traditions,
> Whence these windy moralizings?
> I should answer, I should tell you,
> From the halls of National Law Schools,
> From the Profs and Popularizers,
> From the Legal Intellectuals.

Nowhere is John Maynard Keynes' aphorism about current policy being a reflection of the work of some dead scholar more relevant than in American rights policy. Before Justice Hugo Black could confidently assert that the due process clause of the Fourteenth Amendment was intended by its framers to incorporate the Bill of Rights, there had to be a Horace Flack who announced this under the imprimatur of the Johns Hopkins University Press.[6] To be fair, Flack's writing was better connected to the history of the Fourteenth Amendment than Longfellow's poesy was to the archaeology of native Americans, but that it seriously oversimplified and overstated the historical record has been amply demonstrated.[7] Indeed, Justice Black was never able to marshal much support within the Court for his "historical bullet" theory of incorporation.* Nonetheless, the fact that the theory was abroad in the land,

---

*The application to the states of almost all of the large body of federal law that had grown up by Supreme Court interpretation around the provisions of Amendments One through Eight (which through most of our history had been understood to apply only to acts of the national government) represented a major alteration of the American constitutional order, comparable to that which took place in the so-called "Constitutional Revolution of 1937." However, that earlier alteration (while the work of the judiciary) took place with an attentive country looking on, and in response to something that could be called a genuine popular movement. Nothing like that can be said of the "incorporation" of Amendments One through Eight (*cum* interpretive baggage) into the due process clause of the Fourteenth Amendment (which applies to the states). While rejecting Black's historical theory of incorporation, the Court, largely between the years 1960 and 1970, worked an almost identical result piecemeal. Sometimes there was debate on the Court over the wisdom of extending a particular provision—*Duncan* v. *Louisiana,* 391 U.S. 145 (1968)—and sometimes incorporation was worked in an almost casual fashion —*Malloy* v. *Hogan,* 385 U.S. 1 (1964). What there clearly was not, was any national

and defended by a small but devout faction,[8] made the process of piecemeal incorporation, by which the Court came to the same operational result as Black would have reached with his historical bullet, seem less novel and shocking.

Such is the stuff of constitutional politics in America today. It is a battleground on which the weapons are arguments from history, human nature, and first principles. These are joyfully wielded in the service of the policy outcomes desired by the combatants. Sometimes the history is sound and the arguments right; sometimes they are just plausible; sometimes they are profoundly mistaken but sincerely advanced; and sometimes they amount to nothing more than a kind of intellectual thuggee, undertaken in what its practitioners believe a noble cause. But always the combat takes place in the specialized vocabulary of public law—part legal terminology, part historical, part philosophical. It is a technical jargon which leaves even most educated Americans as outsiders—"laymen" on the sidelines. Beyond the veil of this priestly language many public policy sins have visited upon us on the basis of arguments which, if clearly stated and fairly rebutted would likely be rejected by substantial political majorities. It is to this latter end I hope this book may modestly contribute.

---

debate or even consciousness of what was going on. A variety of arguments can be advanced for "nationalizing the Bill of Rights," but popular approval is not among them. Even today knowledge of what has happened and appreciation of its significance is restricted to the legal community and those few liberal arts graduates who remember something of the course in constitutional law.

CHAPTER 2

Isolating the Churches

—

PERSUADING the Supreme Court to adopt an extreme theory of church-state separation was the first major rights industry victory after World War II, and a close look at it serves as a kind of preview of much that followed, especially in the 1960s and 1970s. Today church-state relations is an area in which there is a growing appreciation that the constitutional law created by the Supreme Court is wrong—wrong in the sense that the arguments advanced (especially the historical arguments) are untenable, and wrong in the sense that policy which results does not represent a sensible adjustment of conflicting values. The unsound foundation on which the Court's doctrine of radically separated church and state rests has been most recently and elegantly exposed by Robert Cord of Northwestern,[1] and there were others before him.[2] Senator Daniel Patrick Moynihan has been moved to publish an article on the subject titled "What Do You Do When the Supreme Court Is

Wrong?"[3] And Nathan Glazer, harkening back to the notorious recalcitrance of the pre-1937 "Nine Old Men," has argued that we need another "switch in time" by the Court in the law of church and state.[4]

The constitutional issue involved is simple. The First Amendment declares that "Congress shall make no law respecting an establishment of religion." Through a series of Supreme Court decisions (never explicitly approved by the peoples' elected representatives) this injunction was "incorporated" into the due process clause of the Fourteenth Amendment and came to apply to acts of the states as well as the national government. The question is the extent to which church-related social service institutions, especially schools, must be excluded from government programs which attempt to benefit the public through the use or strengthening of private sector institutions. The matter hinges on the interpretation given by the Court to the phrase "respecting an establishment of religion." It might be supposed that this interpretation would be linked in some intellectually coherent way to what the framers of the First Amendment (members of the first Congress and the ratifying state legislatures) thought they were accomplishing by their language. It might also be expected that this interpretation would rest on (or at least not contradict) national custom and usage in the relationship between religious institutions and government over the century and a half between the ratification of the First Amendment and the first authoritative explication of the establishment clause by the Court in 1947. In fact, the reverse is more nearly the case.

What the Court Hath Wrought

The foundation for the ediface of radical separation erected by the Court was laid in *Everson* v. *Board of Education.*[5] A New Jersey statute authorized local boards of education to underwrite the transportation of children to and from schools other than private schools operated for profit. The school board of the township of Ewing, a suburb of Camden, voted to authorize the reimbursement to parents of fares paid on regularly scheduled buses for the transportation of their children to public schools or Catholic parochial schools. Arch Everson, a Ewing taxpayer, sued in a state court contending, *inter alia,* that both the statute and the school board resolution constituted laws "respecting an establishment of religion" proscribed by the First Amendment. The trial court sustained Everson on state constitutional grounds, but the New Jersey Court of Errors (the state's highest) reversed this decision, and the case came to the U.S. Supreme Court on the First Amendment issue.

In the Supreme Court, Arch Everson's position was supported in three *amicus curiae* briefs. Nineteenth-century nativism appeared in the form of the durable Order of United American Mechanics. There was an American Civil Liberties Union (ACLU) submission. And E. Hilton Jackson, soon to join Protestants and Other Americans United for the Separation of Church and State, wrote for the General Conference of Seventh Day Adventists. Ewing was represented by William Speer, of the state Attorney General's office, but with him on the brief was Porter R. Chandler, partner in the prestigious Wall Street firm of Davis, Polk. Mr. Chandler and his firm enjoyed a special relationship with the Roman Catholic Archdiocese of New York, and for almost twenty-five years Chandler had a way of turning up with the impressive resources of Davis, Polk in cases in which Francis Cardinal Spellman had an interest. In addition, six other states filed briefs supporting New Jersey and Ewing. These states had school transportation arrangements of their own to protect. *Everson* v. *Board* was, in fact, a textbook example of the modern "public policy litigation" in which the tangible personal interest of the plaintiff is dwarfed by contending interest groups seeking to shape future constitutional law to their liking.

Justice Hugo L. Black delivered the opinion of a Court divided

5–4. He began with a consideration of the background of the establishment clause which relied heavily on certain writings of James Madison and Thomas Jefferson,* but had virtually nothing to say about the actual legislative history of the First Amendment's language in the First Congress. Black concluded that the establishment clause "means at least this":

Neither a state nor the federal government can set up a church. Neither can pass laws which aid one religion, aid all religions or prefer one religion over another. . . . No tax in any amount, large or small, can be levied to support any religious activities or institutions, whatever they may be called, or whatever form they may adopt to teach and practice religion. . . . In the words of Jefferson, the clause against the establishment of religion by law was intended to erect "a wall of separation between church and State."[6]

But after this sweeping separationist pronouncement, Justice Black pirouetted neatly and upheld the Ewing program on the ground that the aid in that case was a public safety measure designed to protect students and could in no way be construed as aid to church-related schools.

Four dissenters were convinced that Justice Black had missed the point. Justice Robert H. Jackson's dissent likened Black's majority opinion to Byron's Julia who, "whispering I will ne'er consent, consented."[7] What could be more helpful to a school, Jackson asked, than depositing the students at its door? Justice Wiley Rutledge, with whom Justices Jackson, Felix Frankfurter, Frank Mur-

---

*A word is in order concerning Jefferson's famous statement, on which Black and his strict-separationist successors within the American judiciary so heavily rely, that the establishment clause was intended to erect "a wall of separation" between church and state. This was not part of the legislative history of the establishment clause, nor was it a comment made at the time of the ratification of the First Amendment. It was made eleven years later in a letter to the Danbury, Connecticut, Baptist Association. Jefferson was responding to congratulations by the Baptists for his having refused to issue the Thanksgiving Day proclamation following the precedents of Washington and Adams. While it surely reflects the third president's opinion as to what the establishment clause should be understood to mean, it is difficult to see why it is entitled to greater respect than the differing views of his equally illustrious precedessors.

phy, and Harold Burton joined, also filed a lengthy dissent. Justice Rutledge, like Black for the majority, made lavish use of the writings of Madison and Jefferson during the controversy in Virginia over the disestablishment of the Episcopal Church in the mid-1780s. But Rutledge pressed on to what he regarded as the logical consequence of these writings, that New Jersey's program violated the establishment clause.

In retrospect, what is interesting, not to say shocking, about *Everson* is that every member of that Court, with the possible exception of Justice Stanley Reed,[8] endorsed a sweeping theory of strict separation, pillared on selective quotation of Madison and Jefferson. The favorite tag line, on which great weight was placed by both Black and Rutledge, was Jefferson's metaphor from his famous letter to the Danbury Baptists concerning "a wall of separation between church and state."

The following year, 1948, the Court began to build on *Everson*. *McCollum* v. *Board of Education*[9] saw the justices, with only Reed dissenting, striking down a "released time" program in Champaign County, Illinois. Here religious teachers had been allowed into the schools for brief periods to offer instruction to students whose parents desired them to receive it. Again Black wrote for the Court and found the Illinois arrangement "beyond all question a utilization of the tax-established and tax-supported public school system to aid religious groups to spread their faith. And it falls squarely under the ban of the First Amendment (made applicable to the States by the Fourteenth) as we interpreted it in *Everson* v. *Board of Education,. . . .*"[10]

In 1952 there was a swing by the Court toward moderation in *Zorach* v. *Clauson.*[11] This upheld a New York released time program which differed from that in Illinois in that the children were released during part of the school day to receive religious instruction at churches and synagogues. Justice Black, in bitter dissent, argued that *Everson* and *McCollum* were traduced; Jackson and Frankfurter agreed. But Justices Rutledge and Murphy had been replaced by Sherman Minton and Tom Clark and neither, at least initially, felt committed to Black's radical separationism. William O. Douglas, who wrote for the majority, and was touted as a dark horse for the Democratic presidential nomination that year, took uncharacteristic note of the diversity and flexibility of the American tradition in relations between religion and the public order:

The First Amendment . . . does not say that in every and all respects there shall be a separation of Church and State. . . . We are a religious people whose institutions presuppose a Supreme Being. . . . When the State encourages religious instruction or cooperates with religious authorities by adjusting the schedule of public events to sectarian needs, it follows the best of our traditions. . . . To hold that it may not would be to find in the Constitution a requirement that the Government shows a callous indifference to religious groups. That would be preferring those who believe in no religion over those who do.[12]

The Douglas opinion was really rather fine, but it proved one of the most famous nonstarters in American constitutional history. It was ten years before the Court returned to the question of the meaning of the establishment clause, but when it did, it was to reaffirm radical separationism with a vengeance. Urged on by a rights industry grown larger and sleeker since 1952, the Court struck down all organized prayer and Bible reading in the public schools—practices which had been in varying degrees traditional since the emergence of the public school system in America.[13] Justice Douglas, his larger political ambitions long since shattered and his rights industry audience augmented, repented of his lapse into moderation in *Zorach*. In a footnote to his concurrence in the New York "Regent's Prayer Case" in 1962 (Black wrote the opinion of Court in the *Everson-McCollum* idiom), Douglas wondered whether there might not be something wrong with the motto "In God We Trust" on the pennies.[14] So much for "we are a religious people . . ."! The lone dissenting voice was Potter Stewart's. He accused the majority of "misapply[ing] a great constitutional principle."[15] Stewart was essentially a moderate on church-state issues and later joined strict separationist majorities because he felt bound by precedent rather than out of conviction that the Court was right.[16]

Economic pressures on independent schools (especially Catholic parochial schools) in the mid-1960s, and the sympathetic response to their difficulties by legislators and governors in a number of states, forced the justices back to the task of interpreting the establishment clause; this time in the context of participation by church-related schools in state-funded programs of education enrichment.

The first such decision was, like *Zorach,* a false dawn. *Board of Education* v. *Allen*[17] involved a New York statute providing that state-purchased textbooks be "loaned" to students in nonpublic schools. While title to the books would continue to vest in the state, the books would not be returned, but would be written off at the end of their normal period of usefulness.

Justice Byron White delivered the opinion of the Court and relied heavily on the "pupil benefit theory," which he purportedly derived from *Everson.* In this formulation, if the beneficiaries of the governmental program were principally the consumers of services, and not the church-related institutions, their participation in the public program could be sustained. White concluded the New York statute had a secular legislative purpose and a primary effect that neither advanced nor inhibited religion.

Unregenerate to the end, Justice Black dissented. *Everson,* Black reminded the majority, had said that bus transportation for students at church-related schools went "to the very verge" of what was permissible under the establishment clause; textbooks were over the verge. Justice Douglas and Justice Abe Fortas also dissented.

The effect of the *Allen* decision was to stimulate optimism among supporters of aid to independent schools in state legislatures throughout the country, and legislation soon emerged seeking to provide other sorts of educational services in nonpublic schools at state expense. The optimism was premature. *Allen* did mark the emergence of Justice White, who, unlike Stewart, has consistently dissented from the separationist orthodoxy according to *Everson* and *Engle.* But it soon became clear (even with the appointments of Warren Burger in 1969 and William H. Rehnquist in 1971) that a moderate majority on church-state questions was not yet. Once states moved from textbooks to other sorts of aids, the conventional wisdom reasserted its power over the "center" of the Court.

In 1971 came the decision in *Lemon* v. *Kurtzman.* [18] A Pennsylvania statute authorized the state to "purchase" certain specific education services from private (including church-related) schools. This was, in fact, a system of state subsidy of the salaries of teachers of certain secular subjects (mathematics, science, languages) in independent schools. Chief Justice Burger wrote the opinion of the Court disallowing Pennsylvania's initiative; only Justice White dissented. Burger reasoned that while the intent of the program was secular, the degree of state supervision necessary to insure that the subsidized teachers did not engage in any religious training (and thus give the program a primary effect of advancing religion), would result in "excessive entanglement" of government and church-related institutions. On its face, the *Lemon* opinion looks like just another strict-separationist result. But this overlooks the potential for accommodation on the school aid issue which the Chief Justice built into the notion of excessive entanglement. Burger's formulation opened the way for indirect state aid to parents and children at church-related schools. In other words, if there was no public money actually going to the schools that had to be directly accounted for, there would be no entanglement and no constitutional problem.

All this was clarified two years later (1973) in *Committee for Public Education* v. *Nyquist.* [19] This involved a New York law, passed after *Lemon,* which had three major provisions. First, it made available direct grants for maintenance and repair of facilities and equipment of nonpublic schools serving high concentrations of pupils from low-income families. Second, it offered tuition grants ($50 for elementary school, $100 for high school, up to 50 percent of actual tuition) to parents of nonpublic school children with incomes of $5,000 per year or less. Third, for parents above the

$5,000 income line, a sliding scale of state income tax credits was established. On the maintenance grants, Burger found an establishment clause violation because the payments were direct to the schools; entanglement would result from the state insuring that chapels and chalices were not among the facilities and equipment repaired with the public money. Burger was prepared, however, to uphold the tuition grants and the tax credits because they were only indirect aids to the schools and would not result in entanglement.

But Burger was undone. He could not carry the Court on his direct-indirect distinction—only White and Rehnquist would join him. Justices Lewis Powell, Harry Blackmun, and a perhaps reluctant Stewart, joined the separationist hardliners, William Brennan, Thurgood Marshall, and Douglas. Justice Powell wrote for this majority and argued that the Pennsylvania program had the "effect of advancing religion." Even though this effect was indirect (prior versions of this text had spoken of a "primary" effect of advancing religion),[20] a substantial benefit was conferred on church-related schools. That was enough. And it was also enough, along with the familiar uncritical references to Madison and Jefferson, to dampen any hope that Powell might be a recruit to moderation in church-state matters.

In the years since the failure of Burger's initiative in *Nyquist*, the Court, deeply divided, has limped through a series of cases in which various justices have sought to determine and explain what kinds of public support could be given to students in church-related schools, and what could not. Or, as lawyers put it, what is "more like" the textbooks approved in *Allen* and what is "more like" the teacher subsidies disapproved in *Lemon*. This has proved a frustrating and confused enterprise.

In 1975, in *Meek* v. *Pettinger*[21] the justices faced Pennsylvania's response to *Lemon*. The program provided (1) textbook loans to children in nonpublic schools; (2) loans of "instructional materials and equipment" (slide projectors, Bunsen burners and so on) to independent schools; and (3) certain auxiliary services (for example, speech therapy) to be delivered in nonpublic schools by public school personnel. The now well-defined moderate block (Burger, Rehnquist, and White) supported the entire package. The essentially equivocal center of the Court (Stewart, Powell, and Blackmun) went only for the textbook loans, and the obdurate bloc of Brennan, Marshall, and Douglas would have denied textbooks (thus overruling *Allen*). Thus only the textbooks survived.

This same division within the Court (with John Paul Stevens replacing Douglas in the radical-separationist bloc) reappeared in 1977 in *Wolman* v. *Walter*.[22] Here, an Ohio statute provided for (1) textbook loans; (2) the supplying of standardized tests and scoring services used in public schools to nonpublic schools; (3) certain diagnostic services for speech, hearing, and psychologically impaired students in the nonpublic schools; (4) certain therapeutic, guidance, and remedial services for students in nonpublic schools, with these services delivered off the schools premises (in a van, a community center, or a public school); (5) the loan to nonpublic school pupils and their parents of instructional equipment such as tape recorders, maps, and scientific gear; and (6) transportation and other services for field trips. The super-separationists combined with the muddy middle of the Court to invalidate elements 5 and 6, but the moderates captured the center bloc to sustain elements 1 through 4. In this tortured rendition the establishment clause becomes, for a delicately balanced Court, a doctrinal razor that passes between diagnostic services, which may be delivered on nonpublic school premises, and remedial services aimed at the disabilities diagnosed, which must take place off school premises; between textbooks, which may be loaned, and maps and cassettes which may not!

In a recent installment of this continuing farce, *Committee for Public Education and Religious Liberty* v. *Regan*[23] in 1980, the moderates and the centerists upheld a New York law that directly reimbursed church-related and secular nonpublic schools for their costs incurred in complying with certain state-mandated testing requirements. This arrangement differed from one previously struck down[24] only in specifically providing for a state audit of school financial records to insure that public funds were used only to pay for secular services. In the concluding sentence of his dissent in *Regan,* Justice Stevens perfectly, if inadvertently, reflected the establishment clause predicament into which the Court has been lured:

> Rather than continuing with the Sisyphean task of trying to patch together the "blurred, indistinct and variable barrier" described in [*Lemon*], I would resurrect the "high and impregnable wall between church and state constructed by the Framers of the First Amendment.[25]

Stevens is as correct about the "Sisyphean task" as he is wrong about the framers of the establishment clause. This is precisely the root of the confusion. It is the continued attachment of at least three of the present justices to the historical myth of strict separation, as first articulated in *Everson,* that produces the curious divisions and frustrates the healthy development of relations between religion and the public order in America today. As Professor Mark Howe of the Harvard Law School put it almost twenty years ago, "in the matters at issue [interpreting the establishment clause] the Court has too often pretended that the dictates of the nation's history, rather than the mandates of its own will, compelled a particular decision."[26]

Original Understandings

What did the framers of the First Amendment mean by separation of church and state, and what is the axial American tradition in the matter?

At the outset it is necessary to separate "the framers" from James Madison. Madison was indeed the prime mover and House manager of what became the Bill of Rights,* but no one would suppose today that the product of a grinding congressional process could be casually equated with the personal views of a single member, no matter how influential. The question is not what Madison "really thought" or might have desired in his heart of hearts, but what he put to his fellows in Congress and what they, and the state legislators who voted for ratification, took his submission and their changes to mean.

Madison's original draft language for the religion guarantees of the First Amendment makes clear what was proposed: "The Civil rights of none shall be abridged on account of religious belief or worship, nor shall any *national religion* be established. . . ."[27] Were the various alterations of this formulation driven by an intention on the part of some legislators to broaden the prohibition?

The most thorough consideration of this textual pulling and hauling of the religion clauses in the First Congress is by political scientist Michael Malbin.[28] He demonstrates that there is support in these debates for an interpretation of the establishment clause as precluding interference by the newly established national government with the existing religious establishments in several of the states. For instance, Samuel Livermore of New Hampshire, specifically concerned about the state establishments, would have altered the language to hold that "Congress shall make no laws touching religion, ..."[29] The intent of this suggestion was to make plain that the states would continue to have perfectly free hands with respect to the relationship to religion and the public order.

Malbin also finds support for an interpretation holding that the establishment clause sought to achieve separation of church and state in the sense of prohibiting those forms of governmental aid to religion which established, or would tend to establish, a national

*Twelve articles were sent by Congress to the states for ratification. Article I (dealing with apportionment of the House of Representatives) and Article II (dealing with the compensation of senators and representatives) were not ratified. Articles III–XII became Amendments I–X on 15 December 1791 when Virginia's approval satisfied the "three-fourths" requirement of Article V. Massachusetts, Connecticut, and Georgia belatedly ratified the Bill of Rights in 1939.

church, or which would discriminate between religious denominations. The dropping of the adjective "national" from Madison's original proposal had nothing to do with what legislators were seeking to proscribe. It was avoided out of deference to Antifederalist sensibilities. Throughout the struggle over ratification there had been objection to the idea that a "national" government was being created—as opposed to a new, somewhat stronger confederation of sovereign states. The word "national" had been avoided in the Constitution itself, and some legislators thought it unwise to risk antagonizing states' rights partisans by raising such a verbal red flag in an amendment. Madison himself continued to urge that the term "national religion" be used in order to clarify the meaning of what was proposed. Mr. Madison, it was reported,

> . . . believed that the people feared one sect might obtain a preeminence, or two combine together, and establish a religion to which they would compel others to confirm. He thought that if the word national was introduced, it would point the amendment directly to the object it was intended to prevent.[30]

And this was the same Madison who had defined religious freedom a year before on the floor of the Virginia ratification convention as the absence of "any exclusive establishment."[31]

Malbin concludes that there is no support whatever in the legislative history for the interpretation of the establishment clause adopted by the majority of the United States Supreme Court—that the clause prohibits not only the establishment of a national church and laws which discriminate between churches, but also precludes nondiscriminatory cooperative relations between government and churches, condemning *any* government aid to religious institutions.

Robert Cord of Northwestern University, who recently reexamined the materials, is equally clear. For the framers of the First Amendment, the language regarding religion was intended to do three things:

Isolating the Churches

First, it was intended to prevent the establishment of a national church or religion, or the giving of any religious sect or denomination a preferred status. Second, it was designed to safeguard the right of freedom of conscience in religious beliefs against invasion solely by the national Government. Third, it was so constructed in order to allow the States, unimpeded, to deal with religious establishments and aid to religious institutions as they saw fit. There appears to be no historical evidence that the First Amendment was intended to preclude Federal governmental aid to religion when it was provided on a non-discriminatory basis.[32]

Indeed, early Congresses and presidents did not behave *as if* the establishment clause effected a radical separation of church and state. Madison himself was a member of the congressional committee that recommended the chaplain system, and, as president, he issued four Thanksgiving proclamations. Late in life, it is true, Madison manifested ambivalence concerning these proclamations. In 1946, a document in Madison's handwriting was discovered in which he articulated a much broader theory of the establishment clause than he had advanced during his career as a public man. Referred to by scholars as the "Detached Memorandum," the fragment may be taken as indicating Madison's most mature view of separation of church and state. But unless we are prepared to assume that Madison casually sacrificed principle to political expediency in his active years (and there is no evidence of such craven behavior on other issues) we must assume that in the period relevant to assessing "the intention of the framers" (the 1790s), Madison did not subscribe to a theory of separation as radical as that expressed in the "Memorandum."

Now what of the famous Virginia debates of 1780s? Is it not possible to argue that in this earlier period Madison, and especially Thomas Jefferson, displayed radical separationist views that they disguised during the years of federal constitution making, but that "surfaced" later in their lives? And may not these views be taken as the originally obscured, but nonetheless valid, animating logic of the establishment clause?

Elegant, but it won't fly, it won't even walk because while the

Madison and Jefferson of the Virginia debates certainly enunciated a theory of the separation of church and state, theirs was not a theory of strict separation. A brief review will suffice.

The Declaration of Rights of the Virginia Constitution, adopted in 1776, contained a broad affirmation of the right of free exercise of religious conscience, consistent with the good order of society. During the revolutionary years, Virginia's required tithes for the support of Anglican clergymen were first suspended and then abolished. In 1784, however, sentiment had developed in the Virginia Assembly, spearheaded by Patrick Henry and Richard Henry Lee, to provide tax support to churches and to shore up the position of the newly organized Episcopal Church (the successor to the old Anglican establishment). Two bills were introduced: the Incorporation Bill, which accorded recognized legal status to the Episcopal Church, and the General Assessment Bill, which would have established Christianity as the official religion of the state and assessed citizens for the support of some church or other. If no choice were recorded by a citizen, the assessment went to support "seminaries" (most of which were Episcopalian) within the counties where the money had been raised. What was involved was close to a classic establishment with a preferred position for one church body.

James Madison opposed both bills. The Incorporation Bill passed in December 1784, but Madison succeeded in having the Assessment Bill postponed to the following year. In the interim, Patrick Henry was elected governor and there were other changes in the membership of the Assembly. In July of 1785, before the Assembly met, Madison drafted his famous "Memorial *and* Remonstrance"—so beloved of Justices Black, Rutledge, Douglas, Brennan, and Stevens. This was actually a petition opposing the establishment of the Christian faith and the assessments for maintenance of churches; it was circulated within the Virginia political elite receiving hundreds of signatures. The central thrust of Madison's argument was that the bill accorded a preferred position to the Episcopal Church. When the Assembly was reconvened and the Assessment Bill was taken up, Madison had the votes to defeat it. While the meaning of the vote in the Assembly is not altogether clear, the combination of the previously passed Incorporation Bill and the General Assessment Bill appears to have struck non-Episcopalians (Baptists and Presbyterians) as constituting not even-handedness, but a *de facto* establishment of the Episcopal church. It was this, not *nondiscriminatory* cooperative relations, that was defeated.[33] (The Presbyterians, in particular, saw the incorporation of the Episcopal Church as conferring on it benefits similar to those enjoyed by the old Anglican establishment. This certainly affected their reaction to the Assessment Bill.)

Clearly the presence of the Incorporation Act on the books was a continuing challenge to Madison and Jefferson, and the former quickly dusted off the draft of a "Bill for Religious Freedom" that Jefferson had originally written in 1779. Madison saw this measure through the Assembly in 1786, and the Incorporation Act was repealed by the same session—thus effecting complete disestablishment in Virginia. Jefferson was so proud of this act (the "Virginia Statute of Religious Liberty") he provided that it be one of three accomplishments listed on his tombstone along with "Author of the Declaration of Independence" and "Father of the University of Virginia." The statute, however, addresses the problem of *interference* by government with individual religious beliefs and practices. It simply does not speak to the contemporary issue of nondiscriminatory cooperative arrangements between government and church-related social service institutions. Furthermore, the overall Jeffersonian performance with respect to this relationship between religion and the public order undermines the notion that the third president consistently maintained radically separationist views. As president, Jefferson, like Washington and Adams before him, signed into law acts of Congress providing federal land grants to a religious body for "propagating the Gospel among the heathen [native Americans]."[34] And in a message to the Senate on 31 October 1803, Jefferson asked that body to advise and consent to an Indian treaty "in which one of the conditions was the use of federal money to support a Catholic priest in his priestly duties, and

further to provide money to build a church."[35] The strongest and
most frequently invoked argument for Jefferson's strict separationism is his refusal to issue Thanksgiving proclamations. But even
here things are not as clear as they appeared to Justice Black and
his ideological associates. In a long and carefully considered letter
to a Presbyterian minister in 1808, explaining his reasons for breaking with the practice of Washington and Adams in this matter,
Jefferson wrote that:

> This results not only from the provision that no law shall be made
> respecting the [sic] establishment or the exercise of religion, but from that
> also which reserves to the States powers not delegated to the United States.
> Certainly no power to prescribe any religious exercise, . . . has been
> delegated to the Central Government. It must then rest with the States,
> as far as it can be with any human authority.[36]

Surely Cord is correct in concluding that, while Jefferson's personal preference may have been for a complete separation of government and religion, he did not elevate that preference into a
conviction that the Constitution mandated such a policy for the
states.

Thus the historical argument for strict separationists is revealed
as an error within a deception. The deception is the insistence that
the intention of the framers and the essence of the American tradition in church-state relations is adequately represented by the
thoughts of Madison and Jefferson. The error is a misinterpretation
(or, at least, overstatement) of their positions. Not even the writings of Madison and Jefferson during the campaign for disestablishment in Virginia will support the sweeping separationism trum-
peted by their partisans as "the American way."

In a telltale aside from his concurring opinion in the Court's
1973 decision holding the reading of Bible passages as part of
public school exercises unconstitutional, Justice Brennan counseled that a "too literal quest for the advice of the Founding
Fathers upon [establishment clause] issues" would be "mis-

directed."[37] Only, one suspects, because from Brennan's perspective the quest would be embarrassing.

Nor can we leave the matter here. It is a weakness of currently fashionable modes of constitutional interpretation (see chapter 7) that they slight not only the intentions of the framers, but also what might be called the intermediate gloss—what our constitutionally literate forefathers conceived particular provisions to mean. In the case of the establishment clause the intermediate gloss is particularly interesting. Was it understood by the "follow-on" generation to the framers that the First Amendment erected a "high and impregnable barrier" between church and state?

Justice Joseph Story was appointed to the Supreme Court by Madison, where he sat from 1811 to 1845. He was concurrently a professor at the Harvard Law School and author of the influential *Commentaries on the Constitution of the United States.* Of the religion clauses of the First Amendment Story wrote:

> . . . at the time of the adoption of the Constitution, and of the Amendment to it now under consideration, the general if not the universal sentiment in America was, that Christianity ought to receive encouragement from the State so far as was not incompatible with the private rights of conscience and the freedom of religious worship. An attempt to level all religions, and to make it a matter of state policy to hold all in utter indifference, would have created universal disapprobation, if not universal indignation.[38]

In the same fashion Thomas Cooley's famous *Constitutional Limitations,* first published in 1868, saw no establishment clause violation as long as the national government treated all churches equally.[39] In his widely used short textbook on *The General Principles of Constitutional Law,* Cooley put it this way:

> By establishment of religion is meant the setting up or recognition of a state church, or at least the conferring upon one church of special favors and advantages which are denied to others. It was never intended that by the Constitution the government should be prohibited from recognizing religion. . . .[40]

Examples could be multiplied but the point is clear. The axial tradition in the nineteenth century understanding of the separation of church was one of pragmatic flexibility which celebrated accommodations between religion and the public order so long as they were nondiscriminatory and not coercive of conscience. Altogether representative is Philip Schaff's treatise on *Church and State in the United States,* published in 1888. Schaff was professor of church history at Union Theological Seminary. Drawing on the opinions of contemporaries such as Cooley, Francis Lieber, and George Bancroft, Schaff concluded that "A total separation of church and state is an impossibility, unless we cease to be a Christian people."[41]

There is, however, one strand of nineteenth-century thought concerning religion and the public order to which contemporary theoreticians of strict separation can correctly appeal—the essentially nativist "Blaine Amendment" movement of the 1870s.

On the origins, development, and forms of American nativism it is sufficient to remind the reader of minor classics by Ray Allen Billington and John Higham[42] and to emphasize the extent to which anti-Catholicism was its unifying theme. The Civil War saw a decline in nativism from the heights to which it had climbed in the 1850s. Catholic fought alongside Yankee in the Union Army, and two-thirds of General Thomas Meagher's Irish Brigade fell before the sunken road at Fredericksburg. In the immediate postwar period, Catholic leaders were emboldened, as Higham puts it, "to open a campaign to secure for their own parochial schools a share of the funds that the states were providing for education, and to get for Catholic charitable institutions public subsidies comparable to those traditionally awarded to Protestant charities."[43] It was a bad tactical mistake. Nativist fears of a "school funds grab," backed by blocs of unwashed immigrant voters in large cities, intensified during the 1870s.

In 1875 the faltering Grant administration, stained by scandal and casting about for a way of reviving Republican prospects before the election of 1876, moved to exploit this resurgent anti-Catholicism. Grant himself delivered a tub-thumping speech before the veterans of the Army of the Tennessee urging them to see that "not one dollar appropriated" for education be spent to support any but "free" (that is, government-run) schools.[44] Rutherford B. Hayes, running for governor in Ohio, lambasted the Democrats (from whom he would steal the presidency a scant two years later) as Catholic coddlers. And that prince of political opportunists, James G. Blaine, Republican of Maine and minority leader of the House of Representatives, introduced an amendment to the federal Constitution which would have added the First Amendment as follows:

> No State shall make any law respecting an establishment of religion or prohibiting the free exercise thereof; and no money raised by taxation in any state for the support of public schools, or derived from any public fund thereof . . . shall ever be under the control of any religious sect.[45]

The approach was not original with Blaine. Several states had already been panicked into modifying their constitutions to specifically proscribe aid to church-related schools. The Blaine Amendment passed the House 180 to 7, but with ninety-eight members not voting. In the Senate, Democrats moved to weaken the language, and the final version fell short of receiving the necessary two-thirds vote. Nevertheless, several more states were emboldened to write such bans into their constitutions—provisions which came to be known as "Blaine Amendment," although the Plumed Knight had nothing directly to do with their adoption and had been gathered to his fathers before some states acted. Impetus was lent to this movement by the ascendance in the last decades of the nineteenth century of the American Protective Association (APA), the most effective nativist lobby in American history. But with the waning of the APA in the new century, popular concern with keeping Catholic schools from benefiting from public funds abated—without, however, entirely dying out.

Looked at straight on, the historical case for strict separation rests on Madison's "Detached Memorandum," Jefferson's belletristic flourish (the "Wall" metaphor) from his letter to the Danbury Baptists, and the Blaine Amendment movement. On the other side is a rich historical record to the contrary. How could it have happened that in the middle decades of the twentieth century successive Supreme Court majorities came so confidently to distort the American past?

The Radical Separationists

The answer lies in the work of loose coalition of lawyers, educators, and interest group activists who, for various reasons, favored a policy of very strict separation of church and state. What happened, largely in the immediate post-World War II period, was that a version of the American tradition in the matter of religion and the public order was manufactured to suit the needs of a network of active and skilled elites concerned with maximizing the provision of human services by the state (especially in education) and confining private sector institutions (especially the churches) to wholly private matters of worship and personal ministering.

Beginning in the mid-1940s and culminating in the early 1960s a series of books, most of them from one publishing house, the (Unitarian) Beacon Press of Boston, presented this distorted but highly serviceable version of the American tradition of church-state relations. Not only did this spurious creation confer legitimacy on the policy arguments of the radical separationists, it provided a pseudoscholarly background for the strict separationism, unjustified by either the history of the First Amendment or by the understanding of that amendment by previous generations. Most importantly, this remanufactured tradition was available in time to provide the appearance of an intellectual foundation for what majorities of the Supreme Court did between 1947 and 1963.

Isolating the Churches

Three different kinds of people came together in an uneasy network of alliances to promote the radical separation of churches from American civic life. First, were the anti-Catholic Protestants, fearful of expanding Catholic power and disturbed by signs of growing Catholic political confidence after World War II.* Protestants and Other Americans United for the Separation of Church and State (Americans United) was their interest group vehicle and Paul Blanshard the most noted publicist. Second were the liberal secularists who were hostile to religion in general as obscurantist and to Catholics in particular because of their "authoritarian" religious heritage and their "unthinking" anticommunism. The ACLU and the American Jewish Congress were the front line groups, and Leo Pfeffer the most prominent advocate.[46] Third, was the public school establishment. These persons, often operating from professorships in teacher training institutions, were determined to advance the monopoly position of government-run schools. The National Education Association contributed to litigation, and several of the leading strict separationist publicists, such as R. Freeman Butts and V. T. Thayer, were closely tied to the public education establishment.[47]

The underlying motivation of the strict separationists sprang from an idealization of the government-run school as the proper training ground for citizenship in America, opposition to independent schools as "divisive," and an hostility to churches, especially the Roman Catholic church (perceived as undemocratic) as purveyors of social services. Since taxes were collected from all, it was an affront to those who reprobated one or all churches to have these institutions participating in publicly funded programs. "Public" was equated with "government."

*There were really two sorts of Protestants in this category: churchmen of the political left such as G. Bromley Oxnam, president of the Federal (now National) Council of Churches, and Guy Emory Shipler, editor of the politically liberal magazine *The Churchmen,* and churchmen of the religious right such as Joseph M. Dawson of the Baptist Joint Committee on Public Affairs and Louie D. Newton, president of the Southern Baptist Convention. The men of the left could not forgive the Roman Catholic church for supporting Franco in Spain; the men of the religious right could not forgive the Roman Catholic church's ancient claim of exclusivity.

The participation of elements of the Protestant left and right in the campaign is only superficially paradoxical. The campaign focused mainly on church-related schools. At the time the principal mischief was done, the late 1940s, the Protestant right was running very few schools and was deeply suspicious of the Roman Catholics who were. As Baptist and other fundamentalist sponsorship of private academies increased in the 1970s, the strict separationism of these groups has been increasingly tempered by realism. On the Protestant left, interestingly, anti-Catholicism ran as deeply as on the right, albeit for different reasons. For the left churchmen, then as now, socialism was as important as salvation; the earthly advancement of humanity was perceived as a government responsibility not properly shared with the private sector. It is one of the major ironies of our time that some of the most reflexive statists and secularists in America are to be found in the ten or so blocks of the upper West Side of Manhattan, which encompass the headquarters of the National Council of Churches at 450 Riverside Drive, the neighboring Riverside Church (William Sloan Coffin, Pastor), and the Union Theological Seminary.

It must be emphasized that this was not a centrally directed campaign, nor were the people involved acting with conscious cynicism to misrepresent the American tradition. They were men of goodwill and considerable intelligence who were convinced of the overriding importance of a policy of strict separation. They went to the past to find support for this policy and by selective perception managed to stand the past on its head. The undertaking was as sincere as it was mistaken.

Among the first of the "new wave" of separationist productions was a doctoral dissertation in political science by Alvin W. Johnson at the University of Minnesota. Published in 1934, it is a curious book, scholarly in appearance, turgid in style, but slippery and even slipshod in analysis. Johnson thought that state provision of textbooks to students in church-related schools was a violation of "the American way," writing that:

The plan of state aid to all students without regard to whether they attend private or public schools has been in general practice for some time in matters of health. The law [in some states] has now been extended to textbooks. It cannot be denied that such extensions should be carefully watched. . . .[48]

And Johnson is at pains to let his reader know that several state courts had disapproved the provision of textbooks to pupils in church-related schools. He cites the New York case of *Smith* v. *Donahue*[49] without making clear that more was involved in the case than textbooks, and that the basis for the decision was that state's Blaine Amendment. Johnson also cites the Maine case of *Donahoe* v. *Richards.*[50] Unhappily for his argument this case had nothing whatever to do with aiding pupils in church-related schools. It was a suit on behalf of a Roman Catholic schoolgirl who had been expelled from school for refusing to read from the King James' version of the Bible. The school committee (of Ellsworth) imported the eminent Richard H. Dana of Boston, and he won the case. The opinion by Judge John Appleton, one of the most highly respected state jurists of the period, upheld the right of the school committee to select the books for the instruction of the pupils and concluded that no deprivation of free exercise of religion, as protected by the Maine Constitution, was involved. A more strident revision of Johnson's volume, in which he was assisted by Frank H. Yost, a Seventh Day Adventist official and founder of Americans United, appeared in 1948.[51]

The year 1948 also saw the publication of the volume two of Irving Brant's biography of Madison.[52] This devoted a chapter ("Freedom of Religion") to its subject's role in the struggle for disestablishment in Virginia. Brant, a journalist and civil liberties activist of distinctly progressive* views,[53] concluded that Madison

*The term "progressive is overworked in America. It is used to refer to the middle-class reform movement of the early decades of this century with its favored devices of referendum, recall, nonpartisan government by commission, and regulation of big business. It also refers to that political persuasion widespread among intellectuals in the 1930s and 1940s which was anticapitalist and antibourgeois,

favored the "principle of total separation between government and religion,. . . ."[54] He quoted the "Memorial and Remonstrance" at length, but appeared unaware that Madison's opposition to forcing "a citizen to contribute three pence only of his property for the support of *any one* establishment" does not add up to "total separation."[55] In his third volume, published two years later,[56] Brant gave the framing of the establishment clause a once-over-lightly—asserting, rather than demonstrating, that Madison was really "aiming at . . . absolute separation of church and state and total exclusion of government aid to religion." And while noting that Madison was forced to compromise with lesser men who did not share his separationist vision—especially with "conservatives" in the Senate—Brant guilelessly ascribes the final product to Madison, suggesting that his personal views are an altogether satisfactory gloss on the constitutional language. While Brant's work appeared after Black and Rutledge had committed themselves to a similar misinterpretation in *Everson*, Brant's *Madison* produced *post hoc* legitimation and reinforced the literary foundation of a consensus-in-error on the meaning of the establishment clause. Later writers, some more careful and qualified than Brant, tracked his error even though· they attempted to return to the primary sources.[57]

---

pro-Soviet in foreign policy, and reflexively statist, utopian, and egalitarian. William L. O'Neill has recently chronicled the decline of this progressivism in *A Better World* (New York: Simon and Schuster, 1982). Here I use the term in a third sense to associate Brant with a school of American historical interpretation of which Charles A. Beard, J. Allen Smith, and Vernon L. Parrington were exemplars. This persuasion, which until quite recently was powerfully influential within the universities, saw the development of the Constitution as a struggle by the emerging forces of light, champions of an egalitarian, secular democracy, over dark, "conservative" or "aristocratic" forces who defended values such as property, order, and religion. To the progressive historians the fact that the framers' commitment to democracy was carefully qualified was unforgivable. But Jefferson and the later Madison appeared more "liberal" and congenial. By their tendency to identify the "real" American tradition with the ideas of these two men, the progressive historians created a hot house historical climate in which the myth of radical separation could flourish.

Most remarkable of the radical separatist apocrypha produced in the 1940s and early 1950s was the freshet of books which poured from the Beacon Press in the years 1949 to 1952. Paul Blanshard's *American Freedom and Catholic Power*[58] was the quintessential expression of the postwar anti-Catholicism of the American left. A lapsed Congregationalist minister, a "free thinker" inclined toward socialism, a one-time field secretary for the League for Industrial Democracy, a lawyer, and a sometime correspondent for the *Nation,* Blanshard was a facile writer with a sense of high moral mission—exposing Catholicism as an authoritarian enterprise aimed at undermining American democracy by securing public support for its parochial schools. It was an irony of his career that the principle source of long-term support for his ideas was the Protestant right, epitomized by Americans United. Perhaps the kindest thing that can be said of Blanshard's demonology is that the pre-Vatican-II church was easier for outsiders to misperceive than the church today, and that many of the old Irish-American clergy were political gut fighters of an unattractive sort. However bizarre Blanshard's views, Beacon Press stuck with him, eventually publishing eight books including his autobiography in 1973.

In 1949 Joseph L. Blau's *Cornerstones of Religious Freedom in America* was also published.[59] This collection of documents with extensive commentary by Blau, a professor of religion at Columbia University, is superficially impressive but ultimately misleading. There are the obligatory early selections from Roger Williams, William Penn, Madison, and Jefferson. But instead of selections from Justice Story or Daniel Webster,[60] or Lieber, or Bancroft, or Cooley, or others with some claim to expertise in American public law, the reader is introduced to such curiosa as Richard M. "Rumpsey-Dumsey" Johnson's demand for mail delivery on Sundays and a report by David Moulton and Mordecai Myers arguing against the appointment of chaplains in the New York legislature in 1832 (they lost). Blau's preface credits *The Humanist* magazine as a source of much of his contemporary material, and Blau's perceptions of reality parallel those of Blanshard and the founders of Americans United. He is particularly scandalized by the rough handling Oxnam and the emergent Americans United were receiving from the Catholic hierarchy.

More pointed was R. Freeman Butts' *The American Tradition in Religion and Education,* which was published in 1950.[61] Prominent in the public education establishment, Butts was a professor at Columbia Teachers College. After the now-familiar misinterpretation of the framing of the establishment clause, the book slogs on to applaud the Court for *Everson* and *McCollum.* Typical of Butts' analysis is his treatment of the religious liberty guarantees of the Illinois Constitution of 1818. These protected freedom of worship, provided that no one could be compelled "to attend erect, or support a place of worship," and concluded "that no preference shall ever be given by law to any religious establishments or modes of worship." These words Butts concludes "show clearly the intent to prevent . . . cooperation between the state and a large number of churches is just as much prohibited as is cooperation between the state and a single church." Twaddle. The language can be read fairly as prohibiting state patronage of some churches over others; it might be read as prohibiting state preference for churches over nonreligious charitable enterprise; but there is no way, especially if considered in historical context, that the words can be read to mean what Butts would have them mean. (Depressingly, the copy of Butts' book from which I worked bore the holograph inscription "Harold H. Burton, 1950.")

A similar autistic separationism is the outstanding feature of Beacon's two church-state offerings in 1951—V. T. Thayer's *The Attack Upon the American Secular School,*[62] and Conrad Henry Moehlman's *The Wall of Separation Between Church and State.*[63] Thayer was a prominent ethical culturist and proponent of progressive education who was honored as "Humanist of the Year" by the American Humanist Society in 1964. Moehlman, a Baptist minister, was professor of church history at the Colgate-

Rochester Divinity School. Both faithfully repeat the errors of their predecessors, and Moehlman goes his determinedly secular yoke fellows one better by titling a chapter "The Splendor of Public Education." In his footnotes he solemnly reproduces part of his correspondence with Wiley Rutledge in which the Justice agrees with Moehlman's views.

The climax of the Beacon Press effort, however, was the publication in 1953 of Leo Pfeffer's *Church, State, and Freedom.* [64] Pfeffer was to become the leading strict separationist lawyer of our time. His views have been developed in dozens of Supreme Court briefs, law review articles, letters to editors, and in four books. He has worked with and for most of the major separationist interest groups, including the ACLU, Americans United, and the American Jewish Congress. He was a catalyst in the formation of the Committee for Public Education and Religious Liberty in New York. While regional in its base, this coalition of city and state groups has been the radical separationist moving force in a number of important establishment clause cases (for instance, this was the "Committee" in *Committee* v. *Regan, Committee* v. *Nyquist,* and *Levitt* v. *Committee*). For two decades Pfeffer, as scholar-advocate, was a key man in selling radical separation. So identified was he with the pseudo-historical argument that Cord cast his own 1982 book in the form of a rebuttal of Pfeffer. Leo Pfeffer, in short, is an archetypical rights professional.

All the Pfefferian sound and fury went into *Church, State, and Freedom.* Despite the fact that two generations of college students have turned to it (or been set on it by innocent instructors) as an "authoritative work" on church-state relations in America, it is, in fact, a skillful brief. It is scrupulously honest, but a work of advocacy rather than inquiry. Consider Pfeffer's treatment of the Northwest Ordinance of 1787 which resolved that Congress should encourage religion, morality, and education in the new territories. Pfeffer notes that the old "Articles Congress" had made land grants to support both education and religion in furtherance of this policy, but concludes "it is important to note that after the Constitution and the First Amendment were adopted no more public land was granted for the support of religion under the Ordinance."[65] This is strictly true; none were made under the Northwest Ordinance. They were made under new legislation enacted by the new Congress.[66] Also telltale is Pfeffer's abridgment of Anson Phelps Stokes' classic two-volume work on *Church and State in the United States,* first published in 1950. The original Stokes work was animated by a moderate separationism, and was a serious attempt to do justice to the variegation of the American tradition. Stokes did not set his face against all cooperative arrangements between the state and the churches. For instance, he concluded that:

> although government may not properly give financial aid to any denominations, there are many things it may do to help them. It may for instance legally continue to exempt from taxation churches (including synagogues) and Roman Catholic parochial schools and similar schools of other bodies conducted without thought of private gain, with a reasonable amount of land about them—as long as the general principle of tax exemption for public-service institutions continues to be approved by a majority of the American people—It may also cooperate in spirit with those of any community who wish to supplement public-school education on the side of the religion of their choice through such strictly constitutional ways as the 'dismissed time' plan seems to provide.[67]

In the 1964 abridgment, however, it is Pfeffer's strict separationism which predominates. "Dismissed time" programs are anathematized, and Pfeffer advocates a federal constitutional amendment specifically forbidding any use of public funds to assist or facilitate any educational, charitable, or civic activities of any church-related institutions.[68]

There is more, but this is enough. The ground for the radical revisionist history of church-state relations in the United States had been prepared by the "progressive" historians of the 1920s and 1930s such as Vernon Parrington[69] and Charles A. Beard—who gracefully rearranged the American intellectual history into a morality play in which the good, "liberal" views of Jefferson and Jackson emerge as the axial American political tradition, triumphing progressively over their bad "conservative" opposition. Charles Beard, for instance, in a fascinating little conceit called *The Republic,* [70] published in 1943, prefigured Justice Black in *Everson* by asserting (there was no argument advanced in support of the point) that Congress can no more "vote money for the support of all churches than it can establish one of them as a national church. That would be a form of establishment."[71] What the Beacon Press books added to Parrington and Beard was a welter of what looks like scholarly supporting detail. Without the protective shield of prestigious pages they produced, the extreme and historically vulnerable theory of *Everson* would certainly have been exposed much earlier than it was—early enough, perhaps, to keep the Court from reinvesting its prestige in the error many times over.

Counting Costs

The misbegotten constitutional law in this area imposes several different kinds of costs on American society. Not only are we substantially deprived of the option of enlisting church-related social service institutions (a large and richly experienced institutional sector) in implementing public programs, but their exclusion often makes it difficult for government to act through private sector institutions at all. As a practical political matter, legislators are often unwilling to vote for programs utilizing private sector institutions if the church-related institutions, which loom large in their particular constituencies must be left out. Coalition building for the use of private sector institutions is made more difficult at a time of quickening interest in public-private cooperation and in the health of what Peter Berger calls the "mediating structures" of

American society. As Berger and Richard John Neuhaus have written, in the public policy areas of "health, social welfare, education, and so on—the historical development of programs, ideas, and institutions is inseparable from the church."[72]

A further cost of the prevailing policy is psychological—the sense of affront and injustice experienced by those who use or staff church-related service institutions and see them disabled—excluded from general programs to improve schools, hospitals, and so on, because of their church affiliation. The argument has been most succinctly put with respect to schools by Professor Donald A. Erickson of the Center for Research on Public Education at the University of San Francisco:

Since most patrons of private schools must "pay twice" for their children's instruction, once through public school taxation and once through user costs at private schools, it is obvious that private schools, though constitutionally guaranteed the "right" to exist, may be put out of business through economic coercion, ... [This] is one of the most basic, pervasive realities in the world of education today. In the light of the constitutional constraints, the nation could easily lose most of its private schools.[73]

Lest it be thought that the imperiled educational sector is of little social value, consider the findings of James. S. Coleman and his coworkers of both superior academic achievement and superior discipline and work habits in private high schools:

[A]chievement and discipline are intimately intertwined. . . . In the Catholic sector and in the schools of the other private sector in our sample, the academic demands as measured by the homework done and the advanced mathematics courses taken by students from comparable family backgrounds . . . , or as measured in the number of standard academic courses taken . . . , are greater than in the public sector. . . .

Similarly, in the Catholic sector and in schools from the other private sector, disciplinary standards in every area measured are higher, and discipline problems, as measured by the absenteeism, cutting classes, threats to teachers, and fights among students, all for students from comparable backgrounds, are lower than in he public schools.[74]

Finally, and ironically, there is an institutional cost accuring to the Supreme Court itself. In his Kline lecture at Northeastern University in May of 1981, Robert Cord argued that "the nation may well be standing at the threshold of the greatest constitutional crisis since Franklin Delano Roosevelt openly attacked the Supreme Court more than a generation ago."[75] He was drawing attention to the rising tide of resistance to the grid of constitutional restriction which the Court has imposed on educational policy making in America. The constitutional law of "establishment" is only a part of that grid (of other parts, more later) but is an important part. By substantially restricting state support to government schools the effect of the Court's decision making is to render educational choice and parental control of the schools, two prime and widely shared American values, accessible only to the affluent. The late Alexander M. Bickel was the first to draw this predicament into sharp focus in his Holmes lecture at the Harvard Law School in 1969:

> The result the courts have reached is hardly sustainable. It confirms and further entrenches the unequal system of private or public, [suburban] parent-controlled schools for well-to-do, mobile whites, and state-controlled, assimilationist schools for the white and black poor; and it forbids the state to alleviate the inequality. . . .
> Under pressure, the insistence on the assimilationist mission of public schools which are unable to perform it cannot be maintained, and it should not be. When it is abandoned, decisions forbidding . . . financial support by the state to church-connected schools must also go.[76]

Bickel's use of the term "assimilationist mission" goes to the heart of the matter. The majority of the Court was captivated by a vision of the public school as universal meeting ground and secular socializer of America. To perform its "assimilationist mission" it had to be rigorously secular, enjoy a dominant if not monopoly position, and be firmly under the control of "professional educators" who would resist parental intervention on behalf of things like prayers or Christmas pageants, which reflected subcultural attachments opposed to the universalistic culture that the school should promote. This was the core teaching of the promoters of strict separation in Jeffersonian and Madisonian wrappings. Since Bickel issued his warning in 1969, the situation has worsened. The Supreme Court has dug in more deeply, and the perception of a need to "do something" about a "runaway judiciary" is by no means restricted to Jesse Helms and the far right. Cord may have been overstating the institutional risk to the Court by invoking the crisis of 1937, but he wasn't overstating by much.*

As against these not inconsiderable costs the architects of the present policy assure us that we are avoiding the "creedal strife" which would result from the participation of church-related institutions in government programs. Perhaps so. But this danger is more frequently asserted than argued; and one wonders whether the anticipated resentment of some determined secularists would really far exceed the present resentment of most Roman Catholics and increasing numbers of Protestants and Jews.

The Court's misinterpretation of the establishment clause is now an open scandal. My reason for leading with it here is that the story is paradigmatic. What most sensible people are now realizing with dismay has happened in one area of constitutional law is replicated

*On 29 June 1983, the Court divided 5–4, decided *Mueller* v. *Allen,* U.S., upholding a Minnesota program of state income tax deductions for parental educational expenses, including tuition payments to independent schools. Justice Rehnquist distinguished *Mueller* from *Nyquist* on the ground that the Minnesota program included all parents—those whose children attended public or private schools —while the New York program had benefited only those whose children attended private schools. This may herald a generally more sensible approach to establishment clause issues, or it may, like *Zorach* and *Allen,* be a false dawn. But rights industry reaction was swift. Professor Robert M. Cover of the Yale Law School, in the *New York Times* of July 11, attacked the decision as Court approval for public "subsidization of white flight," noting that a "national program of private school tuition tax credits is high on the reactionary agenda."

in a number of other areas which we do not yet have in as clear public focus. And the basic components of the rights industry were all present in the establishment clause arena—the ACLU, the NAACP, activist lawyers, committed academics, the National Council of Churches, and the American Jewish Congress. The order of battle was unusual only by the presence of certain elements from the Protestant right which we will not encounter again in such modish company.

CHAPTER 3

Destabilizing the Schools

GIVEN the hostility of the rights industry to church-related schools and enthusiasm for "assimilationist" public schools, it might be thought that civil libertarians would be protective of government-run schools as institutions. Here, however, one encounters a paradox. For while rights professionals have championed the state schools over the private, as the properly "American" arrangement, their steely preoccupation with other issues, such as racial balance and children's rights, have led them to initiatives that resulted in severe damage to their favored educational sector. That the public schools, especially urban public schools, are increasingly troubled and beleaguered is a commonplace. What is not so common is an understanding of the contribution of the rights industry to this disorder.

Rights activists have become involved in the public schools in two major ways: through the urging of heroic measures to achieve racial balance in schools (that is, busing); and through the urging of due process requirements limiting the authority of the teachers and administrators who must run the schools. Initially, the concerns of the activist lawyers were humane and reasonable, provoked by evasive legal manuevers by segregationists and abuses of discretion by school authorities. But the modes of response were sweeping and doctrinaire, employing a spurious constitutional grammar (new "rights" and broad equitable "remedies" for whole classes of persons) rather than the limited grammar of the individual law suit (addressing a particular outrage) or the grammar of democratic public policy making (stressing maximum involvement of elected officials in educational choices, especially choices involving the allocation of scarce resources). Sometimes the public education establishment—through organizations such as the National Education Association and, to a lesser extent, the American Federation of Teachers—have welcomed the legal innovations that have made jobs of their rank and file more difficult and dangerous. In fact, the divergence between organizational elites (who identify with rights industry professionals) and those who teach, administer, and struggle to maintain order, is probably wider in public education than in any other institutional sector of American life.[1] Explanations of this might be pursued in the works of social theorists such as Robert Michels[2] and Mancur Olsen,[3] but the consequences in the classroom, the principal's office, and school committee meeting are of more immediate concern.

Requiring Racial Balance

The requirement of racial balance in public schools (which applies to schools that are part of districts with any history of official racial discrimination) is a relatively recent and exotic growth in the tangled garden of American constitutional law. In 1954 the Supreme Court awkwardly but effectively turned its back on *Plessy* v. *Ferguson*[4] and the doctrine of "separate but equal." The notably opaque opinion of Chief Justice Warren in *Brown* v. *Board of Education*[5] held that separate but equal has no place "in education," and the following year in *Brown II*[6] (the implementation decision) the Court contented itself with the exhortation that state-mandated discrimination in public schools be ended "with all deliberate speed."[7]

In the late 1950s and early 1960s, the years of "massive resistance" to the *Brown* decision, the Court spoke firmly only to reaffirm that decision in the face of direct official resistance in Little Rock, Arkansas,[8] and to hold unconstitutional the action of Prince Edward County, Virginia, in closing its public schools rather than tolerate the enrollment of blacks in previously all-white facilities.[9] It was up to the federal district courts, handling suits by minority parents against local school boards, to determine what constituted compliance with the "stop discriminating" command of *Brown*.[10] And for over a decade, the concern of the courts was precisely with making sure that assignment of children to schools was actually made without regard to race.

The first turn in a significantly new direction came in 1968 in *Green* v. *Board of Education*.[11] The Court rejected so-called "freedom of choice" plans (in effect, minority to majority transfer plans) as an adequate remedy in school districts with a history of racial discrimination. But if "freedom of choice" was inadequate, then what might be adequate? The answer was outlined by Chief Justice Burger's opinion in *Swann* v. *Charlotte Mecklenberg Board of Education* in 1971.[12] The objective of the federal courts, Burger wrote, must be "to eliminate from the public schools all vestiges of state imposed segregation." This meant, in turn, that any system in which there had been purposeful segregative decision making in the past on the part of the school authorities would now be required to become "unitary" in nature. A unitary system was one characterized by racial balance within its schools. This did not mean, Burger explained, that every school in every community must always reflect the racial composition of the school system as a whole. Schools of predominantly one race were not, *per se,* evidence of a lack of racial balance. But courts were enjoined to scrutinize such schools with care and to place "the burden upon the school authorities" to satisfy the court that their racial composition was not the result of past discriminatory behavior.

In other words, some degree of racial balance was required although it need not be arithmetically precise. If the bus transportation of school children within the district was needed to achieve a unitary character (acceptable racial balance) the Chief Justice noted that "bus transportation [is] a normal and accepted tool of educational policy. . . ." Here was the Supreme Court authority for the extensive busing of pupils ordered by district courts in the 1970s and 1980s in pursuit of that statistically elusive quality of racial balance.

The first thing to note about the racial balance requirement of *Swann* is that it purports to be remedial. That is, the obligation of changing the demography of a school system from the *status quo* to a state of "unitariness" falls only on those districts with a history of segregative decision making. Of course the southern and border states that had maintained dual school systems as a matter of law before *Brown* were automatically guilty of such *de jure* segregation. In the North and West the question was whether plaintiffs seeking judicially mandated racial balance could prove some act of purposefully segregative behavior on the part of school officials some time in the past. If they could, the system was considered to have been *de jure* segregated just as if it had been in Georgia. If plaintiffs could not demonstrate such behavior, the existing racial imbalance would be considered to exist *de facto*—the product of exogenous economic or demographic factors unaided by school authorities. The artificiality of this distinction was laid bare by Justice Powell in his concurring opinion in *Keyes* v. *School District No. 1, Denver, Colo.* in 1973.[13] Racial imbalance in schools, Powell argued, resulted from complex social and economic forces operating essentially the same way as the North and South, East and

West. To make the applicability of heroic remedies depend on whether the school was in the South or whether school authorities had been caught out doing something openly discriminatory was patently unjust.

A second, and even more important, thing to note about *Swann* is that the requirement of racial balance was neither required or presaged by *Brown* v. *Board of Education.* In a crucial exchange during the argument of *Brown* in 1952, Justice Frankfurter asked future Justice Thurgood Marshall, the NAACP attorney arguing the case for the nominal plaintiffs, whether a favorable decision for him would "entitle every mother to have her child go to a non-segregated school?" Marshall replied that it would not. Frankfurter pressed on "what will it do?" Marshall's reply was clear: "The school board, I assume, would find some other method of distributing the children by drawing district lines." The only constitutional requirement, Marshall added, was that the school attendance be drawn "on a natural basis," and not be drawn so as purposely to include or exclude black neighborhoods. In other words, what lawyer Marshall envisioned was very different from what Justice Marshall voted for in *Swann.* Marshall envisioned the dismantling of the official structure of separation, which had existed in so many districts, and its replacement by systems of neighborhood schools in which attendance lines would correspond with some natural (presumably topographical or geographical) features of the town or district. As Lino A. Graglia put it in *Disaster by Decree,* the best full-length study of the sequelae to *Brown,* "there was no thought at the time [of the original *Brown* decision] that anything more than neighborhood assignment might be required. . . ."[14]

What had happened between 1954 and 1971? Where along the way was the constitutional command to dismantle artificially imposed segregation by race in schools transformed into a constitutional command to foster equally artificial racial balance based on purposeful assignment of pupils by race? The search for an answer begins with the entry of Congress into the process of school desegragation in the Civil Rights Act of 1964; it leads into the byzantine and largely invisible (to the public) involvement in the politics of school desegregation of what was then the Department of Health, Education and Welfare; and it twists through the pages of prestigious law reviews where elaborate rationales were developed for what was being done.

In the late 1950s and early 1960s, many previously segregated school systems were adopting complicated "pupil placement plans" (neutral as to race in their terms, these usually kept blacks and whites in separate schools). In handling challenges to these evasive maneuvers the lower federal courts seemed clear as to what *Brown* required. Federal District Judge John Parker, one of the most respected jurists of his time, put it this way:

> The Supreme Court has not decided that the states must mix persons of different races in the schools or must require them to attend schools or must deprive them of the right of choosing the schools they attend. What it has decided, and all it has decided, is that a state may not deny to any person on account of race the right to attend any school that it maintains.
> . . . The Constitution, in other words, does not require integration. It merely forbids discrimination.[15]

Both the Fourth and Fifth Circuit Courts of Appeal accepted this view of the matter and, as already suggested, it remained orthodox for over a decade.

In fact, on the eve of the great national and congressional debate leading to the passage of the Civil Rights Act of 1964, the Seventh Circuit Court of Appeals reaffirmed this orthodoxy in *Bell* v. *School City of Gary, Indiana.*[16] "Desegregation," the court held, "does not mean that there must be intermingling of the races in all school districts. It means only that they may not be prevented from intermingling or going to school together because of race or color." *Bell* is a particularly significant case because of the use made of it in the congressional debates that produced the 1964 act. Title VI of the proposed legislation prohibited discrimination on the basis of race "under any program or activity receiving Federal financial assistance." This prohibition was to take on great importance for the public schools with the passage the following year of the Elementary and Secondary Education Act, under which major federal resources began flowing to local school districts. The meaning of the word "desegregation" in Title VI of the act (indeed in all titles of the act) was made unmistakably clear by the floor managers of the civil rights bill on both sides of the Capitol. In the House, Congressman Emanuel Celler of New York declared that "the bill would simply implement the law of the land [the Brown decision]. There is no authorization for either the Attorney General or the Commissioner of Education to work toward achieving racial balance in given schools."[17] And in the Senate, Hubert Humphrey explained that Title VI would do nothing more than mandate that the "local school authority refrain from racial discrimination in treatment of pupils and teachers."[18] When Senator Robert Byrd of West Virginia, now Senate minority leader but then an opponent of the civil rights bill, asked Humphrey if he could give assurance that "school children may not be bused from one end of the community to another end of the community at the taxpayer's expense to relieve so-called racial imbalance. . . ." Humphrey replied, "I do," and made reference to a specific section of the Bill, Section 404, which, Humphrey held, "merely quotes the substance of a recent court decision, which I have with me and which I desire to include in the record today, the so-called Gary case [*Bell*]."[19] The point was made repeatedly in response to persistent questioning: the meaning of "desegregation" in the proposed legislation was identical to that set forth by the Seventh Circuit. As Senator Jacob Javitts put it (in reassuring Senator Byrd) a government official who sought to require racial balance on the authority of the new Civil Rights Act could be "making a fool of himself."[20] The Senator, however, reasoned without the rights industry.

The reality of American rights politics during the late 1960s was that just such "fools" very quickly found their way into the new created positions in the federal bureaucracy where judgments had to be made as to how the new law was to be enforced; and they set about standing the act on its head. As Graglia has observed, to the "professional desegregators" drawn into the newly created positions of civil rights specialists in the Office of Education and the Office of Civil Rights of the old Department of Health, Education and Welfare, "merely ending racial discrimination was far too small a task and too limited a goal."[21]

There is a distinct life cycle to political issues and movements in the United States that is often remarked upon but little studied by poltical scientists. The period from the mid to late 1960s, following upon the passage of the Civil Rights Act of 1964, represented the "peaking out" of the modern civil rights movement that had been given life by *Brown* v. *Board of Education,* that had gathered momentum under Martin Luther King, Jr., in Montgomery, and that had gained national prominence with the Freedom Riders of the early 1960s. The many groups concerned with the legal rights of black Americans had forged an effective lobbying alliance (The Leadership Conference on Civil Rights) to push for passage of the 1964 act. For many freshly minted young lawyers, "civil rights law" was the highest calling to which an idealist could aspire. The intellectual and literary classes of America were united in support of help for black people to an almost unprecedented degree. The prestige of civil rights groups was at its all-time high, and most importantly there was no sense of ambiguity about civil rights issues. There was as yet no cloud over some civil rights activists resulting from their behavior during the riots of the "long hot summers" of the late 1960s; the invocations of violence by the Cleavers and the Browns had not settled into the national consciousness. Most importantly there was no widespread sense that the goals of the civil rights professionals might be in tension with other important social goals and values. The Moynihan Report and "benign neglect" were in the future. It was the high summer of civil rights and the professional desegregators, often fresh from the universities, identifying powerfully with the interest group leadership of the civil rights movement, came to their jobs of administering the act as enthusiasts. Not for them to weigh and balance; it was for them to achieve "social change."

It is in just such periods, when issues or reform movements reach their zenith, before healthy skepticism develops and second-thinking takes place, that mistakes in public policy are often made. They were in civil rights policy. But today many Americans who chaff under these policy mistakes have little idea who made them or how. They were made, in the first instance, by rights industry professionals within the federal government who, concentrating on their overriding moral mission, "became more and more remote from public opinion, and indeed from common sense."[22]

The first step in the administration of Title VI with respect to the public schools was fair enough. In April of 1965 HEW's Office of Education issued a series of guidelines which defined an adequate desegregation plan. While such plans had to include something more than the assignment of pupils on a nonracial basis within bona fide geographic attendance zones, fairly drawn freedom of choice plans were apparently adequate to satisfy this requirement. What was interesting was how quickly the lower federal courts which were wrestling with desegregation suits leaped on the HEW guidelines as indicating the *constitutional minima* which school districts were required to achieve.

On reflection, this is a curious development. Looked at operationally, the requirements of the Constitution of the United States were being set almost invisibly by officials within a federal agency who were presumably operating pursuant to the intent of Congress in implementing a statute. And this became positively sinister the following year when HEW issued a *revised* set of guidelines for adequacy in compliance. The initiative for these new guidelines appears to have come from the United States Civil Rights Commission. Created by the Civil Rights Act of 1957 to study and advise the other federal agencies with respect to race relations, the commission quickly became established as the in-government outpost of the professional civil rights movement. It was then, and is today, regarded as an appurtenance of the rights industry. This explains the scalding fury unleashed in early 1984 when President Reagan altered this status quo by appointing a majority of commissioners whose views of proper rights policy more nearly agreed with those of his administration than with those of the rights industry.

"The Commission," Graglia noted, was "deeply dissatisfied with the fact that Congress had limited the 1964 act to ending segregation. . . ."[23] In 1966 the commission recommended that the HEW "make it clear" that means of "desegregation" which went beyond nonracial assignment and freedom of choice "were permissible and desirable" if greater degrees of integration would result. And the commission went on to urge that revised guidelines "insure" that local plans were adequate not only to "disestablish dual, racially segregated school systems," but "to achieve substantial integration within such systems."[24] This was fateful language—language that sought to have embodied in new guidelines precisely the policy which Congress had rejected in adopting the act.

"Imposing a requirement of integration in the face of the language of the act was a delicate task," Graglia wrote, but the bureaucrats at HEW were up to it.[25] The new guidelines found that simple nonracial assignment was inadequate compliance with the requirement of the act. "No single type of plan," the guidelines explained, "is appropriate for all school systems." In addition to nonracial assignment, "a school may (1) permit any student to transfer from a school where students of his race are a majority to any other school, within the system, where students of his race are a minority, or (2) *assign students on such basis*" (Emphasis added).[26] In other words racial assignment of students was not only licit, but might be required for a plan to be considered adequate. Thus was the use of racial percentages and quotas introduced into the law of "desegregation," and the requirement of a desegregation plan (actually racial balance plan) was set in place of the original statutory requirement.

All that was needed to complete this legal *coup de main* was for similar surgery to be performed on the constitutional desegregation requirement of *Brown*. A willing judicial scalpel was found in the hand of Judge John Minor Wisdom of the Circuit Court of Appeals for the Fifth Circuit. In *United States* v. *Jefferson County Board of Education*, [27] Wisdom wrote that the revised guidelines were not only authorized by the Civil Rights Act of 1964, but constituted "minimum standards" of constitutional law for desegregation. "No army," Judge Wisdom wrote, "is stronger than an idea whose time has come. . . ." And while Judge Wisdom claimed to approach his decision-making task with humility, he "proceeded to deliver a fifty-seven page demonstration of his determination to work his will in spite of all obstacles." [28] Not only the intent of Congress, but fifteen years of prior constitutional law were brushed aside. While the revised guidelines had imposed a requirement of integration without ever using that term, Judge Wisdom held that for purposes of the United States Constitution the words integration and desegregation were *interchangeable*. Wisdom concluded that "the United States Constitution, as construed in *Brown*, requires public school systems to integrate students, faculties, facilities, and activities" and "the law imposes an absolute duty to integrate, that is, disestablish segregation" for the "racial mixing of students is a high priority educational goal."

Particularly outrageous was Judge Wisdom's treatment of the reassurance given by Senator Humphrey to Senator Byrd that "classification along *bona fide* neighborhood school lines, or for any other legitimate reason which local school boards might see fit to adopt, would not be effected by the civil rights law" and that the bill did not seek to go further than the requirements of the *Bell* case. According to Wisdom, Senator Humphrey's references to *Bell* "indicate that the restrictions of the Act [Section 404] were pointed at the Gary, Indiana, *de facto*-type segregation." In other words, the carefully crafted prohibitions of the act on requiring racial balance were meant to apply only in situations where the existing racial imbalance had come about accidentally and not in situations where there was any history of *de jure* (intentional) segregation. There is not a shred of evidence in the legislative history that such a distinction was in the minds of any of the framers of the Civil Rights Act of 1964. The distinction between *de facto* and *de jure* was only beginning to be developed at that time, and Wisdom's use of it was casuistic. District Judge William Cox, sitting with the Fifth Circuit on special temporary assignment, dissented in *Jefferson County* noting that "the English language simply could not be summoned to state any more clearly" than the act did that desegregation did not imply racial balance and that "these so-called 'guidelines' of this administrative agency [HEW] are actually promulgated and being used in opposition to and in violation of" the act.

But the deed was done. The prestigious Fifth Circuit had endorsed the revised definition of "desegregation" and it remained only to be seen whether the Supreme Court would buy it. And beginning with the decision in *Green,* declaring that freedom of choice plans were insufficient, and culminating in *Swann* in 1971, the Court did. The constitutional law of *Brown* v. *Board of Education* was rewritten. Rights-industry activists within the Civil Rights Commission and the Department of Health, Education and Welfare, along with the law clerks of the Fifth Circuit and the Supreme Court and their judicial principals, had wrought what Congress and the original *Brown* Court had declined.*

---

*Congress has rallied on several occasions and attempted to undo the judicially underwritten policy of heroic racial balance measures. The story of its failure is a fable for our times. An amendment to the Higher Education Act in June, 1972, included a "moratorium" on court orders which had "the purpose of achieving balance among students with respect to race, sex, religion, or socio-economic status." And in the 1974 Education Act amendments Congress condemned "excessive transportation of students" to achieve "the elimination of the vestiges of a dual school system." The federal courts, however, have taken the position that since racial balance orders persuant to *Swann* enforce the Fourteenth Amendment, Congress could not have meant to interfere with the judiciary in enforcing the Constitution of the United States. (Even though the interpretation of the Constitution being enforced is the bastard child of a bureaucratic misconstruction of the intent of Congress!) The only recourse remaining open to Congress is to limit the jurisdiction of the federal courts to entertain school desegregation cases. This would constitute an attack on the independence of the judiciary, and despite the way in which this independence has been abused, Congress has wisely refrained from such a radical step.

Bright young lawyers, fired with righteous enthusiasm, passed through the clerkships, the Civil Rights Division of the Justice Department, and other key enforcement positions in the federal bureaucracy, and went on themselves to become middle-aged law professors (and federal judges) perpetuating the cycle. And there was no shortage of academic theoreticians to explain why the sharp departures from previous law in *Jefferson County* and in *Swann* were not really departures at all. Thus in 1975, Professor Owen M. Fiss of the Yale Law School discovered that there were *two* "harmful practices" to which *Brown* had been addressed. One was the assignment of students to schools on the basis of race—the one recognized all along. But the second was "the segregated pattern of student assignments itself." Racial separation per se was asserted to be a distinct violation to which *Brown* spoke, and *Brown* could be used as underpinning for decrees mandating racial balance. The fact that no one had noticed this second dimension to *Brown* until the 1970s, and that the contemporary evidence (that of the late 1950s and early 1960s) is to the contrary, are embarrassments of which Fiss takes no notice. Whatever the divisions within particular communities on the issue, the Constitution requires integration and the courts are the appropriate agency to enforce the requirement. Legislatures, responding as they do to majorities, are simply not reliable.

Whenever a decision is entrusted to a legislature or any body directly responsible to the citizenry, the risk is high that the outcome will only manifest the interest of the dominant group. It may therefore seem that in raising doubts about the ethical superiority of relying on the legislature or the school board, particularly if the board is an elective one, I may also be reflecting doubt not widely shared—about the superiority of the democratic process in general. But I do not believe so. Society's commitment to the ideal of self-government is not so intense or absolute as to preclude an exception for minority rights. The equal protection clause, primarily a restraint on majoritarian action directed at miniorities, is ample evidence of that fact.[29]

Destabilizing the Schools

Ronald Dworkin, an American professor of law at Oxford, is one of the most prolific and one of the most audacious theoreticians of rights and liberties writing today. Dworkin argued that since the process of drawing school attendance district lines was a political process, highly likely to have been "corrupted" by racial prejudice in America, that this "antecedent probability of corruption," unless school districts negated the charge, justified court orders to integrate. Racial balance should be considered required by the Constitution because purposeful segregation *probably* took place *sometime.* [30]

David L. Kirp, professor of public policy and lecturer in the law school of the University of California, Berkeley, was more modest. After a careful review of the transition from desegregation to integration in constitutional law, Kirp concludes ruefully that what the courts are attempting "takes us far from the positivist view of law as a set of propositions susceptible of clear statement. . . ." Yet he cannot turn his back on the enterprise and, after lip service to the concept of judicial self-restraint, concludes that "the courts—and the society—may simply learn to live with the strains on judicial legitimacy which inhere in the contempory race and school cases, cases which are at once political and constitutional events."[31] But such acceptance of "strains on legitimacy" can only be justified on the basis of an assumption: that the goal of racial balance is so obvious and overwhelming a moral imperative that responding to it dwarfs the significance of how the decision to respond is made. Unfortunately for this argument the "rightness" of the goal does not reveal itself with equal force to all (or even most) elements of the polity.

For almost a decade federal district Judge W. Arthur Garrity, Jr., held the school system of the city of Boston in virtual thralldom. In more than 400 rulings over those years seeking to compel racial balance within the system, Judge Garrity referred to "the requirements of the Constitution." The phrase had obviously acquired a totemic significance. Detailed monitoring of teachers' assignments and of expenditures for extra curricular activities could all be justified by the necessity of meeting "the requirements of the Constitution." The phrase calls up visions of the Founding Fathers, the Reconstruction Congresses, and the unanimous Supreme Court in *Brown*. Many conscientious people in Boston who were worried by what was going on, but counseled "support for the law," would surely have been unnerved had they realized the tender age and peculiar parentage of this "constitutional requirement" Garrity so confidently asserted.

Close observers, who have recoiled with shock after studying the process by which a constitutional requirement of racial balance was created within the bureaucracy and the federal courts, have wondered why so many academic constitutional lawyers have either applauded or passively accepted the development. What must not be lost sight of is that by their specialized professional socialization, interlocking career patterns, friendship networks, and shared role models and reference groups, many of the professors of constitutional law were aligned with the fabricators of the constitutional requirement of integration as partners in a common enterprise.

It is not necessary to dwell at length or in detail on the disabling costs to the public schools of heroic measures to achieve racial balance. The ravages of white flight and resegregation on the school systems of larger cities (and many middle sized cities) is now beyond doubt. Despite efforts to impeach the findings of James Coleman and others who began drawing attention to this disaster in the mid-1970s, the reality refuses to go away.[32] Furthermore, work by David J. Armor[33] and Nancy St. John,[34] indicating few positive educational benefits as a result of heroic integration measures, has held up quite well.[35]

Meanwhile, the rights industry response to all of this has been to push for "metropolitan remedies"—that is, court orders which would sequester surbuban school districts and thrust them into new mega-districts to achieve racial balance which has proved elusive in many cities. Presently the Supreme Court's 1974 decision in *Milliken* v. *Bradley*[36] (the Detroit case) stands in the way of such metropolitan engineering, but the energies of the NAACP, the Ink Fund, the Lawyers Conference on Civil Rights, the ACLU, and others are still devoted to circumventing that decision. Diane Ravitch, in a recent review of the social scientific literature on white flight, concludes with a positive note on the Atlanta, Georgia, school system. Here a considered decision has been made, concurred in by the federal district court, to concentrate on improving the educational qualities of the schools rather than expend resources on heroic integration efforts in a district which is 90 percent black anyway. If Atlanta's black-run school system and its black mayor Andrew Young should succeed, Ravitch notes, Atlanta could become a model for urban systems throughout the nation. But "meanwhile, the American Civil Liberties Union is pressing a suit to compel the merger of the Atlanta school district and the surrounding white suburban districts, in order to make blacks a minority within a predominantly white metropolitan district; not surprisingly, the Atlanta district has shown no interest in surrendering its independence."[37]

When Judge Garrity, in Boston, responding in part to the pleas of a new group of black parents, announced that he would begin to relax his judicial hold on that system, perhaps opening the way for a limited use of the old freedom of choice approach, Thomas I. Atkins, general counsel of the NAACP (and sometime lecturer at the Harvard Law School) announced his opposition.[38] When Milton I. Shadur, federal district judge in Chicago, announced approval of a voluntary school desegregation plan that did not include busing, William L. Taylor, former staffer at the Civil Rights Commission, and David S. Tatel, director of the Office for Civil Rights in HEW in the Carter administration, were among the first noting opposition or concern.[39]

What accounts for such persistence in so bad a cause? (And don't say "the requirements of the Constitution.") Certainly an humanitariam desire to help black children (despite the evidence) is part of the answer, along with a sense that after what blacks suffered in America "historical justice" requires that heroic efforts now be undertaken on their behalf. But there is surely a further, deeply veiled, strand of motivation for many in the rights industry —punishment. The segregative sins of the Boston School Committee had been many and grievous. Can it be doubted that some who witnessed the pain inflicted on the white blue-collar parents of South Boston and spoke portentously of "upholding our law" were psychologically fortified to do so by vivid memories of the contorted, porcine features of Louise Day Hicks. American history (especially the history of the Reconstruction period) is rich in examples of the punitive masquerading as the idealistic. And the "Second Reconstruction," as the modern civil rights movement has often been called, is not unmarred in this respect.

Theodore M. Black, former chancellor of the New York Board of Regents and one of the most acute observers of the contemporary American educational scene, summed it up this way:

> To put it bluntly, forced integration, of which massive busing is an integral characteristic, is not worth the price we pay for it. . . .
> Like prohibition, massive involuntary busing for school integration was a noble experiment. Like prohibition, it has failed. Prohibition did nothing to stop Americans from drinking; it kindled a national disrespect for law and law enforcement that persists as a source of our social problems today. Forced busing has not produced significant scholastic improvement among black youngsters, which was its purpose; it has proven tremendously costly in terms of children's time which could otherwise be devoted to study or recreation, in terms of precious dollars which could be spent on improving the quality of education for all kids, and in terms of the disruption and resentment which has set back the cause of interracial amity by years.[40]

At least prohibition was an experiment entered into by the American people through the process of constitutional amendment. The nation, as it were, went in with its eyes open. Busing, by contrast, was foisted on a nation taken unaware by a small set of interlocking interest groups, judicial, academic, and bureaucratic idealists intoxicated by the rhetoric of governmentally managed social change.

Little Litigators

A second axis of assault by the rights industry on public schools involves school discipline and the "children's rights" movement.

In any legal system, and the American system of constitutional law is no exception, there are certain highly functional assumptions undergirding the structure of positive legal rules and precedents. Until they are challenged or overturned, these traditional assumptions often have little by way of case law or legislation to support them. Paradoxically, this very lack of "black letter" law may be an indication of the importance of the assumption. There is little explicit discussion of the assumption because it is taken for granted by everyone—because any challenge to it would be so silly as not to warrant the time of serious men. Such an assumption in America was that while children from the moment of their birth were human beings, certain legal and constitutional rights, including rights as "persons" under the Fifth and Fourteenth Amendments, devolved on them only gradually as they grew to maturity. A parallel assumption was that the state-run school, in its encounter with these all too human children, was very different in legal character from the state acting as policeman or judge in enforcing the criminal law—that the public school was not the polity in miniature.

This is a roundabout way of saying that it was generally understood that in the public school the student stood in somewhat the same relationship to the school authorities as he or she, out of school, stood to parents. Of course the principal and teachers could behave toward the students in ways which, if a policeman or a judge indulged in them, would be patently unconstitutional. The notion that the public school should constitute a microcosm of the adult social and constitutional order would have been laughable thirty years ago, if, indeed, you could have gotten anyone to entertain it.

The traditional assumptions with respect to children's rights began to change in the mid-1960s in an area in which change was probably justified—the juvenile courts. Developed in the early decades of this century, the juvenile justice system sought to provide an alternative to the regular criminal courts for minors in trouble. The idea was that while the juvenile court would operate with the authority of the state, including, if necessary, the power to involuntarily commit a minor to a state institution, the enterprise of the juvenile judge would be very different from assessing criminal responsibility and imposing sanctions. The juvenile judge's primary responsibility was the future welfare of the child. Whether or not a particular child had in fact pushed an old lady in the gutter in the course of stealing her purse was certainly a matter of interest to the judge in reaching a determination as to whether the child should be found "delinquent" and in deciding what rehabilitative strategy was best in that particular case. But the truth as to the attack on the old lady was merely one datum to be taken into consideration along with others in making a decision keyed to the welfare of the child. This was the theory of the matter. The reality, unfortunately, was different. It is beyond the scope of this book to explore the question of why the practice of juvenile courts diverged so far from the theory—why the disposition of cases came to resemble the proceedings of a little criminal court in which questions of "did he do it" and "what does he deserve as punishment" became central. Suffice it to say that by the time rights industry lawyers persuaded the Supreme Court to begin extending certain adult constitutional guarantees to children in the juvenile court setting, the ambience of these places had become in many cases more punitive than helping.

The breakthrough with respect to procedural rights for juveniles came in 1967 in the case of *In re Gault.* [41] Fifteen-year-old Gerald Gault had been found delinquent by an Arizona juvenile court and committed to the state industrial school until he reached the age of twenty-one. It was argued that he had been denied (1) the constitutional right to notice of the charges; (2) the right to counsel; (3) the right to confront and cross examine witnesses; (4) the

Destabilizing the Schools

privilege against self-incrimination; (5) the right to a transcript of the proceedings; and (6) the right to appellate review.* The Supreme Court agreed with the first four of these contentions. What was extended to the juvenile courts by Justice Fortes' opinion was not the full panoply of criminal defendants' rights, but rather some notion of procedural minima derived from adult practice. Not quite three years later, in the case of *In re Winship*[42] the constitutional safeguard of proof of guilt beyond reasonable doubt was added to the list of adult rights which necessarily obtained in juvenile proceedings. (Some jurisdictions had used the civil law standard of the balance of the evidence.)

What was disturbing about these decisions was not their likely impact on juvenile justice, but rather the suggestion which rapidly gained currency, that if new rights for children were justified in the juvenile courts, perhaps new rights should be found to obtain in other settings, principally the schools. Thus an innovation in response to the particular problems of one institutional sector, quickly migrated across boundaries with corrosive consequences.

In the year following *Gault,* the American Civil Liberties Union was issuing a widely influential pamphlet on *Academic Freedom in the Secondary Schools.*[43] The activists of the ACLU advanced a number of novel propositions under the familiar and respectable rubric of academic freedom. It was argued, for instance, that since education involves learning through mistakes, students must sometimes "be permitted to act in ways which are predictably unwise so long as the consequences of their acts are not dangerous to life and property, and do not seriously disrupt the academic process." That such criteria as danger to life and property, and danger of serious disruption, sound more like those properly invoked for calling out the army to quell civil disturbances than for regulating the behavior of teachers and principals toward pupils seems not to

---

*As a constitutional matter there is no such right. But if a state makes appellate review available to some convicted persons but not to others, this is vulnerable to challenge as a denial of equal protection of the laws.

have occured to the ACLU authors. They proceeded on to "a recognition that deviation from the opinions and standards deemed desirable by the faculty is not *ipso facto* a danger to the educational process." Clearly this is true with respect to some kinds of opinions, but if by "standards" it is meant standards of behavior, then the suggested principle becomes subversive of the authority of the school officials. Finally, the ACLU statement warned school officials they must accept the implications of the *Gault* decision (although made in a different context) and turn from their traditional ways of maintaining discipline to a due process model informed by the norms of the criminal trial. "Students and their schools should have the right to live under the principle of 'rule by law' as opposed to 'rule by personality'." To this end rules and regulations should be in writing, and students should have "the right to know the extent and limits of the faculty's authority [so they can figure out how to defy it safely?] and . . . the powers that are reserved for the students. . . ." Professor Gerald Grant, a sociologist at Syracuse University, has noted that students in Boston public schools now receive a twenty-five page document called "The Book." This "contains thousands of words on students' rights but only eleven lines of type referring to the responsibilities."⁴⁴

The process of extending adult constitutional guarantees into the schools gathered momentum in 1969 with the case of *Tinker* v. *Des Moines.* ⁴⁵ The Tinker children had been suspended from school for wearing black armbands in protest against their government's policies in Vietnam. School authorities judged that the excitement and tension which might be produced by the armbands could well interfere with the orderly processes of the school. The Tinker children, represented by a volunteer ACLU attorney, supported by Melvin Wulf from the ACLU national office and Charles Morgan, Jr., soon to be head of the Union's Washington office, sued to enjoin the suspensions on grounds that speech guarantees of the First Amendment protected their right to "symbolic speech" within the schools. Justice Fortas, writing for the Court, held that neither students nor teachers "shed their constitutional rights to freedom of speech or expression at the schoolhouse gates." And while First Amendment rights in school had to be accommodated to the "special characteristics of the school environment," the expression engaged in by the Tinker children was constitutionally protected absent a showing by the school authorities that some disruptive conduct was actually provoked or imminent. The judgment of the school officials as to what *might* result in friction or what *might* interfere with routine was brushed aside, and something akin to a clear-and-present-danger test for school administrators was substituted as a matter of federal constitutional law. The school authorities' "urgent wish to avoid controversy" was insufficient to support their action, and the case came to stand "for the proposition that all students regardless of age have a strong individual interest in expressing their views within the school community."[46] While not involving new "due process" procedures, *Tinker* was a clear disincentive to teachers and administrators in the imposition of discipline.

In 1975, the Supreme Court gave powerful direct impetus to the movement for legalization of school discipline. In *Goss* v. *Lopez*,[47] a closely divided Court ruled in favor of nine students temporarily suspended by their high school principal for spiking the punch at a school dance. Ohio law allowed principals to suspend for up to ten days without conducting a hearing, but the students claimed that a hearing was required by the Fourteenth Amendment, which forbids states to deprive persons of "life, liberty, or property without due process of law." For the majority justices in *Goss* even a temporary deprivation of the "entitlement" to education was encumbered by some form of due process requirement. Defenders of *Goss* have argued that the decision does not unduly burden school officials since it requires only a simple hearing and not a "trial-type" hearing with rights of cross-examination, counsel, and so on. This is less reassuring than it sounds. A "little bit of due process" is rather like a little bit of pregnancy—once the schools get into the business of writing codes, holding hearings, and legalizing discipline, a logical momentum drives them to ever more elaborate innovation in order to stay ahead of what will now (once the process is set in motion) be constant nit-picking and claims for "true fairness" by people whose real grievance is that they are being disciplined at all. *Mala fide* claims proliferate, and rights industry activists from the school board level to the Supreme Court aggressively press for more legalistic kinds of process than actually required by *Goss.* A local school board, faced by an attorney from the state civil liberties union or the "students' rights project" of a nearby law school, will come to view increased proceduralization as protection against future "trouble," with the result of inviting what was sought to be avoided.

This is just where in 1975 a second important public school decision is relevant. In *Wood* v. *Strickland*[48] the Court established the right of school children to bring actions for damages against individual school teachers and administrators under federal civil rights law—specifically, under Section 1983 of Title 42 of the United States Code. (This cause of action was originally created by Congress in the Ku Klux Klan Act of 1871.) In addition, the *Wood* majority narrowed the so-called "good faith immunity" which school officials had enjoyed traditionally from suits by students. This was now to be a "qualified" immunity in which the embattled board member or administrator must not only be convinced he is behaving correctly, but must not be in objective violation of the "unquestioned constitutional rights of his charges."

If the chilling impact of such a statement on the behavior of school officials in maintaining discipline is not sufficiently obvious, consider this. In the Spring of 1983[49] the Court held that defendants found liable in federal civil rights suits could be assessed *punitive damages* (in addition to actual damages) if it could be shown that their conduct was adjudged to be "reckless or callous." Thus a law passed in 1871, aimed at curbing the armed predation of the Klan in the chaotic, postbellum South, is now available to the children of the nation for use against their school teachers with the possibility of punitive damages.

Destabilizing the Schools

On Thursday, 11 November 1982, the *New York Times* carried the story of widespread disorder at the Thomas Jefferson High School in Brooklyn. "For more than two hours," the *Times* reported, "groups of students crowded together on Pennsylvania and Dumont Avenues outside the school, some throwing rocks and bottles and yelling 'Gestapo tactics' when the police tried to disperse them." What triggered this disturbance was a search for weapons in which security guards passed hand-held metal detectors around the bodies of entering students. While there were no arrests, about thirty weapons, mostly knives, were confiscated. Police were called to control the rampage in mid-morning. Some students told the *New York Times* reporter that "they had been touched by security officials during the search." And, the *Times* informed its readers, that "many of the students complained that their rights had been violated."[50] As Gerald Grant puts it:

In many urban schools today, hall guards [hired from security services] or quasi- or actual police officers are expected to maintain order in the halls and to some extent even in the classrooms. The presence of raw power indicates that authority has been lost. . . . Adult authority is increasingly defined by what will stand up in court. . . .[51]

A 1978 National Institute of Education report to Congress detailing the breakdown of order in schools found the problem most acute in large cities, acute in smaller cities, and vexing in decreasing degrees in suburbs and in rural areas.[52] (Can it be an accident that the larger cities have suffered the greatest white flight and also have the largest concentrations of rights industry lawyers?) Professor Jackson Toby, a Rutgers University criminologist, commenting on this report, identified the children's rights movement as one factor affecting the school crime problem. (Other factors were the large size of many American schools and the retention of so many students who, absent legal compulsion, would have dropped out before the statutory school-leaving age.) "A generation ago," Toby writes,

DISABLING AMERICA

it was possible for principals to rule schools autocratically, to suspend or expel students without much regard for procedural niceties. Injustices occurred; children were "pushed out" of schools because they were disliked by school officials. But this arbitrariness enabled school administrators to control the situation when real misbehavior occurred. Assaults on teachers were punished so swiftly that they were almost unthinkable; even disrespectful language was unusual. Today school officials are required to observe due process in handling student discipline. Hearings are necessary. Witnesses must confirm suspicions. Appeals are provided for. Greater democratization of the schools means that unruly students get less protection from their classmates.[53]

Does the rights industry accept any responsibility for the breakdown of discipline and order in so many public schools? Of course not. The Children's Defense Fund, a specialized and especially zany rights industry formation, argues that it is the arbitrariness and repressive tendencies of school officials which create student frustration in the first place and this breeds disorder and violence. There is violence and vandalism because there is not yet enough due process in schools. In the mid-1970s, children's rights advocates captured the staff of the Senate Subcommittee to Investigate Juvenile Delinquency, and the subcommittee's 1975 report contains the following conclusion:

At first glance it might appear that the expulsion, suspension, push out, force out and truancy phenomenon [sic], although certainly tragic for those involved, might also create a somewhat more orderly atmosphere for those remaining in the school as the result of the absence of youngsters evidently experiencing problems adjusting to the school environment. The opposite, however, appears to be the case. [One study] found that in schools where the average daily attendance was lower, the disruptions, violence and vandalism rates were higher. This may be explained by the fact that the vast majority of students who were voluntarily or compulsively [sic] excluded from schools do, in time, return to these schools. In many instances their frustrations and inadequacies which caused the absence in the first place have only been heightened by their exclusion and the school community will likely find itself a convenient and meaningful object of revenge.[54]

Beyond the appalling English of the paragraph, what in the world can it mean? Expulsion, a compulsory process, and truancy, a voluntary withdrawal, are lumped together. The conclusion seems to be that people who do not like school very much will not like it better for having been away from it for a while. A true test of "push out" would be to compare schools where it is possible to permanently remove troublemakers (by expulsion or transfer to specialized facilities), to schools where such children must be received back into the classroom after relatively short periods of time. But the very existence of the former kind of school has been made impossible by the due process revolution in public education.

A Utopian Agenda

What was really going on here? It is clear in retrospect that the enthusiasm for "due process" in schools, as with other rights industry adventurism, was driven by certain basic policy commitments which were usually, but not always, unarticulated.

The first of these commitments was to the idea that the traditional public school was a tyranny of the cynical and fearful middle aged over the uncorrupted, intuitively progressive young. Since it was unreasonable to impute real fault to "the kids," their misbehavior must result from evil inhering in the institutions in which they were held captive. Relax the institutional restrictions and inhibitions and the natural goodness and curiosity of the child would assert itself and the offender would be rehabilitated. Should this not happen in particular cases, well, "nothing else would have worked anyway," and the adults involved would at least be partially redeemed because they had "given the kid every chance."

The second commitment was to a "democratic model of the school."[55] The student's rights thrust was, in a sense, the rights industry contribution to the neo-Freudian and neo-Rousseauian "open classroom" movement of the late 1960s.[56] Telltale asides abound in opinions and in law review articles urging "bold initiatives" on judges. For instance, the editors of the *Harvard Law Review*, in praise of *Goss*, noted with greater accuracy than grace that the

> . . . intrinsic dignitary [sic] values underlying due process clause also underlie a particular understanding of the relationship between student and teacher. . . . Because the Court conceived school governance as properly democratic in form, it adopted the individualistic means of protecting rights so prevalent in the larger society.[57]

Professor Mark Yudof, of the University of Texas Law School, in one of the better balanced articles in the students' rights literature, saw the due process revolution in the schools as an inevitable and generally salutary response to the growing distrust of all authority in the 1960s and 1970s. While confessing to some concern over the extent of legalization and its possible overreliance on it, his prescription is unencouraging:

> Due process requirements must be counter-balanced or supplemented with less formal mechanisms—perhaps mediation or ombudsmen—to restore the openness and personal inter-action so necessary for trust.[58]

What this suggests is not a rebuilding of authority or an effort to restore the eroded capacities for judgment and discretion of teachers and administrators. Rather Yudof would substitute other essentially legalistic processes for the legalism that concerns him. In response one cannot do better than quote the recollection of Edward A. Wynne, a professor of education at the Chicago campus of the University of Illinois:

> Some of my older friends, raised in Chicago, have sometimes asked me, "What has happened to the tough teachers of my youth? The legendary tiny old maids who could tongue-lash adolescent giants into humble submission?" And, my friends then go on to say, "The legends were real. I saw them in operation when I was a child, and they won fear and respect."

Destabilizing the Schools

My answer is that those old maids felt sure that: (1) they would be backed up by the "power structure"; (2) their students, despite their temporary recalcitrance, really wanted to complete school; and (3) if their students did not shape up, they would be quickly expelled. As a result, the students were relatively submissive, the teachers comfortable with their power, and few expulsions—and no armed guards were necessary. In sum, it is not so much the attitudes of students that have changed but those of adults, and the students have responded in a predictable fashion.[59]

From relative moderates such as Professor Yudof to the radicals of the Children's Defense Fund, to the best and the brightest at the *Harvard Law Review,* what one encounters beyond the legal rhetoric is a state of mind; you cannot argue with a state of mind, but you can point out its nature and its portent.

The disappointing contemporary performance of American public education,[60] contrary to the orthodoxy of the 1970s, has almost nothing to do with money and almost everything to do with the erosion of the moral authority of teachers, administrators, and parents. Trendy egalitarianism, abandonment of the fundamental subjects in pursuit of fashionable ephemera, and the inferior educations received by so many teachers in their universities, have all contributed to this erosion; but the contribution of the rights industry, operating through the potent technical language of the "law" and the "constitution," was also significant. The wrong headed and sometimes vindictive pursuit of racial balance and the utopian conception of children's rights were surely factors in the decisions made by many thousands of people like Ruby Bridges Hall. Mrs. Hall, who as a girl risked rocks and insults to integrate the William Franz Elementary School in New Orleans in 1960, gave up on public education. "My son went to the school that I started at," she said, "and I don't like to put down public schools, but he wasn't really learning the way he should have." And so, "I put him in a Catholic school and he was so far behind he had to be tutored for a year." Now all Mrs. Hall's children are in parochial schools.[61]

CHAPTER 4

Enfeebling Law Enforcement

IN no other area of American life has the impact of the rights industry been more disabling than on the interlocking institutions of the law enforcement system. A full account of the mischief worked on law enforcement over the past two decades in the name of civil liberties would be a life's work, not a chapter. Here I shall focus on just one aspect of law enforcement—the criminal trial. And with respect to the trial, only one disabling initiative will be discussed. Bear in mind this is one example from several dozen that could have been chosen.

The extent to which the formal criminal justice system of society (police, courts, prisons) can really do much about controlling crime is a matter of debate among scholars. While the dynamics of crime rates are only beginning to be understood, it is now fairly clear that basic social factors such as the size of the youth cohort relative to the rest of the population, rural to urban migrations, and the extent to which nongovernmental institutions (families, churches, and neighborhood groups) operate effectively and self-confidently on the basis of an accepted morality to discourage deviance, have greater impact on crime rates than the numbers of police, their level of professionalism, or whether judges are tough or permissive. It may well be true that what Thomas Hardy called "mighty necessitating forces" are the most potent determinants of order in a society.[1] But the fact remains that the law enforcement system is, in a liberal society, the only instrument available to the community to use directly to control crime and disorder. We do not tell people where to live and when to move; we understand techniques of birth control but have little control, acting through government, over birth rates—they go up and down and we try to figure out what has happened decades after the fact. And while we should be able to stop ourselves from doing things positively destructive of church institutions, families, and public schools, and so on, it is quite beyond the competence of government to revivify (or, to use Bill Buckley's favorite word, "reprisinate") the inherited morality of a society and to make people once again confident in their adherence to and personal enforcement of that code. Certainly we can and should do things to relieve the sufferings of the poor and provide avenues for self-help to those euphemistically referred to as "the less advantaged members of society." But recent American experience has amply demonstrated that social welfare initiatives, however justified on humanitarian grounds, have no impact as crime control strategies—if anything, the reverse.[2] While it can be argued that the impact of the formal law enforcement system on crime and disorder will be marginal, only an obscurantist few deny that impact at all.[3]

Law enforcement is what a liberal society *has.* It must use what it has in a purposeful fashion to contain crime and disorder within levels tolerable to the community. It is certainly true that we do not have high levels of crime and disorder because law enforcement is weak, but weak law enforcement will make crime and disorder more difficult to live with and ultimately corrode the bonds of trust between people and government.[4] Weak law enforcement will leave the community both psychologically and physically vulnerable to a degree beyond that decreed by demographic, economic, and social forces over which we (properly) have little control. The crime control benefits to be derived from the law enforcement systems working more (rather than less) well may be marginal, but since when, especially in the chancey and little understood inter-workings of huge pluralistic societies, are marginal benefits to be scorned?

Criminal Trials as an Endangered Species

The criminal trial is at the heart of the law enforcement system. But the trial is in sorry state today. It has become so bloated through procedural elaboration and innovation that only a small minority of those arrested and charged with serious crimes can be afforded the benefit and subjected to the discipline of trial by jury. Professor John H. Langbein, of the University of Chicago Law School, puts it this way:

> In our day, jury trial continues to occupy its central place both in the formal law and in the mythology of the law. The Constitution has not changed, the courts pretend to enforce the defendant's right to jury trial, and television transmits a steady flow of dramas in which a courtroom contest for the verdict of the jury leads inexorably to the disclosure of the true culprit. In truth, criminal jury trial has largely disappeared in America. The criminal justice system now disposes of virtually all cases of serious crime through plea bargaining. In major cities between 95 and 99% of felony convictions are by plea. This non-trial procedure has become the ordinary dispositive procedure of American law.[5]

It is a powerful comment on the extent of disarray and demoralization among law enforcement professionals and students of their work that there has arisen a literature arguing, in effect, that "plea bargaining is good for you." As if by literary massage a pathology could be transformed into, if not a positive benefit, at least something with which we must live because the system is so deeply entrenched.[6] At the risk of laboring the obvious, plea bargaining is (1) unjust to society because pleas are "copped" to relatively trivial offenses when it is morally certain that most who do so are guilty of far more serious crimes (for which some, at least, might be convicted if more trials could be afforded); (2) unjust to the occasional but very important innocent who is persuaded to admit guilt to a minor crime he did not commit rather than risk mistaken conviction for a more serious crime at trial; and (3) psychologically corrosive and degrading for all who participate in it—attorneys, accused, and judge. The state is not "put to its proof" as the theory of the adversary system presumes it will be, and for the accused the process becomes a sordid crapshoot (albeit with dice loaded in his favor) rather than a solemn accounting before the community of his degree of guilt or his innocence. It is a business only Fagan could warm to.

In one of the better recent textbooks for law students on criminal procedure,[7] the authors devote a 200-page chapter to plea bargaining. This allocation of space is clearly justified given the centrality of plea bargaining in the contemporary criminal justice process. The chapter is learned, informative, and careful. In this sense it is a model textbook presentation; what is so shocking about it is the utter absence of a sense of outrage. Ample data are presented on the increased "tariff" paid by defendants who are so unwise as to reject a proffered plea and go to trial.[8] And since these rejections are in large part based on an assessment by the defendant that the proferred plea is not "good" (that is, low enough), one is certainly justified in concluding that the tariffs avoided by those defendants accepting pleas that are considered good enough (low enough) would be even higher.

When the reader finally reaches a heading for "on the nose" guilty pleas he might be momentarily encouraged—are these defendants pleading guilty to the charge that actually describes their conduct? Yes, but hope is quickly dashed. The "on the nose plea" is revealed to be one in return for a promise of leniency at sentencing, that is, a promise of probation or a specified short term. If the authors are disturbed by the injustice of all of this they are successful in concealing it. Indeed, they conclude that "the most troublesome problem" with plea bargaining is "the possibility that an innocent defendant may plead guilty because of fear that he will be sentenced more harshly if he is convicted after trial. . . ."[9] Clearly this is a problem, but can it be called the most important problem when only a few pages later the authors blandly note:

> It is equally common for a plea bargaining for reduced charges to be motivated by the . . . goal of [maximizing] the judge's sentencing discretion. In this type of agreement the defendant pleads guilty to a lesser charge than is warranted by the facts, not to reduce the potential maximum sentence, but to avoid a legislatively mandated minimum sentence or a legislative directive precluding the availability of probation.[10]

Let us be clear about what is being said here. It is "common" for prosecutors and judges to connive in a system whereby the judgment of the people's elected representatives as to minimum sanctions for certain sorts of offenses is subverted by inducing guilty pleas to lesser offenses because otherwise the court will not be able to "deal" on sentencing.

The two most powerful arguments offered in defense of the system of plea bargaining (to the credit of the authors previously quoted they do not endorse these) are: (1) the system saves the society the money and trouble that would be involved in giving trials ("after all, we simply don't have the resources"); and (2) that if probation or much shorter sentences than actually prescribed for the conduct at issue were not routinely used, the prison population would quickly outstrip the already seriously overcrowded American penitentiaries. These arguments are as correct as they are contemptible. Even if one assumes (correctly in some cases) that American criminal codes specify unrealistically long sentences, the remedy is to confront society, through the legislature, with the alternatives. Making the system "work" by winks and sharp practice can only be justified as a short-term expedient, certainly not as an institutionalized but never legitimized alternative to the process society anciently established and, on the whole, assumes is functioning.

This brief discussion of plea bargaining only scratches the surface. It is included here as a necessary step in the argument that encumbering the truth-finding function of the criminal trial with more and more procedural strictures is bad policy. It is bad policy precisely because it leads to greater reliance on plea bargaining. Furthermore, when trials become more expensive and the proof of guilt more difficult, the prosecutor's hand is thereby weakened in the bargaining process and the deals which he must offer are necessarily more attractive—easier on the accused. Here is the central paradox of American criminal justice today. The trial is a statistical rarity, but its byzantine complexity and cost resonate throughout the entire criminal justice process rebounding to the advantage of defendants and the disadvantage of society at almost every point. That is why it is still important to consider what has happened to the criminal trial and ponder its reform.

From *Brown* to *Miranda*

Of all the procedural innovations of recent years, none is quite so problematical as the broad exclusionary rule, purportedly based on the Fifth and Sixth Amendments to the Constitution, which governs statements made to the police by criminal suspects. This is not because it detracts more grievously than other innovations from the truth-finding function of the trial (a case can be made that the exclusionary rule covering improperly obtained physical items results in a greater amount of otherwise reliable evidence going down the drain), but because the intellectual rationale for the prevailing approach to suspects' statements is so weak.

In a society which uses the adversary proceeding, at least nominally, as the method of determining guilt or innocence, the basic (not the *only,* but the *primary*) principle with respect to admissibility of evidence should be clear. It was admirably stated, for instance, in the report of the British Criminal Law Revision Committee in 1972. This committee struggled with procedural hypertrophy in the British system, which had progressed to a lesser degree than in the American, but was still worrisome.

> Since the object of a criminal trial should be to find out if the accused is guilty, it follows that ideally all evidence should be admissible which is relevant in the sense that it tends to render probable the existence or non-existence of any fact on which the question of guilt or innocence depends.[11]

The two-pronged canon for the admissibility of evidence at trial should test for relevance and reliability. If proffered testimony or physical evidence fails to satisfy either of these requirements, it is excluded; if not (subject to a minimum of narrowly drawn, legislatively created exceptions), it should be admitted.*

There was a time, and not so very long ago at that, when this was the general approach of American courts to admissibility. This was the approach of Blackstone in his *Common Law of England,* [12] the basic text for the training of lawyers in America in the formative period and for decades thereafter.** And according to

---

*The history of the various sorts of evidentiary exclusions and "privileges" which have been recognized at one time or another in Anglo-American jurisdictions— wife-husband testimony, illegally seized physical evidence, and so on—is long and tangled. And the principle I am suggesting has not been followed in recent decades by either English or American courts. Nonetheless, I think it commends itself. Where the concern is reliability, this goes to the integrity of the judicial process and judicial initiative in rule making is proper. Where the concern is to discourage certain sorts of police conduct or to provide for more humane treatment of suspects, defendants, or witnesses these are matters of more general policy which the community should decide through normal representative processes.

**The transplanted English understandings did, of course, include the prohibition on forcing persons (historically by torture) to "accuse themselves" of crimes.

Enfeebling Law Enforcement

John Henry Wigmore, author of the classic *Treatise on Evidence,* which Felix Frankfurter called "unrivaled as the greatest treatise on any single topic of the law," relevance and reliability were the concepts around which all the rest of the American law of evidence was organized. In a telling passage Wigmore wrote:

> Does the illegal source of a piece of evidence taint it so as to exclude it, when offered by the party who has shared in the illegality? . . . [A]n employer may perhaps suitably interrupt the course of his business to deliver a homily to his office boys on the evils of gambling or the rewards of industry. But a judge does not hold court in a streetcar to do summary justice upon a fellow passenger who fraudulently evades the payment of his fare; and, upon the same principles, he does not attempt, in the course of specific litigation, to investigate and punish all offenses which incidentally cross the path of that litigation. Such a practice might be consistent with the primitive system of justice under an Arabian sheikh: but does not comport with our own system of law.[13]

Today all this is changed, and while the story of that change with respect to physical evidence is not our concern here, it is worth briefly reviewing how the change came about with respect to the admissibility into evidence of incriminating statements made by criminal suspects to the police.

In the beginning, and throughout most of our history since independence from England, the procedural guarantees protecting

---

But this, as we shall see, was a limitation on the power of the court to compel testimony under oath, not a limitation on the admissibility of evidence already available as a result of statements made by an accused to those who had effected his arrest—as long as these statements were voluntary and therefore reliable. In his otherwise admirable history of the privilege against self-incrimination, Leonard W. Levy is carried to excess in concluding that the framers of the Fifth Amendment intended to establish the principle that "in a free society . . . the determination of guilt or innocence by just procedures, in which the accused made no unwilling contribution, was more important than punishing the guilty." *The Origins of the Fifth Amendment: The Right Against Self-Incrimination* (New York: Oxford University Press, 1968). That by "unwilling" Levy meant something more than the common law concept of "voluntary" is clear from the specific approval he gives to *Miranda* on page 439. A sounder conclusion is that "the constitutional protection was originally intended only to prevent return to the hated practice of compelling a person, in a criminal proceeding directed against him, to swear against himself." See McNaughton at Note 51 *infra,* p. 274.

defendants at criminal trials were matters for the states to decide for themselves. Almost all had provisions in their constitutions that persons not be forced to be witnesses against themselves, and the meaning and scope of these guarantees were decided upon by state courts. With respect to the protection against compulsory self-incrimination secured in federal courts by the Fifth Amendment to the Constitution, the traditional doctrine was expressed in 1908 in *Twining* v. *New Jersey*. [14] The Court held, following Chief Justice John Marshall's classic disposition of the underlying issue *Barron* v. *Baltimore* in 1833, [15] that the Fifth Amendment provision did not apply to the courts of the states. The Fourteenth Amendment, ratified in 1868, did apply to the states and forbade deprivation of life, liberty, and property without "due process of law." From 1868 until the 1960s (the decade of the "incorporation" revolution), it was settled that the Fourteenth Amendment altered the original division of criminal justice responsibility between the states and the nation only to the extent that states could not, in the words of Chief Justice Charles Evans Hughes, adopt a procedure which "offends some principle of justice so rooted in the tradition and conscience of our people as to be ranked as fundamental." [16] There were certain principles of core due process fairness, deeply embedded in the Anglo-American legal tradition, that could not be flouted—but the protection against compulsory self-incrimination as interpreted by federal courts was not one of them.

In *Brown* v. *Mississippi*, [17] in 1936, the Court considered a state conviction for murder obtained on the basis of an inculpatory statement extracted from defendants after vicious and repeated beatings. Chief Justice Hughes quite properly held this violated fundamental fairness and stressed the unreliable nature of the evidence contained in such coerced statements. The behavior of the state officers was indefensible, the reliability of the evidence was in question, and the weight of Anglo-American tradition was on the side of the Court. There was nothing in Hughes' short opinion to suggest that *Brown* was anything more than a rare federal intervention against a particularly distasteful instance of state misbehavior.

What Mississippi had done was unconstitutional under the due process clause of the Fourteenth Amendment, not because of compelled self-incrimination, but because of barbarism and the attendant risk of false conviction.

For almost thirty years the uses made by the Supreme Court of the *Brown* precedent were reasonable. By this approach the traditional common law approach to inculpatory statements—ascertaining whether the statement had been made voluntarily or coerced by torture, threat, deception or extreme psychological pressure—was established as an element of core due process fairness. Awkwardly but accurately known as the "voluntariness" approach, it required judges to examine the "totality of circumstances" surrounding an interrogation and the making of a contested statement to determine whether the will of the suspect has been "overborn."

In its origins in Anglo-American law the voluntariness test was concerned only with the reliability of the proffered statement. As it evolved through U.S. Supreme Court decisions, however, coordinate considerations, such as the inhumanity of employing those extremes of pressure or trickery calculated to break a man's will, and a policy of discouraging police resort to such techniques (prophylaxis), were coupled with the risk of unreliability in explaining the test. Some commentators (notably Yale Kamisar, to be discussed in detail later) hold that in later voluntariness cases the Court deemphasized reliability as a justification of the approach. This is mistaken and rests on an overreading of a few opinions, notably in *Rogers* v. *Richmond.*[18] Here Justice Frankfurter wrote that the truth of a statement did not, in and of itself, determine voluntariness. It is perfectly possible to conceive of the suspect's will being overborn by extreme pressure or trickery, *and* the suspect's telling the truth which can then be independently validated. It is the general risk of unreliability in such circumstances which justified the approach. The test is not met just because the truth happened to be screwed out of someone in a particular instance. This is a very different thing from saying that a concern for reliability is no longer a pillar of the test. It is true that in the half dozen years or so before abandoning it, the Warren Court majority was applying the voluntariness test in some curiously tender-minded ways (see *Spano* v. *New York*[19]). But the theory of the approach remained intact, drawing legitimacy from its common law roots, until the end of 1966. Certainly there were differing strands or versions of the voluntariness approach. But with all these differences of emphasis between different justices and successive majorities, the voluntariness approach was susceptible to coherent explanations as an accommodation of conflicting social interests and values—something which cannot be said of what succeeded it.

Early post-*Brown* cases, such as *Chambers* v. *Florida*, [20] held that the will could be overborne even where the evidence of physical threat was ambiguous, as long as an atmosphere of physical threat pervaded the questioning. In *Ashcraft* v. *Tennessee*, [21] the Court held that questioning for an extended period of time (thirty-six hours) was "inherently coercive" and the incriminating statement therefore involuntary. Here, however, there was dissent—from Justice Robert H. Jackson.

In what even critics admit is an important essay on the problems of police interrogation, Justice Jackson suggested that Justice Black, who wrote for the Court, was giving the voluntariness test an unwarranted twist. Jackson insisted that under prior decisions, notably *Lisemba* v. *California*, [22] the question of voluntariness turned on whether, based upon an examination of the whole of the evidence as to the questioning, it could be concluded that the will of the suspect had been overborne. The fatal unfairness inhered in the overbearing of the will with the accompanying risk of unreliability. Jackson was concerned about the majority's characterization of one event (the thirty-six hour session) as "inherently coercive"—during an investigative process which ran over four days. In his view the totality of circumstances revealed in the record needed to be assessed—including factors such as the mental state and capability of the suspect.

Jackson reminded his brethren of the obvious: that all interrogation by the police was inherently coercive. To bring a person to a police station and deprive him of his liberty for one hour was coercive. But surely, Jackson argued, this could not be the touchstone of voluntariness. In common law, he pointed out, "the term 'voluntary' confession does not mean voluntary in the sense of a confession to a priest merely to rid one's soul of guilt." On the contrary, in criminal cases voluntary confessions "are the product of calculations of a different order, and usually proceed from a belief that further denial is useless and perhaps prejudicial." To begin to talk about inherent coerciveness in a situation that was by definition coerceive suggested to Jackson the distressing possibility of police interrogation being foreclosed altogether—unless the Court drew back from the unsound premise that Black had articulated. "Does the Constitution," Jackson asked, "prohibit use of all confessions made after arrest because questioning, while one is deprived of freedom, is 'inherently coercive'?" While noting that the majority did not quite say that, Jackson nonetheless concluded that Black was "moving far and fast in that direction," and that while the length of an interrogation should be one fact bearing heavily on the question of whether the statement produced was legally voluntary, it was a very different thing to hold such a statement inadmissible simply because of the time taken getting it. The voluntariness approach would cease to be a satisfactory balance of conflicting social interests if it focused solely on the inherently unpleasant and stressful nature of interrogation in detention.

Jackson's concern with the direction in which the voluntariness test was being taken flared again in his concurrence in 1949 in the case of *Watts* v. *Indiana.* [23] Watts was held for a week, much of the time in a bare cell, and there were long periods of interrogation—several lasting past midnight. Franklin H. Williams and Thurgood Marshall of the NAACP represented Watts before the Supreme Court. While voting to overturn Watts' conviction, Jackson, in a separate opinion, asked a series of questions about interrogation which seemed almost to anticipate the step the Court would take in 1966.

Jackson began by noting that in *Watts* the police were confronted with a brutal murder which they were "under the highest duty to solve." There were no witnesses; the only positive knowledge on which a solution could be based was information possessed by the killer. There were reasonable grounds to suspect an individual, but insufficient evidence to charge him with guilt. The choice was either interrogation or writing off the crime as insoluble and letting the suspect go his way.

But what happened to Watts was worrisome. He had been confined for six days without being told of his right to consult counsel. He had been confined in an unfurnished cell and questioned at night (but not all night) by teams of detectives. Several times during the day, he was driven around town and asked if he recognized particular locations. Jackson noted that to "subject one without counsel to questioning which may and is intended to convict him, is a real peril to individual freedom." Yet to "bring in a lawyer means a real peril to the solution of the crime, because, under our adversary system, [the lawyer] deems that his sole duty is to protect his client—guilty or innocent—and that in such capacity he owes no duty whatever to help society solve its crime problem." Then Jackson went to the heart of the matter. What view should one take of the claims of a person suspected of crime as against the claims of the community? "Is it his right to have a judgment on the facts, or is it his right to have a judgment based on only such evidence as he cannot conceal from the authorities, who cannot compel him to testify in court and also cannot question him before?" Jackson concluded that our system was veering "close to the latter," and that this was a departure from the traditional Anglo-American approach which was not hostile to confessions as evidence.

Truth-finding and trustworthiness must be served along with humaneness, and Jackson reminded the Court that often a statement, when obtained, "supplies ways of verifying its trustworthiness." If the "ultimate quest in a criminal trial is the truth and if the circumstnaces indicate no violence or threats of it, should society be deprived of the suspect's help in solving a crime merely because he was confined when questioned and uncounseled?"

While this question was asked in the context of an argument for limiting the voluntariness approach to serious police abuses, it survives as a dagger pointed at the heart of *Miranda* v. *Arizona*.[24] It was a decision like *Miranda,* in 1966, that Jackson had feared almost twenty years earlier. For *Miranda* turned its back on all that had happened since *Brown* v. *Mississippi*— and, indeed, on over 200 years of Anglo-American common-law tradition.

In 1964, in the case of *Malloy* v. *Hogan,*[25] the Supreme Court had extended the protection against self-incrimination provided by the Fifth Amendment of the federal Constitution to acts of the states (effectively overturning *Twining* v. *New Jersey*). This altered the technical landscape, for thereafter the Court was no longer effectively restricted to considering what was fundamentally unfair under the Fourteenth Amendment but could now, if a majority willed it, put itself in the position of asking whether state practices violated the specific prohibition of the Fifth Amendment.

The *Miranda* Court did just that, extending the federal Fifth Amendment into the detective squad room. Now the suspect, once in "custody," could only be questioned after he had been advised of his newly minted federal constitutional right to remain silent, his Sixth Amendment right to consult counsel before questioning and to have counsel present during questioning, and his right under Supreme Court interpretations of the Sixth Amendment (now also applicable to the states) to have counsel appointed if he should be unable to afford a lawyer. The suspect must further be advised that if he chooses to waive his rights and make any statement, the statement may be introduced as evidence against him. These are the elements of the now familiar *"Miranda* warning."

The ACLU *amicus curiae* brief in *Miranda* urged that it be constitutionally required that counsel be present in order for there to be an effective waiver of rights, on the theory that the suspect needs counsel to waive, *inter alia,* the right to counsel. While this was not accepted by the majority, it was about the only thing that was not accepted. As one commentator put it, the ACLU brief presents "a conceptual, legal and structural formulation that is practically identical to the majority opinion—even as to use of language in various passages of the opinion."[26]

Furthermore, while Chief Justice Warren's opinion for the Court in *Miranda* is far from a model in clarity, it is certain that the burden of showing that a suspect had willingly and knowingly waived his rights, and submitted to questioning without any inducement or encouragement or pressure to make a statement, rests squarely on the police. If they cannot show willing and intelligent waiver, then the confession will be excluded even though it may be voluntary under prior understandings. This is the crux of the matter. *Miranda* excludes confessions which are, for some reason, "*Miranda*-imperfect." The constable blunders, and it does not matter whether the blunder is large or small. This makes questions of common-law voluntariness and likely reliability altogether beside the point. (Unless, that is, one is prepared to take seriously the argument that all statements made in the "inherently coercive" custodial situation are *ipso facto* suspect for reliability.)

The point of the new rules, as Justice John Marshall Harlan noted in his dissent in *Miranda,* "is to negate all pressures, to reinforce the nervous or ignorant suspect, and ultimately to discourage any confessions at all." The voluntariness approach, Harlan argued, was "an elaborate, sophisticated, and sensitive approach to admissibility of confessions." By contrast, the approach of *Miranda* is highly formalistic (not to say simplistic), abandoning any attempt at striking case by case balances between the interests of society in finding the truth and the humane treatment of criminal suspects. The *Miranda* majority extended such sweeping federal constitutional rights into the station house that all other considerations about what properly goes on there pale into insignificance. This was truly to convey to the criminal suspect the right to have a judgment based "only on such evidence as he cannot conceal from the authorities, who cannot compel him to testify in court and also cannot question him before."

And the pursuit of perfect "fairness" continues.* Today we find rights industry spokesmen laboring to extend the formalism of *Miranda* from custodial interrogation to early, on-the-scene questioning of people who might develop into suspects. There are still some places where cops might ask questions of people who have not been sufficiently discouraged from answering!

Leader of the Mirandistas

On what foundation does such hostility to police interrogation of criminal suspects rest? While there is an unavoidable risk of distortion involved in attempting to trace the intellectual gestation of a new rule of constitutional law through the activity of one man, in the matter of the demise of the voluntariness approach and its replacement with *Miranda,* the risk is worth running. Professor

*It is worth a note in passing that we are on our way to producing a generation of lawyers who will be only dimly aware that *Miranda* was a radical departure from a traditional approach to treatment of incriminating statements. Most law school casebooks today *begin* the section on interrogation with *Miranda.* They proceed to invite students to consider problems of *"Miranda* application"—what constitutes custody? what constitutes interrogation? and so on. I am not suggesting that there is anything sinister or conspiratorial about this. *Miranda* is the law; applying *Miranda* will be the business of the young lawyers; with more material to cover each year, teachers of constitutional law can hardly afford extended discussions of the historical evolution of legal principles. But beginning with *Miranda* means that the students do not consider the terribly important choice of public policy that was involved in that departure. Of the leading books on criminal procedure, only one provides anything like an adequate discussion of the voluntariness approach—the exception is Inbau, Thompson, and Zagel, *Criminal Law and Criminal Procedure,* (Mineola, N.Y.: Foundation Press, 1979) which is generally considered to be the "Tory" book in the field. That textbooks prepared for law students fail to include much of a discussion of voluntariness is regrettable, but understandable. It is more troubling that one of the leading textbooks for undergraduates, Ducat and Chase, *Constitutional Interpretation,* 3rd ed. (St. Paul, Minn.: West Publishing Co., 1983), simply provides *Miranda* and leaves the student in the dark as to where it came from and what choices it embodies.

Yale Kamisar of the University of Michigan Law School is a leading legal intellectual. His extensive and impassioned writing on the evils of police interrogation before *Miranda* were more influential than any other texts in focusing the attention of the law schools, the civil libertarian interest groups, and ultimately judges and justices on what he called the "gatehouse" to the criminal justice process—the police station, and more specifically the detective squad room, where sustained questioning of criminal suspects characteristically takes place.

Certainly Kamisar was not alone in attacking the voluntariness approach. In a passage from his collected works on the subject of confessions, which is by way of being his memoir of his role in the controversy, Kamisar credits Bernard Weisberg as a prime mover. Weisberg was a volunteer ACLU lawyer in Chicago who engaged in a personal crusade against police interrogation and doubted that distinctions could be drawn in the real world between reasonable police questioning and unfair coercive tactics.[27] (Weisberg was later to argue for Danny Escobedo before the Supreme Court in the case that paved the way for *Miranda*.) But Kamisar became so prominent in the struggle, and his writings were so sustained and detailed, that it is fair to confront the issue by confronting him.

In his "memoir" Kamisar recalls that "the root from which I drew the juices of my indignation" was the tape recording of the six-hour interrogation in the 1962 *Biron* case.[28] The disclosure is fascinating. Kamisar notes that in *Biron,* a Minnesota murder case,[29] interrogation did not constitute a wrenching from the accused of evidence, nor were there any third-degree horrors. It was an interrogation which, by the judicial standards of the day, was fair and reasonable. So what horrified Kamisar? That the questioning was insistent. That Biron's interrogators "cajoled and nagged him to confess." At several points Biron appeared to become confused; despite this the police did not stop, but conveyed to him by the pattern of their questioning the message "confess now or it will be so much the worse for you later."[30]

I have not listened to the *Biron* tape. But taking Kamisar's characterization at face value, his reaction can only be described as a trifle precious. Was the length of the interrogation excessive? Apparently not. Do "cajoling" and "nagging" rise to the level of an outrage, demanding new constitutional law? Apparently so. Kamisar concludes that one cannot listen to the tape without wondering "whatever happened to the privilege against self-incrimination . . . ?"[31] Yet it cannot be repeated too often that the issue in this period (the early 1960s) was not whether or not to inform the individual of a right which everyone agreed existed, but what right should be considered to exist. What Kamisar must be saying is that the inhumanity revealed in the *Biron* tape was such as to imperatively require that the Fifth Amendment of the federal Constitution, which had not been held to apply to the states at all until 1964,[32] should be extended to the questioning of detainees by the police. But given the magnitude of the innovation involved, it is fair to ask whether something more than "nagging," "cajoling," and telling the suspect that it would be better if he confessed should not be required.

This brings us to the core of Kamisar's position. The atmosphere of the police station house is inherently coercive; the ambiance is profoundly unsettling to the suspect; sustained questioning that seeks to expose contradictions in the suspect's story is necessarily a stressful proceeding. It may be time consuming. Information which has been proffered has to be checked, persons mentioned must be found and interviewed, policemen come on and go off shifts. Many criminal suspects will be lying, and the efforts to break through the often poorly constructed tissue of lies will involve "psychological tricks," such as suggesting a possible resolution of an inconsistency which may prompt the suspect to invent new and even more vulnerable lies, or sympathetically asking for just a bit more detail, or suddenly turning on the subject and coldly accusing him of lying. These same "psychological tricks" are used by us all in dealing with persons whom we suspect of dissembling. For Kamisar, however, subjecting a criminal suspect to this process in the police station is profoundly inhumane and unfair. We are

DISABLING AMERICA

offered no arguments as to why this is so—it is simply asserted as an intuition with which decent persons may not disagree.

How can it make sense, Kamisar asks, to speak of statements that come out of such a sustained process of nagging and cajoling as voluntary?—there has been pressure! And indeed there has. But most of the important decisions people make are pressured to one degree or another, sometimes severely so, and we do not think that this deprives them of their voluntary character.* What Kamisar has done is to conflate the concepts of voluntariness and spontaneity. No pressure to tell the truth is to be tolerated. While I cannot discover that Kamisar agrees with the tiny band who oppose use of confessions on the principle that it is evil *per se* to convict a person on anything but altogether extrinsic evidence, the professor's loathing of any suasion or encouragement by the interrogator is a pure passion.

Now we are entitled to ask, with a passion matching Kamisar's, why in the world the community should bind itself to a canon of pure spontaneity with respect to police questioning? There are profound social interests at stake and they require more than lip service. While no one advocates a return to the rack and the screw (or even the thirty-six-hour third degree) a certain amount of pressure, stress, and "nagging" does not seem an unreasonable burden for the community to impose on persons being questioned by the police in connection with serious crimes. From a common-sensical point of view, it is the passion for pure spontaneity that seems eccentric. Certainly if it is to be adopted it should be on the basis of clear arguments—not a prissy recoiling from the reality of

*One of the more exotic criticisms of voluntariness was that it implicitly violated the presumption of innocence. By allowing some persistence and pressure in interrogation it assumed that suspects were guilty and dissembling—otherwise why countenance any pressured questioning? This misunderstands the presumption of innocence. That principle enjoins criminal conviction only after the state has born its burden of proving every element of a criminal offense beyond reasonable doubt. It is not a counsel of foolhardiness. Police handcuff or hammerlock potentially dangerous arrestees and question when their suspicions are aroused rather than at random; none of this sensible, prudential behavior lessens the state's ultimate burden of proof.

the station house where the blood and the sweat are still fresh, and the cops understand that unless they can obtain some information from the suspect before he has a chance to gather his wits and work out his story (or have it fabricated by counsel), the possibility of fixing responsibility may be lost.

How do Kamisar's arguments stand up? It is convenient to examine them under three headings: the historical argument; the critique of voluntariness; and the response to objections based on practicality and justice.

1. *The Historical Argument.* In his dissenting opinion in *Miranda,* Justice Byron White stated that the application of the privilege against self-incrimination to police interrogation "has no significant support in the history of the privilege or in the language of the Fifth Amendment".

As to the language of the amendment there is, of course, specific reference to criminal proceedings, and, as a technical matter, there is no criminal proceeding underway in the station house. But Kamisar is quick to point out that the privilege had already been extended from criminal proceedings narrowly understood to legislative hearings, and that even Wigmore, opposed as he was to extensions of the privilege, recognized that it reached certain kinds of administrative hearings.[33] Since the criminal suspect can effectively damage his prospects of ultimate escape by statements made in the course of police questioning, he is genuinely "at risk," and the distinction between forbidden interrogation (when a "proceeding" is underway) and permissible police interrogation is artificial.

This argument has force, although it conveniently overlooks the matters of oath and perjury. Historically, one of the humane concerns underlying the privilege was distaste for squeezing individuals between the likelihood of ensuring punishment for their crimes if they told the truth and risk of punishment for perjury if they lied.[34] In this sense the station house is not just like the courtroom (or the legislative hearing room or those administrative hearings that Wigmore had in mind where sworn testimony is taken). Not all risks are equal and not all kinds of pressure are equally distasteful. It is also worth noting that the architects of the privilege against self-incrimination took seriously the notion of the immortality of the soul. Oaths had, for them, a significance almost forgotten in our time. To force choice between eternal damnation and furnishing evidence for ones own criminal conviction was a rather more serious matter than persistent and even "nagging" questioning without oath.

Kamisar "does not contend" the implications of history "dictate that the privilege apply to the police station, only that they permit it."[35] But this permissive history cannot be recent history; recent history is voluntariness. Kamisar concedes this.[36] What, then, does one find if "one travels back far enough?"

One finds, Kamisar argues, a development in English legal history, stretching roughly from the mid-seventeenth to the mid-nineteenth century (and reflected in America), whereby the practice of judicial magistrates (usually justices of the peace) interrogating arrestees and later attesting to their statements at trial, was abandoned. It was abandoned on the general ground that judicial interrogation, even though the arrestees were not questioned under oath, breached the privilege against self-incrimination. So far so good.

Kamisar then argues that police interrogation is simply the functional analogue to the now proscribed judicial interrogation—and if it was wrong for the justices of the peace to do it, it must be equally wrong for the police to do it. In reaching this conclusion Kamisar relies heavily on law review articles by Paul Kauper of the University of Michigan Law School[37] and Edmund M. Morgan of the Harvard Law School.[38] Both these scholars were unsympathetic to police interrogation (although neither supported anything as radical as *Miranda*), and both assumed that the "function which the police have assumed in interrogating an accused [*sic*] is exactly that of the early committing magistrate. . . ."[39] But the history of the matter is really rather different.

The key is that professional, institutionalized police forces did not arrive on the law enforcement scene until the first half of the nineteenth century. How was the identification and capture of malefactors handled before? Or, to put the question in social scientific terms, how was the "intake function" of the criminal justice process performed? The answer is that it was "diffused," that is, not fixed in a particular institution but accomplished piecemeal by a variety of persons and groups some of whom were government officials but many of whom (probably most) were private citizens. These law enforcers included victims of crimes, outraged relatives and clansmen, the fastest runners responding to the "hue and cry," the leader of the *possé comitatus,* captains of dragoons, officers of the night watch, town constables, freelance thief takers, rural justices of the peace, chief constables, county sheriffs, Bow Street Runners, and the "magistrates" for whom these enterprising characters worked. Together this colorful, if inefficient, assortment undertook "the police of the community." And the justices of the peace (simply politically deserving citizens, not trained lawyers) and other low-level magistrates were really "officials of the police" rather than judicial officers in the modern sense. They combined the roles we today identify as investigation and adjudication of guilt.[40]

To take a famous example, when the novelist Henry Fielding received the commission of the peace for Bow Street in 1748 (becoming the "police magistrate") he organized the Bow Street Flying Squad (the precursor of the Bow Street Runners) and supervised its activities. The Bow Street magistracy came to hold commissions from the counties of Middlesex, Essex, Surrey, and Kent and was senior over seven other police magistrates. On Henry Fielding's death in 1754 he was succeeded by his half-brother, John Fielding, known as the "Blind Magistrate." Sir John, as he later became, greatly enlarged the scope of Bow Street's investigative work. He set up a primitive criminal records system (it was said, probably apocryphally, that he could recognize 2,000 professional criminals by their voices), developed an elaborate informant network of tollkeepers, innkeepers, pawnbrokers, and so on, and managed to tap secret service funds to support some of his work. He also held court and adjudged guilt for all but the most serious crimes.

What happened was that through a process of institutional differentiation characteristic of modernizing societies, the police function and the adjudicative function came eventually to be located in separated, specialized institutional structures. The private citizens, the military, and the justices of the peace were replaced by the "New Police" (the model for which was the London metropolitan police, the "Bobbies" created by Sir Robert Peel in 1829). The lower magistracy floated upward into the judiciary proper—sloughing off the old police role, perfecting the adjudicative role, and adopting the traditional legal constraints understood to govern the latter. When they were more like policemen in function, they interrogated suspects; when they became more like judges, they were restrained by the rule against self incrimination. But the people who were now the policemen did interrogate—just as the outraged relatives had, just as the captain of dragoons had, just as the Bow Street Runners had.[41]

The matter becomes clear if we think of a function—the police of the community—that involves *(inter alia)* apprehension and investigation, and to which certain techniques are traditionally appropriate. Where Kauper, Morgan, and ultimately Kamisar go wrong is suggesting that the modern police adopted a discredited practice of which the judiciary had purged itself as a matter of high principle. To argue this is to focus on form and titles rather than the function being performed. The function remained. It was the people performing it and their titles that changed. As between the professors and Justice White on the lack of historical foundation for *Miranda,* the justice had by far the better of it.

2. *The Critique of Voluntariness.* How effectively does Kamisar argue that the "voluntariness" test was seriously inadequate? In his dissenting opinion in *Miranda,* Justice Harlan called the discarded approach "a workable and effective means of dealing with confessions in a judicial manner," and "an elaborate, sophisticated and

sensitive approach to admissibility of confessions." Since the test was discriminating, attempting to take into account a number of variables in the interrogation situation, and since the new test was formalistic and undiscriminating, it might be thought that Justice Harlan had a point. Kamisar's response is that Harlan's faith in the voluntariness was "extravagant."[42] This is so because under the old approach it was too difficult for criminal defendants to show that the kind of coercion applied to them had resulted in the breaking of their will. Here is Kamisar's key sentence: "A victim of *objectionable* interrogation practices could only satisfy this test *with some regularity* in a utopian judicial world."[43] (Emphasis added.) But this is altogether circular. The point of the voluntariness approach was not that those who had been subjected to "objectionable" (read unpleasant) interrogation practices should be able to have their inculpatory statements excluded with "regularity." The point was the opposite—that statements be excluded only when practices had been engaged in which, given the character of the suspect and other relevant circumstances, were either deceptive or so extremely coercive as to offend common humanity and cast doubt on the reliability of the statement which resulted. Kamisar desires to exclude confessions where *some* pressure has been applied to the subject. But it is not an intellectually persuasive argument against voluntariness to impeach it by suggesting that it doesn't do something that it was never intended to do.

The closest Kamisar comes to a specific argument against voluntariness is when he takes Justice Harlan to task for his vote in the case of *Davis* v. *North Carolina*.[44] This vote, Kamisar suggests, showed that Harlan expected defendants to establish with a vengeance the breaking of their will. But do the facts of *Davis* support this charge? It is important to note that Davis was an escaped convict as well as a suspect in the unwitnessed rape-murder of an elderly woman. He was held, of course, and questioned on and off over a sixteen-day period, but there was no maltreatment, deception, or extended periods of questioning. He was driven about on several occasions and asked to identify places and things, and on one occasion was taken for a long walk down a railroad right of way to see if he coul identify a house from which he was maintaining he had stolen some clothes. But there was no evidence of brutality, threat, or false promises. Davis was uneducated, but in British parlance, an "old lag," in full possession of his wits. Great reliance was placed by the majority on an unsigned annotation on Davis' arrest sheet—"Do not allow anyone to see Davis or allow him to use the telephone." It was never established who wrote this, and there were sharply divergent versions in the record as to whether the instruction had been followed. The dissenting opinion, which Harlan joined, was written by Justice Tom Clark, who criticized the majority for lack of respect for the local triers of fact. Speaking for the majority, Chief Justice Warren had chosen, without any particular reason, to accept a defense version of the interrogation produced only after the trial in a *habeas corpus* petition. At best Harlan's position in *Davis* might be used to argue that he took too narrow a view of the voluntariness approach; it can hardly be used to impeach the approach itself.

Kamisar never really explains why society should exclude inculpatory statements which have been secured in pressured, unpleasant circumstances. The proponents of the voluntariness approach had an answer to the "why question." A confession extracted by breaking the will of a defendant was to be excluded not only because of the inhumanity of the process, but because of the unreliability of the confession. If one wishes to abandon the voluntariness approach in favor of something like *Miranda,* it is obligatory that an equally specific answer be given to the "why question." Kamisar implies that pressure, "nagging," and so on are inherently so inhumane as to require a decent society to refrain from resorting to such pressure regardless of any offsetting costs in injustice. But this argument is never clearly made and sustained. Does he consider all pressured statements unreliable? Is there anything left of concern for reliability in Kamisar's thought or in *Miranda* itself? The answers are unclear.

Instead, we find the following curious formulation:

> The "voluntariness" concept seems to be at once too wide and too narrow. In one sense, in the sense of wanting to confess, or doing so in a completely spontaneous manner, "in the sense of a confession to a priest merely to rid one's soul of a sense of guilt" (Jackson, J., dissenting in *Ashcraft* v. *Tennessee*), few criminal confessions reviewed by the courts, if any, had been "voluntary". On the other hand, in the sense that the situation always presents a "choice" between two alternatives, either one disagreeable, to be sure, all confessions are "voluntary".[45]

This is a play on words. It was precisely the thrust of the voluntariness approach, and the intention of the judges who resorted to it, to discriminate between these extremes—to locate that part of the spectrum of pressure beyond which reliability was, as a general matter, called into question and which should not be countenanced by an humane society. Kamisar wants to locate that range (or point on the spectrum) differently than Harlan. Fair enough, but it takes more than arch references to *Davis* v. *North Carolina* to be persuasive.

3. *Questions of Practicality and Justice.* There is great stress in Kamisar's writing on the desirability of the police developing extrinsic evidence of crime rather than relying on statements secured through interrogation. While this is a laudable objective, there is an obvious difficulty, a difficulty which Kamisar consistently ignores. There are a number of crimes where extrinsic evidence does not exist. In these situations either the evidence of guilt must be forthcoming from the perpetrator or no responsibility can ever be affixed. Justice Frankfurter once put it this way:

> Despite modern advances in the technology of crime detection, offenses frequently occur about which *things* cannot be made to speak. And where there cannot be found innocent human witnesses to such offenses, nothing remains—if police investigation is not to be balked before it has fairly begun—but to seek out possibly guilty witnesses and ask them questions, witnesses, that is, who are suspected of knowing something about the

offense precisely because they are suspected of implication in it. (Emphasis added.)[46]

This is an obvious point, but in a society in which stories of crime and detection have for so long been a staple entertainment, it is necessary to remind ourselves how many cases occur in which there are no witnesses, or fingerprints, or convenient bits of tobacco ash lying around for Holmesian analysis. To escape responsibility in such a situation all the perpetrator needs is to be let alone until mated with counsel (whose unvarying advice will be to shut up) and he is home free.

In another subset of cases, where physical evidence does exist, the only way in which the police are at all likely to find it is if the suspect tells them some sort of a story, inculpatory or exculpatory, which provides indications of where to look and things to check. Neophytic repetition of the old saw about it being "easier to sit under a fig tree rubbing pepper into some poor devil's eyes than to go out into the heat of the sun and look for evidence," will not make this dilemma go away. Energy and resourcefulness in searching for extrinsic evidence will often not suffice. In a persuasive case for a canon of pure spontaneity this matter must be faced. If pressure and "nagging" are evils of the magnitude Kamisar thinks them to be, then he should be prepared to explain why society should pay the price of closing down investigation in the categories of cases just described. I cannot find that he does so. Instead he remarks that at the time of *Ashcraft*, in 1944, "neither the court nor 'the country' was 'ready' for" a set of restrictions on custodial interrogation which would involve these costs. "As we know," Kamisar concluded, "it was not until 1966 that the court, if not 'the country' grew 'ready'." And he concludes: "There is cause to wonder whether 'the country' will *ever* grow 'ready'."[47] Poor country! Will it ever live up to the idealism of its law professors?

At base Kamisar does not balance and weigh and attempt to persuade his readers that they should prefer the formalism of *Miranda* over the more discriminating voluntariness approach.

What he does, rather, is to display certain sensibilities that he assumes his readers must share. He repeatedly refers to the 150 years of U.S. history before the Supreme Court began involving itself massively with state criminal procedure as the "stone age" or the "dark ages" of American criminal procedure—as if striving for justice and sensitivity to the rights of accused persons only became matters of concern in America during the chief justiceship of Earl Warren.

While I cannot prove it, I strongly suspect that the settled sense of the American people would agree with Justice Jackson—"interrogation *per se* is not, while violence *per se* is, an outlaw." Constitutional law has departed far from this fundamental principle, with marginally disabling costs for law enforcement. In using Yale Kamisar as a tracer for this development I have not chosen a simple-minded proponent of the *Miranda* approach but the most sophisticated.

The Two Edges of Justice

Theoretically, we have a choice: we can either modify the privilege against self-incrimination and provide resources so as to allow for immediate postapprehension questioning by a judicial officer, or return to a version of the pragmatic Anglo-American compromise* of allowing police officers (substituting for aggrieved private par-

---

*The English compromise (still in effect) takes a somewhat different form than the pre-*Miranda* American variant. First, police interrogation is regulated by administrative directives, not constitutional law. Second, trial judges are not required to exclude statements which are imperfect under the Judges' Rules. Third, the warning as to the "right of silence" which the Judges' Rules prescribes is not triggered by custodial detention but by suspicion focusing on an individual. As long as the individual is simply "assisting the police in their inquiries," questioning may go forward. But when the intention to "charge with the crime" forms itself in the mind of the investigating officer, the warning must be given. It is commonly assumed that this approach is more fastidious with respect to potential defendants than was American practice under the voluntariness approach. Perhaps. I know of no rigorous comparison in the literature. But it is surely the case that with the more deferential attitude of Britons toward the police (long, "voluntary" visits to the

ties) to undertake such interrogation subject to judicially monitored limitations as to duration and permissible techniques. What we cannot do, both for practical and moral reasons, is continue on the path the *Miranda* majority mapped for us of determinedly discouraging interrogation of suspects in the name of a pure, idealized model of the "accusatorial system" which never existed and is flawed in the abstract as an accommodation of conflicting social interests and values. Ours was never a pure accusational system, any more than the continental systems are pure inquisitorial systems. Kamisar is right in debunking the sharp, self-congratulatory distinctions which Anglo-American lawyers have drawn between accusatorial and inquisitorial systems, but he draws the wrong conclusion from it.

While we have a theoretical choice, reflection should make clear that given the demonological baggage carried by our legal subculture with respect to judicial interrogation, and given the extreme unlikeliness of the kinds of resources being made available which would be necessary to mount a workable system of mobile magistrates, the available option is a return to modified common-law voluntariness. This, indeed, is the direction in which a majority of the Supreme Court appears to be leaning—to the horror of the rights industry of course.[48]

Over sixty years ago Judge Learned Hand wrote that:

Under our criminal procedure the accused has every advantage. While the prosecution is held rigidly to the charge, he need not disclose the barest outline of the defense. He is immune from question under oath or comment on his silence; he cannot be convicted when there is the least fair doubt in the minds of any one of the twelve. . . . Our dangers do not lie

---

station house to "assist" are commonly reported), and with the investigator in a position to psychologically defer the intention to charge, there is more room for interrogation in British practice than under *Miranda.* The absence of a canon of mandatory exclusion is also an advantage of the British arrangement. See "The Judges' Rules and Administrative Directives to the Police," *Home Office Circular* no. 31, 1964. See also Glanville L. Williams, "Police Interrogation Privileges and Limitations Under Foreign Law: England," in Claud R. Sowle, *Police Power and Individual Freedom* (Chicago: Aldine, 1962).

in too little tenderness to the accused. Our procedure has always been haunted by the ghost of the innocent man convicted. It is an unreal dream. What we need to fear is the archaic formalism and the watery sentiment that obstructs, delays, and defeats the prosecution of crime.[49]

Writing in the *Yale Law Journal* in 1960, when the judicially wrought "revolution in criminal procedure" was a cloud no larger than a man's hand, Abraham Goldstein, assistant professor of law at Yale, attacked Hand's characterization, arguing that "both doctrinally and practically, criminal procedure, as presently constituted. . . . gives overwhelming advantage to the prosecution."[50] In almost a quarter century since, proceduralization to protect defendants has proceeded apace. Young Abraham Goldstein rose to become Dean at Yale, and then returned to the bench as professor of law. I do not know whether he would subscribe to the same view today (although some of his recent comments suggest to me he would).[51] But it is clear that the rights industry generally, and those in the law schools who most prominently carry its colors, continue to be obsessively preoccupied with defendants' rights even though the trial is now elephantine, and the criminal justice process is dealing with only a fraction of those who commit offenses.[52]

There seems to be a failure among many gently-reared, socially-sheltered, and comfortably middle-class lawyers, of that portion of the human spiritual range which the Greeks called *thumos*—that righteous anger which stiffens the will so that men may undertake unpleasant and even dangerous tasks to protect the community and sustain its values. Furthermore, there is a huge black hole in the conception of "justice" subscribed to today by many legal intellectuals and activists. It is thought an "injustice" if the nicest points of investigative or trial procedure are not observed; to admit any evidence (no matter how useful to the truth-finding function of the trial) that is "illegally obtained" is unjust. But for morally guilty persons to walk away from their crimes in massive numbers or "cop out" for suspended or minor sentences is not perceived as revolting. It will be admitted as a kind of theoretical injustice with "society" as the offended party, but does not seem to have the same emotional stopping power for rights activists as the police asking a suspect questions on the scene, before he is technically in custody and, therefore, before he has received the *Miranda* warning.

Part of this extreme solicitude for defendants (and accompanying indifference to social claims) is a function of the fact that defendants are "real human beings" and society a "bloodless abstraction"; but a more important explanatory factor is that many of the real human defendants are poor or members of ethnic minorities. While one rarely encounters a specific argument that an adverse socioeconomic background should be held to dilute individual responsibility under the criminal law, many within the rights industry argue and work as if they believed this. For others, a debilitating embarrassment seems to inhere in a process by which what they perceive as a substantially unjust society lays forceful hands on persons whom they view as society's economic and psychological victims. Feelings of general social guilt are relived by a determinedly prodefendant, anticop address to criminal justice policy making. While the law review article or the brief may employ the language of liberty or fairness, it is guilt over social inequalities in America which often drives the reasoning.

The late Professor John T. McNaughton of Harvard, an authority on the law of evidence and a close student of the history, uses, and abuses of the privilege against self-incrimination in America, once told the story of how the screw driver was used in his household: it was "used to pry tops off cans, to gouge holes in wood, to dig pits for tulip bulbs, to score lines and occasionally even wrong-end-to to drive tacks." "Once," McNaughton reported, "after hearing strange noises, I searched the house for a prowler who was not there, clutching a screw driver in my fist." But these uses are not what a screw driver is *for*. In the same fashion McNaughton saw the privilege being resorted to for a variety of purposes other than that which it properly served, and he worried that "it may in most applications be an example of man's casuistic insistence upon being civilized to a fault."[53] While McNaughton wished to see police interrogation replaced by some more professional and better regulated type of early questioning, he did not favor extending the Fifth Amendment privilege to the detective squad room and would have left "the witness abuse problem entirely to the due process clause . . . and the offspring of *Brown* v. *Mississippi* [voluntariness]." While he did not live to write of *Miranda* (he was killed in a plane crash in June 1967 several days before he was to be sworn in as secretary of the Navy), it is safe to say he would have regarded it as the ultimate misuse of the screw driver.

Justice Walter V. Schaffer of Illinois, in an influential essay on these problems almost twenty years ago, wrote that "the quality of a nation's civilization can largely be measured by the methods it uses in the enforcement of its criminal law."[54] It is a widely shared and echoed sentiment, but it cuts two ways. The system must be fair but it must also work. Ultimate judgment must be rendered not only on its humaneness, but also on its efficacy and accuracy in truth finding. Sir Basil Thompson, one of the most thoughtful men ever to head the London Metropolitan Police, wrote with stunning prescience over half a century ago:

> The first object of any civilized penal system is the protection of society. It does not very much matter whether the protection proceeds from reform of the criminal in prison or from deterring him, provided that he goes and sins no more. The fact that the length of sentences and their severity have been declining side by side with the falling off in the volume of crime [in England in 1925] seems to indicate that it would not matter what sentences were pronounced provided that our punishment for every crime were swift and sure.
>
> We have only to turn to other countries to see what happens where criminal justice is neither sure nor swift. In the United States a year or two ago, homicides worked out to 1 in 12,000 of the population against 1 in 635,000 in England and Scotland. It was not only that the police are only half the number considered necessary in this country in proportion to population, but that even when a murderer is detected and arrested there are so many delays in the way of extradition from state to state and in appeals that no one feels sure that the sentence will be carried out. Crime has become a great game in which the dice are loaded against the police.[55]

Down through all the discussions of interrogation and exclusionary rules a familiar slogan echoes: "It is better that ten guilty men go free than that one innocent man be convicted." This, presumably, is intended to suggest that you cannot do too much to insure reliability. But in the *Miranda* example, we have an exclusionary rule which is almost completely unhinged from considerations of reliability (whether the defendant is really guilty or not). And it is not ten, but tens of thousands of the guilty who, if not going free, are "walking" with probation or trivial sentences after plea bargaining. Long ago in a "Peanuts" comic strip, Charles Schulz has Schroeder ask Charlie Brown about his philosophy of life. With the cheerful simple-mindedness that has endeared him to so many, Charlie Brown replies, "The secret of happiness is having three things to look forward to, and nothing to dread." Sadly but firmly Schroeder replies, "There's a difference between a philosophy and a bumper sticker, Charlie Brown."

CHAPTER 5

Undermining
Order Maintenance

ANOTHER EXAMPLE of the disabling impact of rights industry involves the ability of the police to perform routine tasks of order maintenance in America. In recent years "civil liberties victories" in the courts have provided a powerful disincentive to police to patrol aggressively in our public spaces. This has coincided, unhappily, with the rise of a conception of police professionalism that views the proper objective of policing as catching criminals and places patrolmen in cars and in centralized tactical units to be rushed to the scene of disorders—ignoring traditional, mundane policing chores such as checking doors, helping citizens in difficulty, and breaking up youth gatherings which are becoming annoying to merchants and passersby.

Within the contemporary clerisy, one frequently encounters the notion that order maintenance is not a very important aspect of police responsibility, especially compared to law enforcement. It is even sometimes argued that the order-maintaining and crime-combatting functions of the police are distinct spheres of activity and should not be the responsibility of the same force. This is wrong. Routine order maintenance in public places and the control of crime are linked in a variety of ways. Roger Starr once remarked, half in jest but whole in truth, that police were most successful in catching criminals "when they stumble onto them committing other crimes."[1] And they are most likely to do this when engaged in a style of patrolling that stresses inquiry and intervention in what is perceived on the street as potentially disorderly or out of the ordinary. The objective is defeated to the extent the police adopt a passive, "buttoned-up" style of patrol in which they float through the community waiting to see or hear by radio of something "really serious" before they get out of their cars and intervene.[2] Routine order maintenance by the police also matters deeply to ordinary people who do not live in monied enclaves where private security guards and electronic systems take care of such things.

Behavior in Public Places

In the contemporary debate over law enforcement attention was focused on the importance of order maintenance by Professor James Q. Wilson of Harvard over fifteen years ago in a widely noted article titled "The Urban Unease: Community vs. City."[3] Wilson's piece came at a time of almost frenzied concern within academia over "the urban crisis." Poverty, inadequate tax bases, declining smokestack industries, and a variety of other ills were being suggested as the answer to the question "what is wrong with our large cities?" On the basis of inner-city opinion sampling,

Undermining Order Maintenance

Wilson argued that these commonly mentioned urban afflictions were not the things that most concerned ordinary urban dwellers. "Only nine percent mentioned jobs and employment," Wilson wrote. "The issue which concerned more respondents than any other was variously stated—crime, violence, rebellious youth, racial tension, public morality, delinquency." But however the issue was stated, "the common theme seemed to be a concern for improper behavior in public places." At first blush this seems just too Victorian—until it is remembered that the Victorians enjoyed much more orderly streets than we do today.

Wilson's opinion research established that order maintenance was important because people, including black people, cared about it.* It made them nervous and fearful to be in public places where they sensed that organized society had lost control and that the law was flouted routinely, even if most of the offenses committed were minor. And the way people feel in public places is an important element in their quality of life, especially if fear leads them to avoid certain public spaces altogether.

Nathan Glazer, in a sensitive article in 1979, argued that New York subway graffiti, far from being an endearing manifestation of the creative spirit of the city's impoverished youth, was a significant public safety problem. As a subway rider himself, he found that while not "consciously making the connection between the graffiti makers and the criminals who occasionally rob, rape, assault, and murder passengers, the sense that all are part of one world of uncontrollable predators seems inescapable." The subway rider is "assaulted continuously, not only by the evidence that every subway car has been vandalized, but by the inescapable knowledge that the environment he must endure for an hour or more each day is uncontrolled and uncontrollable, that anyone can invade it and do whatever damage and mischief the mind suggests."[4]

*Indeed, urban working and middle-class blacks have the worst of it. Many live in high-disorder neighborhoods which for reasons both obvious and complex are worst served by the police.

Graffiti powerfully contributes to the sense that the subway is a dangerous place. What we are now coming to understand is that when people sense a place as dangerous it contributes to the reality of dangerousness. A recent study by the Police Foundation is pertinent in this respect. In the mid-1970s New Jersey undertook a "Safe and Clean Neighborhoods Program." The state provided money to localities to help them assign more officers to foot patrol. After five years, researchers supported by the Police Foundation in Washington, D.C., studied its impact in downtown Newark.

While in no sense conclusive, this report is richly suggestive. A review of the findings by Wilson and George L. Kelling, one of the authors of the Police Foundation study, makes these points.[5] While the Newark data do not show the crime rate to have been reduced by foot patrol (in the sense of violent street attacks, armed robberies, and burglaries having been reduced), area residents had a strong sense of themselves as being "safer." It is possible to interpret these results as indicating that the people had been fooled—that the cop on the beat was a kind of civic placebo. But Wilson and Kelling are clear that the people were not fooled at all. A neighborhood can be safer, even if the "big-C" crime rate has not (yet) gone down, when one understands the multiple sources of fear in public places. Certainly there is the fear of violent attack, but there is also "the fear of being bothered by disorderly people. Not violent people, or, necessarily, criminals, but disreputable or obstreperous or unpredictable people: panhandlers, drunks, addicts, rowdy teenagers, prostitutes, loiterers, the mentally disturbed." This the foot patrol did a great deal about by establishing through daily custom and usage an operational code of behavior—of what would be tolerated on the streets and what would not. Police were able to distinguish between "regulars," which category included both "decent folk" and deviants who knew the rules and abided by them, and "outsiders," who required special attention until they moved on or were socialized into the acceptable street ways of the particular neighborhood. "Persons who broke the informal rules, especially those who bothered people waiting at bus stops, were arrested for vagrancy." If a "stranger" loitered, he was asked by the patrolman "if he had any means of support and what his business was; if he gave unsatisfactory answers, he was sent on his way." The people of downtown Newark, apparently, felt "relieved and reassured" when the police helped them maintain order.

Further, the Newark experience reinforced our understanding that "at the community level, disorder and crime are usually inextricably linked in a kind of development sequence." The sense of a neighborhood as "untended" stimulates disorder and vandalism; as this happens people withdraw from public places and the collective confidence and willingness to assert shared norms of behavior erodes. As the inhabitants pass quickly and furtively, averting their eyes and not "getting involved," the preconditions of more serious dangers are created—the classic pattern of the high crime areas.[6]

Another strand of Wilson's work is also relevant here. Along with Barbara Boland he has argued that police may affect crime rates less by how many of them are on patrol but by what they do there. Wilson and Boland distinguish between what are called "aggressive" and "passive" styles of police patrol. The aggressive style of patrol does not imply that the police on the street are harsh or brutal, but rather that they maximize the number of interventions and observations of the community.

> An officer follows a passive strategy when he rarely stops motor vehicles to issue citations for moving violations or to check for stolen cars or wanted fugitives, rarely stops to question suspicious persons, and does not employ decoy or stakeout procedures in areas with high crime rates. When an officer acts in an opposite manner he is employing an "aggressive" strategy.[7]

Wilson and Boland describe a particularly well-designed experiment in San Diego, California, that tested one component of the aggressive style of patrol—field interrogations or "street stops."[8] In one area of San Diego where a policy of frequent street stops had been in force, street stops were suspended—"whereupon the number of 'suppressible crimes' rose by about a third; when field interrogations were resumed the number of such crimes dropped."[9] "Suppressible crimes" included robberies, burglaries, common thefts, assaults, sex crimes, malicious mischief, and disturbances of the peace. And Wilson and Boland further conclude, comparing thirty-five large American cities, that the aggressiveness of patrol style appears to depress the robbery rate after controlling for other variables.[10]

Putting this together, a picture begins to emerge of successful police order maintenance that contributes not only to public amenity but also to containing suppressible crime. In this picture the police will intervene routinely against the loud and the obscene, the panhandler and the vagrant, the street corner group which has been growing for an hour and ignores requests by merchants to move on. Police will also do a great deal of stopping of suspicious persons to ask for identification. It is an interventionist style that people who depend for the quality of their lives on public spaces around them (who are not simply hailing a taxi or pulling out of an underground parking garage heading for a month at the Vineyard) determinedly desire. So let us recruit, train, and deploy police for aggressive patrol. Ah, but there are problems.

The interventionist style has been under fire from the rights industry for its assertedly dubious legality. An aggressive style of police patrol rests on a legal foundation of half a dozen or so ancient common law offenses which have been, in various ways, codified by the states. Crimes such as "disturbing the peace," "disorderly conduct," "use of obscene and abusive language," and "vagrancy" are of ancient lineage and are relied upon by police in mid-twentieth century America to maintain order and as authority to ask suspicious persons to identify themselves and explain their presence at particular times and places. Both the ancient disorder crimes and the modern requirement of identification have been attacked lately with considerable success in the courts.

"Vagueness"

On 2 May 1983, for instance, the Supreme Court struck down a California vagrancy law that required a person to "identify himself and to account for his presence" when asked to do so by a police officer. The California courts had interpreted the law to require a person to produce "creditable and reliable" identification that would enable an officer to check its authenticity. Justice Sandra Day O'Connor wrote for a Court divided 7 to 2 that the law was unconstitutionally vague.[11] "Vagueness" is a constitutional doctrine which has been directed with telling effect at the ancient common law misdemeanors upon which the police must rely in performing normal order maintenance and conducting aggressive patrol.

Clarity in criminal law is a matter of core due process fairness under the Fifth and Fourteenth Amendments. The evil of a vague criminal statute is two-fold: people are not given adequate notice that certain behavior is forbidden, and too much discretion is vested in the police in deciding when and against whom to apply the law. Vagueness in statutory articulation is one aspect of those dragnet laws used by authoritarian regimes to enforce political orthodoxy—"crimes against the state," "anti-socialist behavior," crime by "analogy" to other crimes, and so on—and in this sense we have done well to elevate the prohibition against vagueness into our constitutional law. But in applying the vagueness doctrine to the common law order maintenance crimes (and to modern variations of them such as the California identification requirement), caution is required.

There is a great difference in language and law between clarity and specificity. Clarity is always required, but specificity, while desirable, is not always possible or necessary. There are large areas of human misbehavior that can only be addressed by the legislature in general terms. "Reckless driving" and "driving to endanger" are familiar examples, as are "cruelty to animals" and "neglect of children." In each case the ordinary usages of language and the

113

common experience of a culture provide perfectly clear notice of a range of behavior that is criminalized. Simply because erratic lane changes or backing down the "up ramp" are not specified in the statute does not mean that notice is inadequate. With such clear but general laws there is always the possibility of bizarre applications to behavior that no one could really have foreseen was prohibited (for example, wheeling onto the freeway with a poodle on your lap). Here there is a problem of insufficient notice and of overboard discretion for the officer in applying the statute to behavior not clearly violative of the law. But the problem does not exist for the core of obvious offenses covered by the statute. Neither the persons who beats the poodle to death nor the officer who issues the summons is adrift in a sea of ambiguity or discretion over the concept of "cruelty." And certainly it does not ask too much of our courts that they discriminate between the legitimate applications of clear but general order maintenance laws, and marginal, problematic applications.

In most of the cases that have come to American appellate courts, where the applications of order maintenance laws at issue have been ambiguous or marginal, the courts have quite properly found them unconstitutionally vague as applied to those particular defendants.[12] Unhappily, the Supreme Court of the United States has recently been less careful.*

An example is *Papachristo* v. *City of Jacksonville* in 1972.[13]

*In 1966 Charles Reich, then a professor of law at Yale, published a widely read and quoted article on his nocturnal wanderings, arguing that no matter how suspicious the circumstances, police should not be allowed to stop and ask questions of someone absent some indication of specific criminal conduct—"Police Questioning of Law Abiding Citizens," 75 *Yale Law Journal* 1161 (1966). As the author of *The Greening of America* (New York: Bantam Books, 1970), Reich enjoyed a brief season of notoriety as the country's leading anti-authority figure. "If I choose to take an evening walk to see if Andromeda has come up on schedule, I think I am entitled to look for the distant light of Almach and Mirach without finding myself staring into the blinding beam of a police flashlight." But it all depends on when and where, doesn't it? English common law allowed night watchman "to detain 'suspicious nightwalkers' until the morning at which time the watchman would either release the suspect or arrest him if grounds for arrest were discovered." Loren G. Stern, "Stop and Frisk: An Historical Answer to a Modern Problem," 58 *Journal of Criminal, Criminology, and Police Science* 532 (1967).

Undermining Order Maintenance

Jacksonville boasted a picaresque vagrancy ordinance which in splendid Elizabethan cadences spoke of "rogues and vagabonds, or other dissolute persons who go about begging, common gamblers, persons who use juggling or unlawful games . . ." and so on. This had been applied to an oddly assorted dozen folk, several of whom were suspected pushers and burglars but several others of whom had committed no greater offense than interracial dating. The point was that none, at the time of arrest, were doing anything that a reasonable person could have imagined to be an offense under the ordinance. The police had simply abused their discretion under the law to take in charge persons of whom they disapproved or whom they suspected, without any immediate circumstantial support, to be up to no good. But Justice William O. Douglas, writing for the Court, struck the Jacksonville ordinance as unconstitutional on its face, rather than as applied.

Now it clearly would be desirable for Jacksonville to modernize its vagrancy ordinance, making clear it was directed at panhandlers, derelicts, and hustlers, and substituting, say, three-card-Monte artists for jugglers. Nevertheless, even though the language of the Jacksonville ordinance was archaic, members of the community certainly understood that a core of clearly proscribable public behaviors (begging, sleeping it off on the curb, and so on) were proscribed as "vagrancy." Archaic language may still be entirely functional—precisely because of the patina of understandings and associations that it acquires over centuries of cultural development, custom, and usage. However, Douglas, the aging Acquarian, concluded his *Papachristo* opinion with a celebration of loafing and loitering, bolstered by a quotation from the ubiquitous Anthony Amsterdam:*

*If the reader is tending to the conclusion that Professor Amsterdam qualifies as a rights industry superstar, the reader would be right. In addition to the areas already mentioned, Professor Amsterdam has written an influential article urging that police use of informants be subjected to the Fourth Amendments warrant requirement—"Perspectives on the Fourth Amendment", 58 *Minnesota Law Review* 349 (1974). In December, 1981, Amsterdam delivered a public lecture at New York University on how the rights industry should cope with the Burger Court, the Reagan administration, and the conservative political turn taken by the country.

If some carefree type of fellow is satisfied to work just so much, and no more, as will pay for one square meal, some wine, and a flop house daily, but a court thinks this kind of living subhuman, the fellow can be forced to raise his sights or go to jail as a vagrant.[14]

That such Dickensian sentimentalization of street life was to have serious consequences is made clear by the California identity check case.

The facts of the case, *Kolender* v. *Lawson,* were simple. When requested by a California peace officer, under circumstances which would justify the stopping and brief questioning of a person under the controlling Supreme Court decision of *Terry* v. *Ohio,*[15] such person might be required to produce "credible and reliable" identification. This, in turn, had been interpreted by the California courts to mean "carrying reasonable assurance that the identification is authentic and providing means for later getting in touch with the person who has identified himself."[16] Edward Lawson, a person of eccentric appearance given to nocturnal rambles, was detained or arrested on several occasions between March 1975 and January 1977 under the provisions of the California law. He was prosecuted only twice and convicted once. The law suit which ultimately came to the Supreme Court was an action by Lawson under federal civil rights law (the Ku Klux Klan Act again) for compensatory and punitive damages against the officers who had detained him. While the record is not entirely clear on the point, it seems that Lawson's practice when stopped was to refuse the request for identification altogether.

While the Supreme Court majority declined to overturn that portion of the decision below holding that Lawson could not re-

---

The lecture was extensively reported in the *New York Times* ("On Liberal Law in the Reagan Era," 10 December 1981). Professor Amsterdam quipped that he "thought William French Smith was a pharmaceutical company"; he warned that a more conservative judiciary "is a very frightening prospect"; and he offered the following reflection on taking cases to the Supreme Court: "It once was, during the Warren Court years, that you would take a case to the Supreme Court even if you won, to get a broader and more authoritative ruling. The name of the game today is, 'If you win it, hold it'."

cover damages (on the grounds the officers had acted in good faith), Justice O'Connor did hold the California requirement unconstitutional, not as applied to Lawson, but on its face. This means that even if the stops of Lawson were perfectly good *Terry* v. *Ohio* stops (based on reasonable suspicion), and even though it was perfectly clear to Lawson that, by refusing to respond at all, he was violating the law, and even though there was no exercise of undue discretion by the police who arrested Lawson (that no identification fails the test of "credible or reliable" identification is not really a judgment call), the law might be vague as applied to hypothetical others and must be struck.* An ominous slide into a novel doctrine.

In dissent Justice White, joined by Justice Rehnquist, argued the traditional approach—that a law should not be held unconstitutionally vague on its face "unless it is vague in all of its possible applications." In other words, simply because police might begin demanding birth certificates from middle-aged stockbrokers in three-piece suits in the financial district at high noon is no reason to hold that the statute could not constitutionally be applied in ways in which the vast majority of reasonable persons would see as responsible—say, to a lone, youthful male, disreputably attired, abroad at three o'clock in the morning in a residential district who can satisfy the requirement with a driver's licence. For the dissenters, the evils of lack of notice and overbroad discretion did not require a statute be declared unconstitutional on its face where there is a class of what might be called "Al Capp Cases" under the law—cases where "any fool would know that a particular category of conduct would be within the reach of the statute. . . ." As long as there is an "unmistakable core that a reasonable person would know is forbidden by the law," it is enough for the courts to be alert to possible bizarre (and therefore unconstitutional) applications.

A nicely crafted minority argument; but the important point is

---

*Justice Brennan, in a concurring opinion, rested not on vagueness but on the argument that the requirement of identification was an "invasion of privacy" in violation of the Fourth Amendment. This may not be persuasive, but at least it is coherent.

that the order maintenance interest has lost again, and unless *Kolender* v. *Lawson* can be contained as a doctrinal anomoly it will be a costly loss.

"Overbreadth"

And the homely common law codifications upon which order maintenance depends have been attacked from a second direction. Closely related to the vagueness doctrine, which is derived from the due process clause of the Fourteenth Amendment, is the "overbreadth doctrine," which is derived from the First Amendment's protection of free speech. The notion here is that a statute bearing on utterance, which employs a broad descriptive term in its prohibition, may be applied in ways which burden protected speech. But unlike vagueness, where the "usual rule" (at least until *Kolender* v. *Lawson*) is that the unconstitutionality of an allegedly vague law must be judged in the light of the conduct to which it is applied, the Court, prodded by rights-industry activists, has held repeatedly that a defendant whose utterance admittedly falls outside the protection of the First Amendment may still challenge the statute for overbreadth as hypothetically applied to some other defendant at some other time. By this approach statutes which have both legitimate and illegitimate (constitutional and unconstitutional) applications can never be applied at all.

To make this curious doctrinal twist clearer, let us take an example of the overbreadth doctrine in action. *Gooding* v. *Wilson*[17] is dolorously typical. Here a Georgia defendant was convicted under a statute forbidding a person "without provocation, to use to or of another, and in his presence . . . oppropious words or abusive language, tending to cause a breach of the peace." The options open to the Court in *Gooding* go back to 1942 and the pivotal case of *Chaplinsky* v. *New Hampshire*.[18] Here the statute in question, based on the ancient common law doctrine of "fighting words," provided that "no person shall address any offensive, derisive or annoying word to any other person who is lawfully in any street or other public place, nor call him by any offensive or derisive name." The New Hampshire courts had further interpreted the law to reach only such "words likely to cause an average addressee to fight," that is "face-to-face words plainly likely" to cause a breach of the peace. Justice Frank Murphy concluded that the prohibition was addressed precisely to words likely to produce violence, that is, to "fighting words," and was consistent with the First Amendment's protection of free speech. Fighting words are not constitutionally protected.

How does the situation in *Gooding* v. *Wilson* look through the lens of *Chaplinsky?* The defendant was attempting to block access to an army recruiting station as part of a draft protest. To one police officer attempting to restore public access to the building, defendant shouted "white son of a bitch I'll kill you" and "you son of a bitch, I'll choke you to death," and to another officer he declared, "you son of a bitch, if you ever put your hands on me again I'll cut you to pieces, . . ." The Georgia statute, recall, proscribed the use of opprobrious or abusive language, tending to cause a breach of the peace. This formulation is very close to the language used by Murphy and the New Hampshire courts in establishing what constituted fighting words and was unprotected by the First Amendment. The successful constitutional attack in *Gooding* v. *Wilson,* however, was not that the defendant's words were protected or that they were not fighting words, but rather that the Georgia statute was overbroad because it might be applied to utterance that did not constitute fighting words.

In such cases as *Gooding* the Court could follow its usual procedure when faced with a statute that might have both constitutional and unconstitutional applications. It could follow "its duty to adopt the construction [of the statute] which will save the statute from constitutional infirmity."[19] To put the matter differently, the Court itself could separate the constitutional from the potentially unconstitutional applications of the statute. This the Court declines to do on the grounds that separability or saving construction of a statute is inappropriate in the First Amendment context. As Justice Brennan explained in *Gooding,* given the transcendent value of constitutionally protected expression "a larger public interest" was served by allowing attacks on statutes employing general terms by persons with no requirement that those persons demonstrate that their own expression is protected by the First Amendment and could not be regulated even by a statute "drawn with the requisite narrow specificity." "Facial challenge" for overbreadth, without examination of the application of the statute to the particular utterance at issue, is justified because statutes using general terms might inhibit future persons in their choice of protected epithets and imprecations.[20]

A second option, available to the Court in *Gooding,* was simply to hold that the Georgia statute which spoke of language leading to a breach of the peace was not overbroad as interpreted by Georgia courts and was limited in its reach to fighting words. This the *Gooding* majority declined to do. Despite the explicit connection in the statute between abusive language and breach of the peace, the Court found that Georgia courts had interpreted the statute as reaching language which, while harsh and insulting, was not within the conception of fighting words as defined by *Chaplinsky.* Doing this required a strained reading of Georgia cases which, even as manipulated by Justice Brennan, evince a continuing concern on the part of Georgia judges with the relationship between abusive language and physical violence. Brennan leaned heavily on a 1914 Georgia decision holding that the law could be properly applied in a situation in which the party to which the putative fighting words were addressed was physically unable to retaliate at that moment. "Suppose", said the Georgia court,

. . . that one, at a safe distance and out of hearing of any other than the person to whom he spoke addressed such language to one locked in a prison cell or at the opposite bank of an impassable torrent, and hence without power to respond immediately to such verbal insults by physical retaliation, could it be reasonably contended that, because no breach of the peace could [immediately] follow, the statute would not be violated?[21]

That was enough for Justice Brennan. Georgia had not consistently insisted upon a close nexus between abusive language and the physical response. This meant that Georgia's statute might encompass something more than the fighting words.

Such wordplay is even more serious than the refusal by the Court to apply normal canons of separability and interpretive narrowing in the First Amendment context. For what the majority does in *Gooding* v. *Wilson* and similar cases is to operationally eliminate the category "fighting words" by construing it so narrowly that almost no actual abusive language statute, applied by actual state courts, has much choice of constitutional survival. That this is the game afoot is made clear by the progeny of *Gooding.* In *Rosenfeld* v. *New Jersey,* the defendant had harangued an open school board meeting describing teachers and board members, *inter alia,* as "motherfuckers."[22] In *Brown* v. *Oklahoma,* the defendant in a public meeting referred to "motherfucking fascist pig cops," and to a particular policeman as a "black motherfucking pig."[23] And in *Lewis* v. *New Orleans*, the defendant addressed a policeman who was arresting her son as a "god damned motherfucker."[24] Until this line of doctrine can be grasped by a new majority and bent back in the direction of *Chaplinsky* v. *New Hampshire,* we will continue in a situation in which the doctrine of fighting words (which "by their very utterance inflict injury") is preserved as a form but not a reality; we will continue in a situation in which the Court strikes down the kinds of public deportment statutes on which police order maintenance in part depends because it cannot be made absolutely plain that these might not apply to some language that is simply insulting but not so insulting as to likely provoke physical response.*

*The story of the depressing impact on public morals of the sustained rights industry campaign for relaxation or abandonment of standards of obscenity is too long and complicated to be addressed in this book. Whether the effort within the Court to protect the concept of obscenity from the nihilism of Justice Brennan will succeed remains to be seen, but the continued prominence in the media of what

But the heavy intellectual guns of the rights industry are positioned to discourage any reform. Consider Professor Laurence H. Tribe of the Harvard Law School, who is the author of an influential textbook in constitutional law which asserts that traditional philosophical and constitutional understanding of the relationship between the state and the individual have been "ruptured beyond repair" and that the task facing our generation is to replace them with conceptions of "personhood" and constitutionally required levels of government social services." "Ultimately," Professor Tribe writes, "the affirmative duties of government cannot be severed from its obligations to refrain from certain forms of control; both must respond to a substantive vision of the needs of the human personality."[25] (This seems to mean that treating protections of the individual against government as matters of constitutional law while treating levels of governmental social services as matter of ordinary policy is somehow illegitimate.) It is the notion of personality development ("personal growth and self-realization") on which Tribe bases his prescriptions for constitutional law.* Thus in the matter of First Amendment speech protection,

---

might be called the "Larry Flint Theory of Free Speech" (if anything can be censored, everything is in danger) does not make for optimism.

*Professor Tribe is the very model of an activist professor. His most recent triumph in the Supreme Court was in an establishment clause case, *Larkin* v. *Grendel's Den,* No. 81–878, 13 December 1982. This involved a Massachusetts statute which provided that state liquor licenses should not be issued to establishments located within 500 feet of a church or school if the governing body of such a church or school filed written objection. Grendel's Den, an overpriced but underinspired Harvard Square eatery, was within 500 feet of the Holy Cross Armenian Catholic Parish, which objected to the issuance of a license. Despite the traditionally broad powers of the states to regulate (or proscribe) traffic in liquor within their borders (a distinguished if incautious Maine judge once called this power ". . . the most fulsome embodied in the concept of sovereignty"), Chief Justice Burger held that for a state to allow religious institution such a power of decisive objection was a "establishment of religion." Justice Rehnquist in dissent recalled the truism that great cases and hard cases make bad law. "Today's opinion," Rehnquist wrote, "suggests that a third class of cases—silly cases—also make bad law." In the fall of 1983 Professor Tribe submitted a bill for $332,441.00 to the Attorney General of Massachusetts under the Commonwealth's analogue to the federal Civil Rights Attorney's Fees Award Act of 1976. Such statutes provide public payment for

Tribe argues that verbal expression is an end in itself because it enhances personal growth and self-realization.[26] Traditional theorizing about free speech requires some answer to the question why the utterance in question should be protected—to allow for the vigorous mounting of political opposition necessary to republican government, to inform the electorate, to advance the search for truth, or some such. Or, to put it another way, the traditional approach requires us to consider whether the utterance in question rises to the level of dignity and significance to be classed as "speech" for First Amendment purposes. For Professor Tribe the "why question" is not necessary; in fact, it is wrong headed. Any utterance is justified (and thereby protected as "speech") because it pleases the speaker to utter it; it expresses his personality. Earlier approaches to free speech, Tribe writes, were "far too focused on intellect and rationality to accommodate the emotive role of free expression. . . ."[27]

Tribe's approach to the problem of abusive language laws is predictable; he rejects the whole notion of saving constructions of such statutes by reference to *Chaplinsky* v. *New Hampshire.* He rejects the concept of "fighting words" as criminal standard because it "is obviously not precise and focused enough to give advance warning of the exact reach of the statute. . . ."[28] Passing over the point that no criminal statute can give warning of its "exact" reach, and that only certain types of statutes can achieve precision, is it altogether backward to ask whether Professor Tribe seriously thinks that ordinary people are not given fair notice of an offense when they are forbidden to employ such epithets as would likely lead to a breach of the peace? And is it not also fair to ask, as traditional speech analysis would prompt us, what value is served by "freedom of imprecation" beyond the momentary sense of emotional release experienced by the "speaker" and the satisfaction he

---

attorneys handling certain sorts of "civil rights" and "public interest" cases. Thus far, Massachusetts has resisted Professor Tribe's claim.

may feel in giving pain to another person in a fashion which cannot be punished? In other words, for those who are not persuaded by a neo-Freudian theory of the American constitution, some arguments as to the value of the speech being protected and some colorable connection to the world view of the framers and prior interpreters of the First Amendment are still required.

Radical Libertarianism

Beyond all this nice constitutional quibbling there are important moral issues at stake. What underlies the hostility of the rights industry and many judges to legal requirements for minimum standards of deportment and language in public places? The answer I think is the attachment of many mid-twentieth century American intellectuals to an extreme libertarian social philosophy.* Beneath the commitment to exaggerated notions of vagueness and overbreadth is a primary anxiety that society may be intruding itself in illegitimate ways on the freedom of individuals when it sets minimum standards of public behavior. No serious person can really argue that it is a grave infringement on anyone's liberty to be asked

*There can be little doubt that concern over race was also a powerful, if largely unacknowledged, factor in the Court's hostility to common law disorder crimes in the 1960s and 1970s. Since some police discretion is inevitably involved in enforcing these laws (indeed, this is so for many kinds of laws), and since it was likely that this discretion was being abused in some instances by racially prejudiced officers, the response was to strike the laws themselves rather than to seek narrowing interpretations. This is another example of an underlying concern over equality moving judges to delegitimate law enforcement practices wholesale—even though on their faces such practices are serviceable accommodations between individual liberty and the needs and interests of the community. The fear of racist abuse of discretion by police is quite well founded, and there is no wholly satisfactory "solution" to the problem. Few would deny, however, the progress made in this area in the past decades. Police may resocialize slowly (in some departments more slowly than others), but it does happen and the progressive integration of forces helps. We must not, however, allow ourselves to be gulled into divesting police of order-maintenance discretion because that is the only way we can think of keeping them from abusing it. See Kenneth Culp Davis, *Discretionary Justice* (Baton Rouge: Louisiana State University Press, 1969), pp. 52–96.

to produce identification or to be told by the legislature to avoid the earthier Anglo-Saxon expletives in addressing police officers or public meetings. The anxiety derives from the fact that we are intruding on people at all absent some immediate danger of physical injury to person or property. What business does society have regulating words or conduct when there is no "victim"? This is what moves Justice Brennan to waffle and Professor Tribe to embrace the preposterous as obvious. They accept a radical libertarianism with respect to language—a doctrine that has been sedulously propagated by both academic and journalistic elements of the rights industry with increasing success since the early 1960s.

In its classic form the doctrine is derived from John Stuart Mill's essay *On Liberty,* first published in 1859. Mill urged a "simple principle" which he claimed should "govern absolutely the dealings of society with the individual in the way of compulsion and control." The principle was:

> That the only purpose for which power can be rightfully exercised over any member of a civilized community, against his will, is to prevent harm to others.[29]

Not striking out of context; but in context it becomes clear that by "harm" Mill (as an old Benthamite) really means tangible and immediately apparent physical harm to persons or property. And since speech by its nature almost never entails such immediate physical harm, "punishing words" can almost never be justified. This denies language power—the potential for harm. Intangible, subtle, long-term harms, and the sorts of emotional pain that result from the loss of amenity in public places are simply not provided for in Mill's calculus. He dismisses efforts to protect such interests through law as "the tyranny of the majority." It is harsh but fair to observe that Mill's "principle" is mimetic of a schoolyard taunt, but most of us grew up to understand that "names" can sometimes hurt a great deal.

In the introduction to a new textbook for university undergraduates on the hoary subject of "the law enforcing morals," Professor

Thomas Grey of the Stanford University Law School takes as his point of departure that, as to speech, "Mill's views have achieved orthodoxy in the century since he wrote *On Liberty.* "[30] While Grey is certainly correct that Mill's position as to speech is ascendant in law schools today, it may be doubted that it is generally ascendant in American society. For Mill's extreme libertarianism has no traditional roots in American law and culture.

We all remember the famous dissent of Oliver Wendell Holmes, Jr., in the case of *Lochner* v. *New York.* [31] In under two pages, Holmes exposed the judicial activism of his day as an intellectual shambles and snapped off one of the most famous quips of American constitutional history by remarking that "the Fourteenth Amendment does not enact Mr. Herbert Spencer's *Social Statics.* " But Herbert Spencer was not the only social theorist taken to task by Holmes in the *Lochner* dissent. A few sentences earlier Holmes had written:

> It is settled by various decisions of this court that state constitutions and state laws may regulate life in many ways which we as legislators might think as injudicious. . . . Sunday laws and usury laws are ancient examples. A more modern one is the prohibition of lotteries. The liberty of the citizen to do as he likes as long as he does not interfere with the liberty of others to do the same which has been a shibboleth for certain well-known writers, is interfered with by school laws, by the post office, by every state or municipal institution which takes his money for purposes thought desirable whether he likes it or not.[32]

The well-known writer Holmes had in mind was surely John Stuart Mill.

Holmes was correct. We have not as a people either written or legislated or behaved as if we thought that individuals should be at liberty to act or speak as they like as long as their action or words resulted in no immediate physical harm to their neighbors. We have assumed that actions and words can have deleterious effects other than the immediately physical. We have also assumed that majority sensibilities qualified for some protection through criminal law. If we had not, how on earth did all these statutes that the Supreme Court now finds fault with get on the books? Vagrant, offensive, obscene, disrespectful, inflammatory, and so on are terms which generations have thought to have sufficiently clear meaning to use in law. The academy, with its elevation of Mill's libertarianism to the position of canon, would have us now conclude those legislative majorities who thought these terms meaningful and legally appropriate were wrong. Passing over the problem of democratic theory posed by this position, is it fair to ask whether Mill's position is itself sufficiently coherent and persuasive to deserve the reverence it is now accorded by the *illuminati?*

Mill's views on liberty were subjected to whithering contemporary examination by Sir James Fitzjames Stephen, as eminent a Victorian as he was a lawyer and judge. While it is impossible to fairly represent the richness of Stephen's attack on Mill's libertarianism in this space, one argument, which bears on the problem of routine order maintenance, will convey its flavor. Stephen comments on the "odd manner in which Mr. Mill worships mere variety, and confounds the proposition that variety is good with the proposition that goodness is various."[33] He then quotes Mill:

Eccentricity is much required in these days. Precisely because the tyranny of opinion is such as to make eccentricity a reproach, it is desirable; in order to break through that tyranny, that people should be eccentric. Eccentricity has always abounded when and where strength of character has abounded, and the amount of eccentricity in a society has generally been proportioned to the amount of genius, mental vigor, and moral courage it contained. That so few now dare to be eccentric makes the chief danger of the time.

And Stephen responds:

If this advice were followed, we should have as many little oddities in manner and behavior as we have people who wish to pass for men of genius. Eccentricity is far more often a mark of weakness than a mark of strength. Weakness wishes, as a rule, to attract attention by trifling distinctions. And strength wishes to avoid it.

It is even unclear that Mill himself consistently subscribed to the extreme position expressed in *On Liberty*. The argument that people should be allowed to behave as they please unless their behavior inflicts tangible, immediate injury on someone else is a position with which it is easy to flirt but difficult to wed and support. Gertrude Himmelfarb has demonstrated that far from being a core idea of Mill's, the extreme libertarianism of *On Liberty* was something close to an intellectual aberration.[34] In writings both before and after *On Liberty*, Himmelfarb finds a more balanced, serious-minded Mill stressing the importance of society's claims on individuals, the importance of shared fundamental principles which are "above debate," and the superiority of existence in a stable social state over "miserable individuality."[35]

Finally, Mill's most distinguished modern critic, the British jurist Patrick Devlin, has effectively scouted the facile distinction between immediate physical and long-term moral harms.[36] Lord Devlin's ultimate judgment of the "simple principle" advanced in *On Liberty* is finely honed:

> As a tract for the times, what Mill wrote was superb, but as dogma it has lost much of its appeal. For Mill's doctrine is just as dogmatic as any of those he repudiates. It is dogmatic to say that if only we were all allowed to behave just as we liked so long as we did not injure each other, the world would become a better place for all of us. There is no more evidence for this sort of Utopia than there is for the existence of Heaven and there is nothing to show that one is any more easily attained than the other. We must not be bemused by words. If we are not entitled to call our society "free" unless we pursue freedom to an extremity that would make society intolerable for most of us, then let us stop short of the extreme and be content with some other name. The result may not be freedom unalloyed, but there are alloys which strengthen without corrupting.[37]

While radical libertarianism with respect to public manners and morals does not comport with either the Anglo-American cultural tradition or with good sense, it certainly does accord with a master trend in intellectual fashion of the past twenty years. This does not validate Mill. It calls the trend into question.

In the wake of the attempted assassination of Ronald Reagan, historian Peter Shaw recalled that in the weeks before firing the shots outside the Washington Hilton John Hinckley "repeatedly evidenced disturbed or suspicious behavior in public."[38] In Lakewood, Colorado, Hinckley had attracted the attention of a policeman who recalled him as deeply suspicious. He was briefly questioned but nothing more. At the Nashville airport Hinckley was arrested and briefly detained for attempting to carry firearms and cartridges onto an airplane. And outside the Hilton several observers noted his agitated behavior; a reporter who overheard his mutterings realized that Hinckley did not belong in the press section where he was standing but did nothing. Shaw argues that Hinckley's easy passage through all these incidents and more was the product of a widespread change in elite views on social deviance. "The pendulum has swung so far from a rigid conception of propriety in public that for the crowd gathered outside the Hilton, bad manners would have consisted in objecting to behavior like Hinckley's." Even the traditional terminology of opprobrium—"nuisance," "undesirable," "antisocial"—has, for many, come to sound quaint if not positively sinister. Commenting on the attack on Reagan, Gerald Ford referred to "loners, kooks, screwballs" with reference to Hinckley, but in fashionable circles "it was Ford himself who gave the appearance of being in violation of a social norm."

Such radical libertarianism trickling down through the universities, the salons, and the media reinforces the passive or legalistic style of police order maintenance and discourages focusing on deviant behavior until there is blood on the street. As Shaw put it:

Acquiescing in the contempt of its critics, the middle class has come to accept the deviant as hero and learned to view mental disturbance as a sign of divine grace (at the same time regarding the policeman as villain and superintendents of the mentally disturbed as signifying a penchant for cruelty).[39]

It is instructive to recall that Sir Robert Peel's establishment of the uniformed London police was opposed as a threat to civil liberties—as, in fact, "unconstitutional." Consider Peel's reply:

I want to teach people that liberty does not consist in having your house robbed by organized gangs of thieves, and in leaving the principal streets of London in the nightly possession of drunken women and vagabonds.[40]

The '83 Good Cop's Manual

The relationship between cops and constitutional lawyers in contemporary America has become ludicrously lopsided in favor of the latter. One reason is simply the exponential growth of constitutional law bearing on the criminal justice process. As Lloyd Weinreb puts it:

The few pages of "black-letter law" that once sufficed to state the constitutional principles have been amplified by a mountainous outpouring of cases and commentary. Virtually all of the currently applicable law has its main exposition in opinions of the Supreme Court written since 1960.[41]

Before me as I write is a document of a thousand mimeographed pages issued by the Attorney General of the State of Maine titled *Law Enforcement Officer's Manual.* This production covers everything from "probable cause" through "handling child abuse and neglect situations." In between are such categories as "information obtained through the officer's own senses," "open fields and abandoned property," and "legal considerations pertaining to roadblocks." On the problem of the "effect of corroborative information

on probable cause" the manual devotes seven full pages to a detailed discussion of the leading Supreme Court decisions in the
area,[42] with liberal reference to lower court interpretations of these
precedents. In concludes with the following injunction:

> The main point of advice for the law enforcement officer was that he
> must satisfy the two-pronged requirements of the Aquilar and Hawkins
> cases before [informant] information can be considered toward establish-
> ing probable cause. . . . By keeping these items of advice in mind and
> carefully following the guidelines presented in this manual, the law en-
> forcement officer should have little difficulty justifying any arrest or
> search, whether conducted with or without a warrant.[43]

No doubt.

The manual is a third-year law student's delight; as public policy
it is a disaster. Even if it could be assumed (which it cannot be in
Maine) that at least one member of every force in the state is a law
school graduate or the product of a first-class graduate program in
criminal justice, and therefore equipped to approach the *Manual*
critically and defensively and interpret it for his fellows, it remains
unclear exactly how the people of the state can expect to be better
protected by ordinary officers who are trying to find their way
through the maze of appellate court decisions and listings of factors
which might or might not, under varying circumstances, authorize
or prohibit them from making what are necessarily split-second
decisions on the highways and byways. How, precisely, is the
average sea-and-shore fisheries warden to benefit from a four-page
discussion of the *Carroll*[44] doctrine (searches of vehicles) nuanced
à la Professor Tribe, when he must make a quick decision whether
to stop and search Clarence Moody's pickup truck on the basis of
rumors around the wharf that Clarence has been less than scrupulous lately in the matter of short lobsters? After reading about the
Carroll doctrine, and being reminded that it requires probable
cause, the warden could then refer back in the *Manual* to the
discussion of *Spinelli* v. *U.S.* to enlighten him on the subject of
informant's information and probable cause. Should he do so con-

scientiously he will be misinformed because a month after the *Manual* was issued the Supreme Court effectively overruled *Spinelli* and altered the ground rules in this highly controversial area.[45] Clarence's "shorts" are on their way to becoming salad for the tourists.

The *Manual* can only have the effect of further inhibiting initiative (the temptation to say "chilling" is almost irresistible) by law enforcement officers in the field. But this is not the limit of the *Manual's* potential mischief. It could have the long-term effect of further compromising the truth-finding function of the criminal trial. We have noted examples (see chapters 3 and 6) of how courts in this activist age often look to guidelines produced by bureaucrats to determine what they will hold the Constitution to require. The *Manual,* of course, purports to state what the law now is. In many instances, however, these statements are tendentious, or represent the law to be clear where in fact it is unsettled (the *Spinelli* example). But it is not hard to imagine that such statements, massaged by "right thinking" judges and law clerks could become self-fulfilling prophecies.

Certainly police officers need to be trained to behave lawfully. Of course we need to educate them as to proper and improper investigative techniques, if for no other reason then to protect the admissibility of evidence so that the possibility of successful prosecution is preserved. Certainly the chief law enforcement officer of a state should be concerned with the quality of this training and education. The question is how? The choice of modes in training and education is crucial. What is so wrong with Maine's *Manual* is that it is a hideously legalistic document, written uncompromisingly in the idiom of appellate courts, with no attempt whatever to "translate" for the street or develop the kind of simple operational rules which give meaningful guidance—and more important, confidence—to working cops. The unrelenting theme of the *Manual* is what officers may not do. Its tone is hectoring and negative. The young lawyers who wrote it might well reply that the constitutional law bearing on law enforcement is, in fact, vast, complicated and limiting. That is precisely our dilemma. But why should these bright young men and women assume that their job is simply to pass this numbing doctrinal substance on to police forces? Surely it is not beyond the wit of skilled lawyers genuinely sympathetic to law enforcement to serve as buffers between cops and constitutional law, stressing the positive and seeking to find ways of encouraging aggressive professionalism rather than cringing uncertainty? The role "lawyer" as learned in law school today includes scrupulous concern for constitutional complexity, and very little concern for the operational problems of those who must enforce law and maintain order. The point is not that the Maine *Manual* is extreme or unique, but that it is typical of the direction being given by constitutional lawyers to cops in contemporary America.

CHAPTER 6

Preempting
Private Outcomes

IN 1976 the late Professor Herbert J. Storing published an article titled "The Constitution and the Bill of rights."[1] Its thesis was simple; to a nineteenth or early twentieth century scholarly readership it would have seemed trite. Coming when it did, it doubtless struck many as novel or even eccentric. Storing reminded us that there is more to the tradition of civil rights and liberties in America than the specific prohibitions on government contained in the Bill of Rights.

We all learned in school that a set of limiting amendments had been insisted upon by Antifederalist critics of the new Constitution who feared a too powerful national government. The Federalist proponents of the new charter answered with the plausible, if not ultimately persuasive, argument that the new central government was already a limited one. It could exercise only the powers delegated to it, and it would be redundant, for instance, to prohibit its legislature from intermeddling in religion when it was not empowered to act with respect to religion in the first place. The answer to this is that legislatures often interfere with things beyond the scope of their authority in attempting to legislate for things that are. And we may thank the Antifederalists for their persistence and James Madison for his sound political judgment in seeing the limiting amendments through. But the point remains that for the framers, basic civil liberties were seen as inhering most importantly in the structure of the government they set up. We have just noted Federalist opinion on the point, and certainly the Antifederalists thought similarly—by definition.[2] Their insistence on a bill of rights was a matter of desiring further insurance against an overreaching central authority. All could agree with Thomas McKeen of Pennsylvania who declared that "the whole plan of government is nothing more than a bill of rights. . . ."[3]

Without detracting from the importance the Bill of Rights has taken on over the course of American development, a proper perspective on our institutions can be restored by accepting Storing's invitation:

> . . . to consider what our constitutional law would be like today if there had been no Bill of Rights. Its focus would presumably be to a far greater extent than it is today on the powers of the government. We might expect more searching examination by the Supreme Court of whether the federal legislation that seems in conflict with cherished individual liberties is indeed "necessary and proper" to the exercise of granted powers. We might expect a fuller articulation than we usually receive of whether, in [John] Marshall's term, "the end" aimed at by given legislation "is legitimate." Might this not foster a healthy concern with the problems of *'governing,'* a healthy sense of responsible self-government?[4]

For Federalists and Antifederalists alike, however divided they were on other issues, the most important guarantees of civil liberty lay in the three principal, structural features of the system which was taking shape under their leadership: the federal arrangement itself, democratic control at the state and local levels, and limited government—or, as I shall refer to it, the primacy of the private sector. Federalism issues are beyond the scope of the book.* The threat posed by the rights industry to democratic control of the state and local levels is a constant theme of the preceding chapters and need not be labored further here. The concern of this chapter is with the carelessness of the rights industry toward the third great structural feature which the framers saw as assuring the liberties of Americans, the principle of limited government.

The framers (excepting perhaps a few of the more extreme Antifederalists) appreciated the need for vigorous government; they were neither laissez-faire enthusiasts (this doctrine dates from a later period) nor callow libertarians of the contemporary variety. They appreciated what government could do to protect people. The *raison d'être* of the constitutional convention was, after all, more government. But it was universally assumed that government, however vigorous, would be limited to certain areas and spheres of human activity; that government would be the creature of society, not the reverse. The idea that the primary networks of commercial, social, and even familial intercourse—the complex and highly inflected hierarchies of private association, power, and achievement—would be generally available for governmental manipulation in pursuit of "social change" is a very recent heresy. So is its corollary—that the rules and procedures appropriate to restraining governmental power are equally appropriate to restraining private power.

---

*It is argued by some these days that federalism has nothing to do with civil liberties because it involves the relationships between governments and not the relationship of government to the individual. Jesse H. Choper, Dean of the Boalt Hall School of Law at Berkeley, is particularly influential in this respect. See "The Scope of National Power Vis-à-Vis the States: The Dispensibility of Judicial Review," 86 *Yale Law Journal* 1552 (1977). "There is," Choper suggests "a qualitative difference that separates constitutional issues of federalism from those of individual liberty." Explaining all that is wrong with this will have to await another day.

The Public-Private Distinction

Ours, the civic books tell us, is a "government of laws and not of men." The idea which is struggling toward expression over these slippery words is that our public officials are constrained to behave toward us, as citizens, in accordance with certain rules. These rules are impersonal; they apply equally to all; they are positive; and they are knowable in advance of their application. This binding of government by general rules is the essence of what political scientists call "constitutionalism," and the perfection of techniques for such limited government has been the major preoccupation of liberal politics for 200 years.

The American Republic was conceived in fear of unbridled governmental power, and its architects derided kings and princes who made their rules as they went along—who justified capricious and arbitrary treatment of subjects by appeals to divine right or the "real" or "ultimate" welfare of their subjects. But the small group of aristocratic politicians to which we reverently refer as "the framers," drew a very sharp distinction between the public and private spheres of human life. They regarded the state as a unique and distinctly dangerous social institution, and it was this peculiarly potent danger they sought to confine. Government was something special, and the rules that defined man's relationship to it were properly quite different from those which applied to private contexts. Failure to grasp this fundamental eighteenth-century distinction has been the source of considerable confusion in historiography and recent political thought. The founders, for instance, favored public equality, not private equality.[5] Men, confronting government, were to be equals, and the state was to treat all according to the same specific rules.[6] One reason for this requirement of public equality was precisely that it would limit the state's power and prevent it from trespassing too far into the private sphere, which it would surely do if it were allowed to make fine distinctions between rich and poor, gentle and base, and so on. In a very real

137

sense public equality was thought desirable because it protected private inequalities.

Modern political science has generally supported the framers in distinguishing sharply between the state and other social institutions. Adopting Max Weber's terminology, most students have agreed that while many social institutions exercise power over people (that is, induce them to behave in accordance with institutional decisions), only the state possesses the capacity (1) to make authoritative choices for the society as a whole, and (2) to underwrite these choices with a monopoly of legitimate violence.[7] The Roman Catholic Archdiocese of New York and the DuPont Company have "power"; at times this power is more dramatic and visible than that of obscure public officials. But they are not "just like" government. Potentially, the state can make an authoritative choice, binding on everyone in its society, and, in the extreme case, legally destroy those who refuse to comply. This is the state's defining characteristic. Stating it starkly is useful from time to time to restore perspective. Alongside the inherent power of the state, all other sorts of social power are fractional. This is why constitutionalists spend so much time worrying about the state and thinking of ways to hedge it round with rules.

I dwell on these fundamentals because so much of our public law has been developed to deal with the special danger presented by the state. As the Republic has grown, increasingly scrupulous rules have evolved to regulate the encounter between the individual and the single agency which can legitimately take his life or put him in a cage. But these rules have been fitted to the distinctive nature of the institution they were created to confine and are not automatically good in other contexts. And yet constructing arguments for the extension of public sector norms, models, and controls further and further into the private sector has been a major growth area within the rights industry.

At first blush it seems odd that persons who think of themselves as civil libertarians, who would forbid the police asking lone males on residential streets for identification at three in the morning, have become adept in using the coercive machinery of the state to alter the social, commercial, and professional practices of their fellow citizens. This is the result, I suggest, of an attachment to a profoundly alien conception of equality—one with even shallower rooting in American culture than John Stuart Mill's radical theory of liberty. As Michael Novak has pointed out:

> Within the American tradition of political economy, whose formative years lie before the origins of socialism, [it] was widely recognized that human beings differ in talent, temperament, application, and virtue. It was also widely recognized that in the societies known to the past many people lacked the opportunity to prove themselves. There was great expectation that liberty under law would provide a sort of equality the human race had never before experienced. In this sense, liberty and equality would go together. Neither one would be perfect. Liberty would be constrained by both law and circumstance. Equality under the law would not mean that the lad born poor would begin life as an equal—in capital, experience, schooling, culture, or contacts—to the lad born to an aristocratic family. Yet in a single lifetime, it was believed and—much more important—it was experienced, a lad born poor might outstrip in his accomplishments, in fortune, and in fame many who had been born in "better" circumstances. Life was not imagined to be a morality play about equality of results. It was believed to be a morality play about the opportunity of all to better themselves and their condition, according to their own efforts and their own luck.[8]

And Novak is surely right, as a matter of intellectual history, in locating the origins of the newer, quite different ideal of equality in late nineteenth- and early twentieth-century European socialism with its leveling emphasis and unhesitating statism. Cast in this mold, equality becomes antithetical to liberty, for in a free society it is impossible to assure either equality of results or perfect equality of opportunity. Free men must accept responsibility for their own destiny even while not possessing complete control over it. The "new equality" rejects this paradox as incoherence, and sets out to put things right through government action. It is this passion for the new equality (a new human rights agenda if you will) that drives rights professionals to extend the dominion of the state. But as Walter Berns reminds us, while traditional understanding of human rights "required government to protect and respect the private realm; to secure the new human rights will require government to intervene in the private realm and eventually destroy it."[9]

Paul Johnson has written recently of the "loss of faith in the state as an agency of benevolence" and considers this an intellectual master trend of the 1980s. Johnson argues that fifty years ago "most intelligent people believed that an enlarged state could increase the sum of total human happiness. By the 1980s, the view was held by no one outside a small, diminishing and dispirited band of zealots."[10] Perhaps he is right; one hopes so. But contemplating a sleek, altogether confident, and deeply entrenched rights industry, I confess to doubt. The lead article in the May 1983 *Harvard Law Review,* concerned with equalizing domestic and child-rearing chores between men and women, suggests that government "could mandate a shortened work week for all people, in order to force everyone to take leisure time sufficient to raise children," and impose "a large fine or surcharge on anyone wishing to work longer hours. . . ."[11] Cities are badgered by activists to legislate against all-male clubs under the once honorable banner of "anti-discrimination." Governmentally mandated hiring quotas are euphemized as "goals." There are a number of different avenues of public law along which the rights activists have pressed seeking to extend government control over private sector choices in the name of advancing equality. In some campaigns they have not altogether succeeded, in others they have.

They have laid siege to the "state action limitation" on the application of the equal protection clause of the Constitution. Even though the Fourteenth Amendment manifestly speaks to acts of the state governments ("No state shall . . .") it is argued that if a state does not employ its general police powers to forbid private discriminatory behavior, it effectively condones that behavior. Since the state condones the behavior, it is party to it, and therefore the equal protection clause applies![12] And there is a corollary to this. The fifth and concluding section of the Fourteenth Amendment (the "implementation clause") empowers Congress "to enforce, by appropriate legislation, the provisions of this article." If the rationale of private decisions becoming state decisions through state inaction is accepted, then the national Congress would be in a position to regulate any behavior it found offensive. Congress already has the power to regulate nonstate behavior with an arguable effect on interstate commerce. This was the rationale on which the public accommodations provisions of the Civil Rights Act of 1964 were upheld by the Supreme Court in *Heart of Atlanta Motel* v. *United States.* [13] And the commerce power might seem sufficient to allow the national government to reach discrimination which is, in any meaningful sense, "public." But many of the new egalitarians continue to be uncomfortable with the commerce clause approach and believe Congress could regulate private choices more boldly and comprehensively under the implementation clause of the Fourteenth Amendment—were it only freed of the state action limitation. However, after wobbling dangerously in the late 1960s, the Supreme Court has declined to abandon or substantially dilute the doctrine.[14]

While the effort to emasculate the state action limitation has thus far failed, other paths into the private sector have been followed with considerable success. Nondiscrimination requirements have been piggybacked onto federal contracts, grants, and financial support of all kinds, so that he who takes the "king's shilling" takes the king's social policy—at least as far as the activity being supported, and arguably for all dimensions of activity of the receiving firm or institution. Given the expansion of federal aid programs since 1960—the ubiquity of "federal funding" today—the reach of this technique is very long indeed. And this reach may be further extended if courts and legislatures can be persuaded that a tax exemption (government deciding for one reason or another to collect a particular tax differentially) is "just the same as a grant." This has, in fact, begun to happen.* Finally, a majority of the

---

*In *Bob Jones University* v. *United States*, 103 S.Ct. 2017 (1983), the Supreme Court upheld a bureaucratic interpretation of a section of the Internal Revenue

Supreme Court has been persuaded to bless an interpretation of the old Civil Rights Act of 1866 (which forbids states depriving persons of the capacity to enter into legal contracts because of race) as forbidding private persons to decline to enter into contracts with other private persons because of considerations of race.[15]

As long as the private sector conduct proscribed by governmental civil rights outreach was racial or ethnic discrimination there seemed little cause for worry, especially when the discriminating behavior addressed was that of large employers of skilled and unskilled labor or of businesses inviting the custom of the public. There was a stable, if regionally uneven, consensus in that racial discrimination was morally wrong, and even the most hidebound reactionaries must have felt a little foolish arguing for a "private right to discriminate." Protecting racist restauranteurs and personnel officers from the governmental coercion was not a matter about which persons of good will could be very concerned, and rightly so. But this changed as the "antidiscrimination" agenda of government was progressively expanded in the late 1960s and early 1970s. To the classically forbidden criteria of race and ethnicity, about which there was at least considerable consensus, was added sex (or "gender," as the lawyers say) about which, as shown most dramatically by the failure of the Equal Rights Amendment, the national consensus is much less clear.* This was followed by carelessly

---

Code to the effect that schools do not have a "racially nondiscriminatory policy as to students" could no longer qualify as charitable organizations to which, as a class, the Code permits taxpayers to deduct contributions. This is *not* the same thing as accepting the argument above that tax exemptions and grants are legally and morally congruent, but it is a step in the wrong direction. While it is wrong in principle to extend a no-racial-discrimination rule on the strength of a tax exemption, it is not, in and of itself, very worrying. (A private capacity to discriminate racially is not a claim with great ethical stopping power.) What is worrying is the likelihood that, once extended and judicially blessed, the simple no-racial-discrimination rule will swell to include "gender," age, handicapped status and God knows what else. And result-oriented affirmative action will follow in the wake.

*Of course there are kinds of discrimination on grounds of sex which are morally wrong in the same sense as racial discrimination is wrong. Violations of the principle of equal pay for the same work is an example. The difficulty is that while discrimination on the basis of race is almost always irrational and wrong, many kinds of discriminations on the basis of sex are reasonable, moral, and (to the horror

drawn provisions proscribing "age discrimination,"[16] and finally, in many jurisdictions, by prohibition of discrimination against the handicapped, including the mentally handicapped (retarded or disturbed). As with sex, these latter human characteristics are very different from race (in the sense of presenting more situations where they are appropriately taken into account), and different from one another in the issues they pose and in degrees of supporting consensus. But the error involved in ill-considered additions to the list of outlawed characteristics pales into insignificance next to error involved in moving beyond prohibitions on acts of discrimination to the requirement of "affirmative action." For just as the constitutional requirement that public schools cease discriminating was superseded by the requirement of racial balance (chapter 3), so government's command to private sector decision makers has changed from cease discriminating to "show results."

Origins of Affirmative Action

The effort undertaken in the 1950s to overrule *Plessy* v. *Ferguson*[17] and dismantle the apparatus of governmentally enforced racial discrimination was a cause of profound moral importance to a generation of American reformers. The merits of the issue were clear; the forces defending Jim Crow were simply, unarguably wrong. Such a situation breeds a fine fighting spirit, and this was needed because the battle was savage and hard things had to be done. The claim of stable political majorities in a cohesive region of the country to continue managing their local affairs in a fashion long accepted had to be firmly overridden. Alterations were ac-

---

of fulminating feminists) continue to be regarded as licit by large numbers of persons of both sexes in all regions of the country. Trying to treat sex just like race in antidiscrimination law results in the intellectual compromise of the enterprise.

cepted in the principles of American federalism which had served the Republic well for a century and a half. The cause was genuinely noble, but along the way rhetorical excesses—"Freedom Now!"— were tolerated by people who should have known better and should have said loudly that freedom is an elusive, partially subjective quality which cannot be simply delivered "now." To countenance such slogans was to underwrite a corrosive disillusionment among blacks and many of their elite white defenders. This, however, was a minor error; two others had more evil breeding power. The first was that racial discrimination was acceptable as long as it was meant to work in favor of groups discriminated against in the past. The second was that American society was full of groups which had been abused and subjugated in essentially the same way as blacks.

How did the American national government become committed to a policy that reaches deeply into the private sector to insure equality of social results according to race, ethnicity, and sex? How, in short, were we committed to the policy of affirmative action? As with the evolution of school busing to achieve racial balance, the answer involves interpretation of the Civil Rights Act of 1964 and the implementation of that act in a set of executive orders, departmental directives, and bureaucratically crafted guidelines.

In its original and best sense "affirmative action" meant that an institutional actor (a government agency, a university, a business, a labor union) had an obligation to do something more than cease discriminating on grounds of race. It had an obligation actively to seek minority persons for its work force. Since minorities have been discriminated against in the past, it cannot be assumed that minority persons will be found by following normal hiring practices. Therefore, the institution must reach out—it must advertise in new places, it must seek to tap new wells of "person power," and it must undertake training programs aimed at bringing minority persons up to the levels of qualification at which they can compete for positions. Finally, the institution must examine its hiring standards to see if these include criteria that operate against hiring of minority persons without any relation to job performance. However, this original conception of affirmative action was quickly superseded by an alternative conception which focuses on results. By this second approach, satisfactory affirmative action must be demonstrated in terms of quotas or percentages of new employees or "goals" for the over-all work force and specialized parts thereof. If racial goals or quotas are going to be set and taken seriously, however, this inescapably involves using race, or ethnicity, or sex, at least to some extent, as a criterion of selection.

Titles VI and VII of the Civil Rights Act of 1964, as we known, have to do with government employers, private employers holding government contracts, and private employers engaged in interstate commerce. On their face these provisions seem to contemplate affirmative action in the first sense of aggressively seeking minority employees, and we saw in chapter 3 how congressional supporters of the 1964 civil rights bill assured skeptics that far from requiring the use of racial and other proscribed criteria for "benevolent" purposes, such use was expressly excluded by the "no-discrimination" command, which was the heart of the bill. One cannot reread this legislative history fairly and come away with any other conclusion that (so much as one can ever speak of Congress "intending" anything) Congress intended the act to establish a color blind rather than a color conscious policy both for government and the private sector.

This was also the sense in which the term affirmative action was used in the crucial executive orders of the Johnson administration, which fixed the bureaucratic responsibility for enforcing the non-discrimination provisions of the Civil Rights Act among government contractors. This conception of affirmative action, however, was reshaped in successive Labor Department and Department of Health, Education, and Welfare regulations which emphasize goals, numbers, and minority "set-asides."

Executive Order No. 11246 (the beginning of bureaucratic policy making under the act) was issued in 1965.[18] It required that government agencies and private contractors* undertake "affirmative action" and "insure that applicants are employed, and that employees are treated during employment, without regard to their race, creed, color or national origin." A prohibition of discrimination on grounds of sex was added by Executive Order No. 11375 in 1967. So far so good. .But as with the application of the act to public schools, rights professionals were strongly of the opinion that a prohibition of discrimination was not enough. And just as an HEW guideline crucially altered the original desegregation policy of *Brown* and of the 1964 act with respect to our schools, so the original understanding of affirmative action was altered in the bowels of the bureaucracy. The new approach was ratified by the then obscure Order No. 4 of the Department of Labor:

> An affirmative-action program is a set of specific and result-oriented procedures to which a contractor commits himself to apply every good faith effort. The objective of these procedures plus such efforts is equal employment opportunity. Procedures without effort to make them work are meaningless; and effort, undirected by specific and meaningful procedures, is inadequate. An acceptable affirmative-action program must include an analysis of areas within which the contractor is deficient in the utilization of minority groups and women and further, goals and timetables to which the contractor's good faith efforts must be directed to correct the deficiencies and thus, to increase materially the utilization of minorities and women, at all levels and in all segments of his work force where deficiencies exist.[19]

In the twinkling of a Washingtonian eye this approach migrated to the Office of Civil Rights at the old HEW, and the new "result-oriented" doctrine was applied to all private colleges and universities receiving federal support (which, by that time, was almost all of them). By 1970 one particular visible rights activist, J. Stanley

---

*It is worth reflecting on the way in which the mental images triggered by particular words may affect our thinking about a policy initiative. "Contractor" tends to conjure up lines of concrete mixers and assembly lines turning out fighter bombers or canteen covers. In fact, a "contractor" may be a university department, an independent art gallery or museum, or a charitable agency delivering social services on an Indian reservation.

Pottinger, head of the Civil Rights Office at HEW, could make deans, chancellors, and chairmen—the nation's most hardened academic infighters—tremble before him. When Mr. Pottinger, a Harvard law graduate and future trustee of the Lawyers Committee for Civil Rights under Law, made his triumphal progress from HEW to take over the Civil Rights Division of the Justice Department he was well and truly the "Hammer of the Universities."

Goals quickly began (in all but name) to operate as quotas, and often very rigid ones. Following the school busing pattern, judges began issuing sweeping "affirmative" remedial orders in suits under the 1964 act. Thus, for instance, in January of 1980 former NAACP staffer, Judge Robert L. Carter of the Federal District Court for the Southern District of New York, forbade New York City's using its existing test to screen applicants for the police force unless 50 percent of the recruits selected were black or hispanic; the Court of Appeals for the Second Circuit modified Carter's order by simply requiring that one-third of those hired off the existing list of eligible candidates had to be members of the designated minorities.[20]

Putting aside (again) the question of the legitimacy of such bureaucratic/judicial policy modification, the use of racial quotas and goals as public policy raised a constitutional question.* There was, lurking in the constitutional background, the argument that the equal protection clause should really be understood as forbidding the use of race as a criterion of choice for any reason—that the Constitution of the United States should be "color blind." And while the Supreme Court in *Swann* had licensed the use of racial classifications in school assignments as an appropriate device for remedying the evils of past state-enforced segregation, it was not

---

*It is sometimes argued that Congress in later enactments, such as the Equal Opportunity Act of 1972 and Title IX of the Education Amendments of 1972, gave retrospective endorsement to result-oriented affirmative action. I think, however, that a fair-minded reading of those statutes will reveal that they track the "no-discrimination" principle of the 1964 act. A subtler version of this argument suggests that by not explicitly rejecting the result-oriented style of implementation of its prior enactments, Congress was, in some meaningful sense, approving it. The weaknesses of this type of argument are treated in the following chapter.

altogether clear to what extent other governmental agencies could discriminate on racial lines in an effort to achieve benign ends. Did the Constitution permit "reverse discrimination"—did it allow for "color conscious" policy outside the area of school integration orders? The academic division of the rights industry was quick to proffer rationales for color consciousness in hiring.[21] And while approval did not come from the Supreme Court as easily as it came for school busing in *Swann,* it came.

The Court first confronted the reverse discrimination question in the case of *University of California Regents* v. *Bakke.* [22] Here the medical school of the University of California at Davis had set aside sixteen places in an entering class of 100 for minority students. Minority status was operationally defined in racial terms, and in the course of the litigation it was stipulated by the regents that Bakke would have been admitted to the entering class had it not been for the minority "set aside."

The Court was deeply divided in its response, as it has been in succeeding responses to questions of reverse discrimination. One group of four justices including Brennan, Marshall, White, and Blackmun, argued that the Davis affirmative action program violated neither the equal protection clause of the Fourteenth Amendment (the school is a state institution) nor the Title VI ban on discrimination by institutions receiving federal funds. Another group of four justices, Chief Justice Burger, along with Justices Stewart, Rehnquist, and Stevens, thought that it was unnecessary to consider the constitutional question since they believed that the Davis program contravened the no-racial-discrimination provision of Title VI.

There was no opinion for the Court. Justice Powell cast the deciding vote and announced the judgment of the Court in an opinion which argued that Title VI and the equal protection clause imposed essentially identical obligations, and that by making race alone the dispositive criterion for admission under the minority set aside, Davis had acted illegally. But Powell went on to suggest that had Davis used race along with other factors (for example, poverty) in determining who would be eligible for the relaxed admissions standards applied to the set-aside slots, the program would have been both constitutional and legal under Title VI. Powell cited the minority admissions program of Harvard College as an example of one in which race was used in a permissible fashion. While opponents of reverse discrimination as civil rights policy could take some comfort from Powell's opinion, they were quick to note that the difference between Harvard's permissible program and Davis' impermissible one were only cosmetic.

While commentators were still trying to unsnarl the implications of *Bakke,* the Court, in 1979, confronted the case of *United Steel Workers* v. *Weber.*[23] This involved an affirmative action plan worked out under Labor Department pressure by a private employer (Kaiser Aluminum) and its principal employee union. Under the terms of the plan half of the openings for certain in-plant timing programs were reserved for minorities, racially defined. The question here (since, technically, there was no state action involved) was whether this violated the no-racial-discrimination provision of Title VII of the Civil Rights Act, which covers employers engaged in interstate commerce. Justice Brennan wrote the majority opinion and held that, since the underlying purpose of the 1964 act had been to advance the economic and social position of blacks in America, the no-discrimination language had to be read against that background, and that the program before the Court was therefore not a violation of the statute.

Perhaps the best way of characterizing Justice Brennan's opinion for the Court in *Weber,* is to say it rivals John Minor Wisdom's performance in *Jefferson County* (see chapter 3).* Brennan's task

---

*This parallel is strengthened by the fact that in the Court of Appeals for the Fifth Circuit, where a majority concluded that Kaiser's set-aside violated Title VII, John Minor Wisdom wrote a dissenting opinion. Wisdom argued, among other things, that a presumptive showing of actual discrimination at the Kaiser plant in question had been made based on statistical disproportionality. He disposed of the problem presented by the language and legislative history of Title VII with the argument that at the time of the passage of the Equal Opportunity Act of 1972 Congress knew about result-oriented affirmative action and had, with that knowledge, failed to adopt an amendment proffered by Senator Sam Ervin of North

was to sustain a racial set-aside by an employer covered by the 1964 act. But Title VII, just like Title VI, seemed to proscribe choices between persons based on race. And even if Justice Brennan looked beyond the words of the statute to the legislative history, which by traditional canons of craftmanship is only proper when the words themselves are unclear, that history was dead against him. In chapter 3 we listened to Senator Humphrey; now listen to Senators Joseph Clark of Pennsylvania and Clifford Case of New Jersey, who were specifically responsible for the defense of Title VII on the Senate floor:

Any deliberate attempt to maintain a racial balance, whatever such a balance may be, would involve a violation of Title VII because maintaining such a balance would require an employer to hire or to refuse to hire on the basis of race. It must be emphasized that discrimination is prohibited as to any individual. . . .[24]

Undaunted, however, Justice Brennan, looked past both the clear language and the unambiguous legislative history, and resorted to sophistry built upon platitude. While Title VII did not *require* reverse discrimination to achieve a racially balanced work force, it does not explicitly forbid reverse discrimination to such an end! And since the concern of Congress was to open employment opportunities to blacks and other ethnic minorities that had suffered historically from invidious discrimination, it would betray the larger purpose of the legislature to be bound strictly by its words.* Thus the judiciary approved an executive branch interpretation of what began as a congressional policy, and Congress, once again, was odd branch out.

Carolina, which would have specifically barred any "preferential treatment." Weber v. Kaiser Aluminum and Chemical Corp., 563 F.2d 216 (1977).

*It is worth noting that the most careful and devastating analysis of Brennan's *Weber* opinion was not written by a lawyer, but by a philosopher. See Carl Cohen, "Justice Debased: The Weber Decision," *Commentary,* September 1979. See also "Equality, Diversity and Good Faith," 26 *Wayne Law Review* 1261 (1980).

The third case in the terrible trilogy of affirmative action was *Fullilove* v. *Klutznick* in 1980.[25] Here, however, the question did not involve the Civil Rights Act at all, but what was permitted to the Congress itself by the "equal protection component of Fifth Amendment due process." A federal law, the Public Works Employment Act of 1977, provided that a certain share of federal construction business should be set aside for minority contractors. *Bakke* there was no opinion for the Court. Chief Justice Burger announced the judgment of the Court that the congressional use of a racial classification was not unconstitutional in this instance. His opinion was joined by Justices White and Powell. Burger argued that benevolent racial discrimination by Congress was constitutional as long as it was carefully limited and tailored to remedy some past discrimination. The chief justice rejected the contention that "Congress must act in a wholly 'color-blind' fashion," but suggested that there were strict limitations on the use of racial classifications for benevolent purposes.

Justices Marshall, Brennan, and Blackmun concurred in the judgment. Justice Stevens dissented on the grounds that the 10-percent minority set-aside adopted by Congress in the 1977 act did not meet the criteria for limited and precise action directed at particular past discrimination which the chief justice himself had set forth in the plurality opinion. Justices Stewart and Rehnquist dissented, taking the position that color-blindness is an essential requirement of equal protection.

Such is the state of constitutional law of affirmative action, and if the reader entertains suspicion that much of the tapestry of argument just described is a kind of "law magic," the reader would be correct. The practical effect of all this, however, is that reverse discrimination may be practiced by government and required by government of private sector decision makers—as long as it's not done too openly or crudely. We shall have to look to public policy arguments to succeed where constitutional arguments have failed.

Dimensions of Mischief

Nowhere are the disabling costs of rights industry innovation clearer than in the area of affirmative action—the added administration burden on large employers (many universities now allocate scarce educational resources to the maintenance of separate "affirmative action offices"), and the prohibition of useful devices for personnel selection (there is, at the moment, no test for determining eligibility for employment in the civil service of the United States) *sautant aux yeux*. The less obvious costs are moral and psychological. Affirmative action in the sense now established mocks the merit principle and casts an ugly shadow over the achievement of deserving minority individuals. It may even, in a quite perverse way, hold back talented blacks, women, and hispanics—as attractive candidates from "protected categories" are passed over by employers who fear that if the appointment does not work out the mistake will be locked in. It is precisely the case that the word "rights," used to mean equality of results by demographic groups, now signals "a clear and present danger" to individual liberties. As others have written eloquently of these dangers,[26] I will confine myself to three others which, if more subtle, are none the less real.

Serious, but less effectively scouted than the aforementioned mischiefs, is the fact that result-oriented affirmative action depends for both its intellectual justification and its administration on a palpable falsehood—a widely and casually accepted falsehood, but no truer for that. This holds that when women or minorities turn out to be statistically under represented in a particular labor force, or within a specialty, or in managerial ranks, this underrepresentation can be assumed in some meaningful sense to be a result of discrimination by the employer. Set out in cold print this may seem too obviously faulty a proposition to be widely and casually accepted, but listen to Edward Hoagland, one of our most literate essayists. Reflecting on the goals of the "Women's Movement"

Hoagland observed that these have been divided between matters of simple justice and matters of androgyny. Fair enough. But Hoagland goes on to say that the "simple part is that any fair-minded person who walks into a bank and sees that all the tellers are women and all the officers are men is going to cast a vote for women's rights."[27] But as Will Rogers once remarked, ignorance is not nearly so bad as what we know "that ain't so." And Hoagland's assumption that the sexual asymmetry between tellers and officers results from management discrimination ain't necessarily so.

In fact, a variety of other factors may account for observed demographic disproportionalities that regnant intellectual fashion encourages us to ascribe to discrimination. Carl Hoffmann and John Shelton Reed have reported one particularly illuminating study of promotion differentials between men and women clerks. Men were promoted more frequently than women, but as soon as the employee subpopulation actually demonstrating "promotion-seeking behavior" was identified, the gender difference disappeared —men and women were promoted in proportion to their numbers within the relevant subpopulation. The fact was that more men than women manifested promotion-seeking behavior. Why? The answer lies in the realization that employment means different things to different people, and Hoffmann and Reed found that considerably more married men than married women placed job advancement ahead of home and child rearing concerns.[28] As Thomas Sowell puts it:

> "Representation" or "under representation" is based on comparisons of a given group's percentage in the population which might make sense if the various ethnic groups were even approximately similar in age distribution, education, and other crucial variables. But they are not.[29]

No matter how many times the fallacy is exposed, it pops back again: the rights industry needs to justify the imposition of affirmative action controls, and the need is so powerful that no mere intellectual embarrassment deters.* Thus it was, for instance, that the joint *amici* brief of the ACLU and the Society of American Law Teachers in *Weber* asserted, on the basis of simple statistical disproportionality, that Kaiser had discriminated against minorities in hiring skilled craft workers.

Another danger attendant on the established version of affirmative action is that its internal logic leads the believers on to ever deeper incursions into the realm of private institutions and private choice. An example of this is the argument which has surfaced within the rights industry over the last few years that it is possible and desirable to develop standards for determining the "comparable worth" of quite different jobs.

As data accumulate showing that the principle of equal pay for the same work is beginning to take hold, the fact remains that many types of jobs in which women predominate pay less than many types of jobs in which men predominate.[30] Opening opportunities in previously male-dominated occupations is slow work, and many women appear to prefer traditionally female jobs for very good personal reasons. But if the forces of the market can be overridden might not the cause of women be advanced by a system

*There is a fallback position, but it is even more unsatisfactory; it is risible. This holds that since massive discrimination took place in America historically, the descendants of the "majority" which generally benefited from this discrimination owe compensation to the descendants of the "minority" which was generally disadvantaged. Imposing result-oriented "remedies" is justified not because in any contemporary sense Kaiser Aluminum or Columbia University can be found to have engaged in any actual discrimination against identifiable people, but out of a concern for historical justice. However, once one applies the least analytical pressure to the notions of majority and minority in this argument it collapses. Is the majority composed of "Anglo Saxons"? But they are not a majority, and while some of this ethnic cohort did very well in the course of American economic development, others (e.g., in Appalachia) did rather poorly. What about later arriving white ethnics? The earlier ones benefited more than the later arrivals, but many of these groups also suffered from discrimination and this would have to be taken into account in any attempt to establish what particular groups "owed" historically. And what of intermarriages? How do you score a person named Donovan who grew up in a New England mill town but had a Yankee grandfather named Chauncey? To attempt this seriously would be obscene (one thinks of the Nuremberg Laws). But without such ethnic accounting the historical equity rational collapses. The argument is simply too weak to carry legal or moral weight.

154

which analyzes jobs and rationally (by awarding points for skill, stress level, exposure to the elements, and so on) determines their respective value? The employer would then be directed to establish levels of compensation corresponding to the "real" value of his jobs, regardless of who was prepared to work for what, or what skills were in long or short supply. This does not involve regulation of the market mechanism, but its abandonment. The idea of free economic acts between consenting adults is radically discounted. More importantly, the actual task of valuing existing jobs would create new jobs for rights professionals in state human rights commissions, departments of labor relations, and consulting firms. The foxes would not only guard the chicken coop, they would design it.

The disabling and statist potential of this idea needs no further elaboration. To the costs in efficiency and productivity already resulting from the abandonment of "non-job-related" screening instruments, would be added huge nonmarket costs.[31] That establishing comparable worth would be an expensive proposition for the regulated employers can hardly be doubted. Would any existing jobs really be reduced in pay? Is it not likely that the only direction would be up? Yet the litigating, and lobbying, and propagandizing work of groups such as the National Committee on Pay Equity, NOW, and the Women's Legal Defense Fund goes forward, accompanied by a train of well-tailored "equality consultants" seeking to make a capitalist buck by doing capitalism down. My morning's mail brings a flyer from the junior senator from Maine informing me delightedly that the effort to establish comparable worth will "challenge our society on some of its most fundamental perceptions. . . ."[32] Indeed it will.

But surely the most corrosive affect of the campaign by new egalitarians to preempt private choice is on the capacity of the regulated institutions to pursue their distinctive excellences as the reason and instincts of their leaders and managers dictate (which, as a moment's reflection will reveal, is the only way excellence can be pursued). The long-term danger to a free society in overly circumscribing the discretion of private elites is difficult to over-state. "Civilization," as we have recently been reminded, "depends upon the recognition and the cultivation of excellence and superiorities; the maintenance of a civilized society, therefore, would be made impossible by a thorough-going egalitarianism."[33] Competition in excellence is the prime civilizing force—a force that is diminished and diverted and marginally neutralized by affirmative action. My point is not that unfettered discretion should be accorded to private sector decision-making elites—doctrinaire libertarianism is as alien to America as egalitarian statism—but the kinds of restrictions placed on private sector leaderships by result-oriented affirmative action programs are destructive of creativity, and of organizational standards and tone, in a way that health and safety regulations, or labor relations laws, or governmental financial filing requirements are not. This is because affirmative action programs seek to control the most intimate dimension of leadership—decisions as to the proper human mix to advance the group's ends.*

The mischief, let me hasten to add, is not being forced to choose "unqualified" people. This often happens today in the haste of institutional leaders to appease affirmative action inspectors but it is not inherent in such efforts. The danger that is inherent is that leader discretion will be limited or chilled in choosing the most appropriate of the "qualified" candidates. Here is how Antonin Scalia, former professor of law at the University of Chicago and presently a federal appeals court judge, puts it:

> Affirmative action requirements under Title VI and VII are said repeatedly "not to require the hiring of any unqualified individuals." That gives one a great feeling of equal justice until it is analyzed. Unfortunately, the world of employment applicants does not divide itself merely into "qualified" and "unqualified" individuals. There is a whole range of ability—from unqualified, through minimally qualified, qualified, well-qualified, to

---

*I suspect that for commercial institutions, state control over investment decisions may be similarly threatening, but the matter of the relative magnitudes of threats need not detain us here.

outstanding. If I can't get Leontyne Price to sing a concert I have scheduled, I may have to settle for Erma Glatt. La Glatt has a pretty good voice, but not as good as Price. Is she unqualified? Not really—she has sung other concerts with modest success. But she is just not as good as Price. Any system that coerces me to hire her in preference to Price, because of her race, degrades the quality of my product and discriminates on racial grounds against Price. And it is no answer to either of these charges that Glatt is "qualified." To seek to assuage either the employer's demand for quality or the disfavored applicant's demand for equal treatment by saying there is no need to hire any unqualified individuals is a sort of intellectual shell game, which diverts attention from the major issue by firmly responding to a minor one.[34]

Nor can this point be evaded by flight into obscurantism—by suggestions that quality has "many dimensions," or is "perceived differently by different people" or that it is "really impossible to make fine distinctions between human beings" once certain objective, job-related criteria have been met (can La Glatt sight read and sustain high C?). Persons who have not learned that the fine distinctions are always the most important ones in human affairs have scant claim on the attention of serious people. With respect to the fine distinctions in the world of production and exchange, here is Ralph K. Winter, formerly of the Yale Law School and now, as well, a federal judge:

[Many] . . . intangibles influence business decisions because we subjectively place value upon them, even though, apart from that preference, they seem to have no productive worth. Questions of style and beauty as well as other even less easily defined considerations constantly shape business (and employment) decisions. Matters of individual taste are involved and cannot be eliminated without gross impingement on individual freedom and quite intolerable substantive results. For this reason, if no other, there ought always to be at least a presumption in favor of leaving private conduct free of governmental coercion.[35]

And so it is, from volunteer fire departments[36] to history departments. As regards the universities, Paul Seabury wrote prophetically in 1972 (when result-oriented affirmative action was really shifting into high gear) that:

Compliance with demands from the federal government . . . would compel a stark remodeling of their criteria of recruitment, their ethos of professionalism, and their standards of excellence.[37]

And so it has. Amherst philosopher Thomas R. Kearns faces the underlying issue without flinching:

> Of course, [leadership] discretion remains a familiar and reasonable basis for concern since it is, experience shows, a powerful temptation to wrongdoing. But the crucial point is this: there is no way to eliminate the danger or even to monitor it effectively without destroying it, for discretion is most valuable in connection with matters that are not easily or wisely subjected to rules.[38]

Rules, "objective" criteria, "systematic decision-making"— these are the ultimate traps which egalitarianism lays for excellence.

Protecting the Private Sector

Those who advocate increased governmental restriction of private choice in the name of increased equality frequently parry criticism with the argument that they do not want to regulate those things which are "truly private." By this reasoning the kinds of incursions into the private sector now taking place really involve matters which are part of the "public life of the society." Law firms, university departments of art history, local country clubs, and so on, are places in which commercial transactions or conversations relating to the exchanges of goods or services take place. Such activity, it is suggested, is "public" in the same sense that theaters, restaurants, and hotels are places of "public" accommodation. The latter sorts of businesses solicit the custom of the public generally and are, therefore, in a very poor position to oppose a state requirement of nondiscrimination in service by pointing to the fact that they are privately, rather than governmentally owned.

The difficulties with this defense are manifold. The fact that a store opens itself to "the public generally" certainly deprives it of any meaningfully private character as respects its choice of clientele, but this is much less clear as regards the store's personnel choices. And the rationale is quite attenuated by the time one reaches the golf links and clubhouse where two of the store's executives may, of an afternoon, talk shop or entertain a branch manager to lunch. It can be maintained, I suppose, that an art history department is in some sense "open to the public," but this does instant violence to nature and proper function of this highly specialized association. And law firms, even very large ones, cannot without insult to good sense be characterized as "public" in the same sense that a regulated utility company might be. Human associations, even those involved in commerce, distribute themselves across a spectrum of "privateness." Even partisans of increasing state control to promote equality recognize that as

. . . between public and private there will remain a gray area presenting hard cases. Is a church part of the public life or is it merely a private association? What of the "society" so large that it encompasses the entire relevant public, such as the medical association or the bar association? How about the "private" college open to the general public?[39]

But the tilt is always toward the desired answer, "public"; and if public for any aspect of the institution's activity, then public for it all.

When one ponders this, something very interesting begins to emerge. Following the approach of the new egalitarians the only things which would remain "truly private" are forms of association capable of exerting little or no social, economic or political power. The realm of the private is reduced to the privacy of the priest hole. In the house, with the blinds drawn, a person may be "unaccountable" or even make governmentally disfavored choices—just as the

Mass in Elizabethan England could be said in family chapels but not "in public." When so radically constricted, however, the private realm is no longer the countervailing power to government which, in the American tradition, it is assumed to be. To put the finest point on it, if you argue that any association exercising significant social, economic, or political power is, by that fact alone, morally and legally available to be subjected to government regulation of its most important internal choices, you have traduced the concept of a private sector capable of containing government; you have undercut a major section of our constitutional foundation. From a constitutional viewpoint it is only those non-governmental associations which can exercise some significant external ("public") power which contribute to the maintenance of liberty.

The hour is late and the water riseth. As Senator Moynihan has written:

> The conquest of the private sector by the public sector, of which Joseph Schumpeter wrote a generation ago, continues apace. If the private institutions of America are to be preserved, we are going to have to learn to defend them.[40]

But there was one before Schumpeter who foresaw the danger, and Tocqueville put a name to the evil: "the principle of equality."

> After having thus successively taken each member of the community in its powerful grasp and fashioned him at will, the supreme power then extends its arm over the whole community. It covers the surface of society with a network of small complicated rules, minute and uniform, through which the most original minds and the most energetic characters cannot penetrate, to rise above the crowd. The will of man is not shattered, but softened, bent, and guided; men are seldom forced by it to act, but they are constantly restrained from acting. Such a power does not destroy, but it prevents existence; it does not tyrannize, but it compresses, enervates, extinguishes, and stupefies a people, till each nation is reduced to nothing better than a flock of timid and industrious animals, of which the government is the shepherd.[41]

160

What is so hard for us to understand as a people who have reverenced "the law," is that it is now law against which many important social institutions must be protected—law as the instrument of egalitarianism, law as the statist chilling of excellence. Indispensable as it is in ordering some of the relations between us (our behavior toward one another in the streets and other really public places), law is, in other contexts, at war with the kind of subtle discriminations that advance excellence.

Law requires specifying certain gross features of human situations and treating these alone as decisive. Rules, useful as they are for many purposes, are stupid, mindless, undiscriminating things. Either all who cheat on examinations (or expense accounts, or performance specifications) are canned or they are not. Either all pop-offs (or lushes or eccentrics) are punished or they are not. Rules cannot be inflected to pick up the endless variety and shades of cheaters, pop-offs, and eccentrics, and to attempt to make what are properly discretionary choices "rulefully," runs the risk of turning every institutional decision into a debilitating bazaar haggle.

Ultimately, the matter of protecting the private sector involves protecting it from governmental imposition of rules, and protecting it from itself—from modeling itself on government. Democracy, as the framers understood, is an acceptable form of political organization only when the government so organized is limited and substantial societal space is left for a universe of private associations operating in terms of their own distinctive organizing principles. Disraeli once remarked

> If I were asked, "Would you have Oxford with its self-government, freedom, and independence, but with its anomolies and imperfections, or would you have the University free of those anomolies and imperfections and under the control of the Government?" I would say, "Give me Oxford, free and independent with all its anomolies and imperfections."[42]

It is a sort of sentiment which thoughtful Americans are coming to appreciate.

CHAPTER 7

Corrupting

Constitutional

Interpretation

IN AMERICA the landscape of civil rights and liberties is perpetually fogged with legal terminology and legalistic argument. This cannot be otherwise but it carries with it a danger. It cannot be otherwise because of our commitment to a written constitution protecting certain individual rights, and to statutory protection of others. Our written constitution is law, as John Marshall explained to us; and like any other law it is interpreted by courts—the province of lawyers:[1] Courts followed by lawyers, as the night is followed by the day—elementary and obvious. This is the more so with statutory guarantees which have become much more numerous and complicated in recent years. But what is not so obvious, and is anything but unimportant, is the change in the role of lawyers and in the sociology of the legal profession in America in this century. At the time of the ratification of the Constitution the professional distinction between lawyers and other educated men of affairs was much less sharp than today. Legal training, most frequently, was informally acquired. One bought a copy of Blackstone, read law in an office briefly, and was admitted to a "bar," which was really a local club of those who happened to be practicing at the moment. Movement in and out of practice was easy and frequent. For over a century after *Marbury* v. *Madison* (1803) it was very common, at least outside a few major commercial centers, for successful persons to practice a little law in the course of their careers—along with teaching school (usually early on), farming, lumbering, land speculation, and, perhaps, launching a manufacturing venture. When the large old houses of the nineteenth-century Americans were sold off in the twentieth century (after the third generation went to the state university and moved to New York) there were usually some law books in the ill-assorted library. The rise of the law schools as gatekeepers of the "profession" was a gradual business. The Harvard Law School was established in 1817 to meet the competition of Judge Tapping Reeve's school at Litchfield, Connecticut. And while each place produced outstanding early and mid-nineteenth century alumni (Oliver Wendell Holmes, Jr., from Harvard, John C. Calhoun from Litchfield), Harvard, and other schools modeled on it, did not come to exercise great power over legal education and lawyering generally until after Charles William Eliot appointed Christopher Columbus Langdell Dane professor of law and first dean of the law school in 1870.[2]

While the contours of the present system of high professional specialization (with admission by law school diploma) were taking shape in the late nineteenth-early twentieth centuries, much significant constitutional scholarship and commentary was generated by "laymen." Thus in 1915, Henry Cabot Lodge, trained as an historian, published his influential essay on *The Democracy of the*

Constitution.[3] At Columbia, John Burgess, working within an emerging discipline, had produced in 1890 his two volume treatise on *Political Science and Constitutional Law.*[4] And following in the footsteps of George Bancroft,[5] writers such as Charles Grove Haines,[6] and Albert J. Beveridge in his magisterial biography of John Marshall,[7] spoke directly and powerfully to questions of doctrine—questions of what was correct and incorrect in constitutional law. Even in the last generation Edward S. Corwin of Princeton, a political scientist, was an unembarrassed and widely respected commentator on questions of constitutional interpretation.

Now this is greatly changed. With a few distinguished exceptions, political scientists have relinquished the turf of constitutional policy making to lawyers and have retreated into more abstract, social scientific (but arguably less relevant) studies of judicial behavior. "Doctrine" (that is, constitutional policy) and debating the rightness or wrongness of outcomes are "what lawyers do," and they should not be "aped." Neither historians (again with a few distinguished exceptions), nor men of letters generally, have felt comfortable in monitoring the work of the Supreme Court. What are the consequences of this?

One consequence is that today's near monopoly by lawyers and law schools over questions of public law has hastened the decline of interest in structural protections of liberty (discussed in chapter 8), which were a central concern of writers such as Lodge and Corwin. Concomitantly, there has been increasing preoccupation on the part of our contemporary lawyer-interpreters with the strictures of the Bill of Rights, which lend themselves to legalistic elaboration into subtly nuanced rules. But the greater danger lies in the fact that the task of policing the interpretation of the Constitution by the judges has largely passed from being the common intellectual responsibility of the social, economic, and academic leadership of the country, and has come under the control of an increasingly closed guild, with a specialized language and a claim to special expertise not only in the traditionally lawyerly and technical areas of private law, but in public law as well—including the law of the Constitution.

How well are the lawyers, and especially the law schools, doing as keepers of the canons of constitutional interpretation? Not very well. And the reason for this is the extensive interpenetration of legal education and the rights industry. We are witnessing today the widespread practice of a kind of interpretive brigandage which ranges over the entire world intellectual landscape in search of "sources" for the new constitutional law which is desired. "Interpretation" itself has become a suspect concept.

"Interpretivism" Embattled

It marks the dominance of rights radicalism in the law schools that the traditional approach to deciding what the Constitution means has been assigned an ugly, unsatisfactory name ("interpretivism") and that the ascendant persuasion rejoices in describing its approach by a term which is nothing less than a damning admission ("noninterpretivism").* That these rubrics were initially suggested by one of the relatively moderate mandarins, Dean John Hart Ely of the Stanford Law School, does not take the curse off. Ely, then a professor at Harvard, defined interpretivism as requiring "that judges deciding constitutional issues should confine themselves to enforcing norms that are stated or clearly implicit in the written Constitutions." The approach is distinguished by "its insistence that the work of the political branches is to be invalidated only in

---

*I do not suggest that the law schools are monolithic in this respect. A few redoubtable critics of rights industry excesses have honorable lodging in the legal academy (e.g., Professor Joseph Bishop at Yale). A number of others, while not as rebellious as one might wish, exercise some quiet restraint over their colleagues and students. Nonetheless, the political tropism is sharply to the left—towards advancing those forms of "noninterpretive" constitutional interpretation which make the judicial creation of new rights and liberties easier.

accord with an inference whose starting point, whose underlying premise, is fairly discoverable in the Constitution." Noninterpretivism, by contrast, argues "that courts should go beyond that set of references and enforce norms that cannot be discovered within the four corners of the document."[8] Ely's statement of the matter is fair enough, but some elaboration is useful.

Interpretivism does not insist that the meaning of a constitutional provision is fixed forever by the immediate concerns of the framers or bound in hoops of steel by history. It does mean that to qualify as constitutional interpretation an argument must give weight to what can be known of the intent of the framers and must take into account what previous generations of constitutionally literate persons conceived the words at issue to mean. While interpretivism is restrictive of innovation in constitutional law (that, after all, is the essence of constitutionalism) the two most frequent charges leveled against it by its opponents are untrue.

The first is that interpretivism would necessarily sweep away *Brown* v. *Board* and the constitutional prohibition of governmental racial discrimination which has come to rest on it. It is suggested that since the framers of the Fourteenth Amendment did not specifically intend the equal protection clause to forbid *all* state discriminations based on race (and they clearly did not), then interpretivists must doubt the legitimacy of *Brown.* Therefore, because support from the dismantling of Jim Crow which resulted from *Brown* is a litmus test for men of good will, and because interpretivists must doubt *Brown,* interpretivism is not a position open to men of good will. Slick, but the premise is false. Given the clear antislavery motivation of the framers of Fourteenth Amendment, given the fact that they were reacting swiftly and decisively against one form of state imposed discrimination in the Black Codes, a perfectly good interpretivist opinion could be written for *Brown* (and almost anything would be an improvement on what *was* written), pointing out that while the framers of the Fourteenth Amendment, and Justice Brown who wrote in *Plessy* v. *Ferguson,* were able to conceive of trivial state imposed separations based on race, almost a century of experiences made clear that such state discriminations substantially undercut the specific (not the general) and manifest (not the underlying) purposes of the equal protection clause. Just as in the Fourth Amendment context interpretivism can justify substitution of "zones of privacy" for physical premises in order to preserve the purposes of the framers against the potential of electronic surveillance which they could not have foreseen,[9] so "separate but equal" could have been jettisoned.*

The second common canard concerning interpretivism is that it insists on a strict, and therefore pre-modern, distinction between the judicial and the legislative (including constitution making) functions. In the same way that the result of *Brown* is a test of good will, so the "revelation" of the legal realists that judges make law is a test of good sense.[10] But again, care is in order. Certainly judges make law. Interpretivism allows for controlled innovation, and the sixth-grade-civics-book conception of Congress "legislating," the president "administering," and the courts "adjucating," is not implicit in it.

To learn from the realists is not to be possessed by them. To recognize that the law-making function is shared is not to say that it is shared in equal parts. And it is quite misleading to suggest, as Dean Harry H. Wellington of the Yale Law School recently did, that courts and legislatures are "engaged in a common enterprise of governing the future wisely."[11] The legislature (or the constitutional convention) decides *de novo* on certain policy provisions; such choices (while always less than perfectly clear) represent continuing compacts which the losers in the process agree to accept as legitimate because of the authority conferred by the process itself. Law, constitutional and otherwise, is composed of *compacts,* and judges should approach these compacts on their knees. Usually the compacts will involve ambiguities; often the judge must reason by analogy from the situation to which the framers or the legisla-

---

*The fact that a few interpretivist fundamentalists such as Raoul Berger and Justice Black might not allow this much flexibility should not be seized upon to impeach the entire approach.

tors were responding to a new and unforeseen situation. (Consider the example, beloved of law professors, of an ordinance banning "vehicles" from the parks: is a bicycle a "vehicle"? is a baby carriage?) But the policy provision (not the "value preference") being enforced must be discernibly that embodied in the relevant compact whether it be a constitution or a statute. Otherwise there is simply no legitimate moral basis for judicial decision. When tightly reasoned inferences can no longer be drawn from a compact, the judge must stop—in constitutional cases the governmental rule or practice under attack must be allowed to stand. The legislature or the convention may alter policy for any reason that seems compelling, courts may not. And if this distinction is buried under an avalanche of spuriously tough-minded realism, or hopelessly blurred by endless repeated references to judges as "the nation's conscience," then, invisibly but surely, legitimacy will bleed away from the courts and an important structural aspect of our constitutional system will be imperiled. This is disabling with a vengeance!

Of course, the judges will be cheered along the way to disabling excesses. That is what is happening now.* Unless it is stopped, writes Judge Robert Bork:

> . . . there will occur what I have called the gentrification of the Constitution. The constitutional culture—those who are most intimately involved with constitutional adjudication and how it is perceived by the public at large: federal judges, law professors, members of the media—is not composed of a cross-section of America, either politically, socially, or morally. If, as I have suggested, noninterpretivism leads a judge to find constitutional values within himself, or in the values of those with whom he is most intimately associated, then the values which might loosely be described as characteristic of the university-educated upper middle class will be those that are imposed.[12]

*Reagan administration judicial appointments have so depleted the already thin ranks of interpretivists in the law schools that Judge Robert Bork, formerly professor of law at Yale and now of the U.S. Court of Appeals for the District of Columbia, quipped that the faculty members of the dominant persuasion "who don't like much else about Ronald Reagan regard him as a great reformer of legal education."

But while the gentry can lionize, and justify, and stimulate, and socialize the judges, there is one thing it cannot do; it cannot ultimately protect them from the political consequences of what they do. And however offended we may be by particular decisions without roots in covenants, this mortgaging of judicial legitimacy is the graver danger.

Illegitimate Modes of Constitutional Decision Making

Legislatures, within very broad limits, can create *statutory* rights and liberties as they see fit. They must be persuaded by policy arguments on the basis of which temporary coalitions of political forces can be mobilized. But judges, and especially the justices of the Supreme Court of the United States, must (if they are faithful to their trust) create new *constitutional* rights by interpretation of the text or some known (or discoverable) tradition of prior understanding of what the text means. What happens when the policy result one's heart desires simply cannot be justified by the text, or any discernible intention of the framers, reference to any intermediate gloss on the text, or appeal to any traditional understanding? In this situation the activist judge (or the law professor engaged in "advocacy scholarship") must resort to some verbal formula which allows him access to other sources for the law he would make— sources beyond the document and its history, often beyond the American political tradition itself. I call such verbal formulas illegitimate modes of constitutional decision making and it is useful to catalogue them. They are the intellectual stock in trade of my rights industry and Bork's gentry—the grammar of noninterpretivism.

I apologize in advance for dragging the reader through so much sectarian logic chopping, but this is an area in which an appreciation of what is being done to us depends on seeing how it is being done. What follows are not distinct schools of thought, but interrelated intellectual devices to which persons resort who desire to find their vision of the good in the Constitution when there is no real evidence that it is.

THE "OPEN TEXTURE" SCAM

The original six articles, and Amendments One through Eight (the operational Bill of Rights), and the Fourteenth Amendment are written in a majestic and general idiom—not the language of a corporate charter or a municipal bond issue. And everyone, across the spectrum of constitutional politics, agrees that this choice of idiom was meant to afford flexibility to future generations in applying the language to ever changing circumstances. The general language was meant, in other words, to allow for "a living Constitution." As Justice Rehnquist put it "merely because a particular activity may not have existed when the Constitution was adopted, or because the framers could not have conceived of a particular method of transacting affairs, cannot mean that general language in the Constitution may not be applied to such a course of conduct."[13] So far, so good. But the generality, or "open texture" of the constitutional language is a continuing source of temptation to contemporary constitutional lawyers. They itch to fill up the loose fabric with social policy not remotely related to anything the framers were concerned about.[14]

Take Professor Paul Brest of the Stanford Law School. Brest rejects interpretivism (which he prefers to call "moderate originalism") on the grounds, *inter alia,* that it entails abandoning *Marbury* v. *Madison* and judicial review of acts of Congress (even though all but a few eccentric students of the problem are agreed that a reasonably clear framer intention existed on this point).[15] He goes on to suggest that the legitimacy of constitutional decision making cannot properly be understood to rest on popular consent, or on fidelity to the constitutional text, or on concern with original understanding. Having thus removed all elements of the compact theory of law from the judge's path, Professor Brest would have the legitimacy of his decisions depend on his "competence" as a policy maker and suggests certain "designedly vague" criterion for assessing policy-making competence. It should

> . . . (1) foster democratic government; (2) protect individuals against arbitrary, unfair, and intrusive official action; (3) conduce to a political order that is relatively stable but which also responds to changing conditions, values, and needs; (4) not readily lend itself to arbitrary decisions or abuses; and (5) be acceptable to the populace.[16]

These criteria deserve most careful consideration. Take the prohibition against "arbitrary" or "unfair" treatment. These are qualities notoriously in the eye of the beholder. How, without reference to some discernible compact defining a particular kind of arbitrariness or unfairness can the judge escape the swamp of subjectivity? Furthermore, most official action is perceived as "intrusive" by somebody. The question is always which actions are allowable and to what ends? Again, compacts, enriched by traditional understandings of their meaning, must guide us. But it is the fifth provision that is most interesting. The locution is crucial—"acceptable to the people" rather than in any, even extended sense, the "will" of the people. It must be this way because Brest is talking about holding unconstitutional the policy preferences of the people's however imperfectly elected representatives. But how, given that their elected assemblies are being overruled, and given that Brest will not bind himself to rely on any anterior constitutional compact by which the people have agreed to restrain themselves, can one tell that the people are "accepting" something? Is it their failure to rally behind Court-curbing measures which Brest, along with most responsible constitutional lawyers, would deplore? Is it that they do not revolt, coming after judges with dirks drawn? Is it ignorance and passivity? These are the shoals toward which the sirens of "open texture" beckon us.*

*It is the fashion among noninterpretivists to refer to what used to be called discerning the meaning of statutes and constitutions as "legal hermeneutics." This

THE "GENERAL INTENTION" FIDDLE

Closely related to the open texture evasion is one that asserts that the best we can do in applying the "broad and majestic" constitutional language is to identify the general intention of the framers and then apply this to our reality according to our own best lights. This is a plausible heresy, but heresy nonetheless. It is plausible because at first glance it looks interpretive—examining the circumstances to which the framers were responding, discerning what they intended to accomplish, and reasoning by analogy to new circumstances. What separates this from real interpretation, however, is the *level* of generality of intention that is insisted upon. While a few interpretivist fundamentalists refuse to proceed at all beyond the specific, discernible intention, most of the sadly diminished tribe are ready to reason from generalities, but only low level generalities.

The concern with protecting persons in their homes against intrusions into their privacy by agents of the government is an example of an acceptably low-level generalization. We have moved beyond the specific intention of the framers of the Fourth Amendment in response to an altered technological environment, but not so far beyond as to doubt we are still in touch. Such a general intention may be employed in changed circumstances to create new law. But when intention is stated at a high level of generality, then interpretation ceases and something much more like legislating begins. Thus, "the framers were concerned to further liberty"; reading the First Amendment to protect live sex shows protects somebody's liberty, therefore by doing so we are "true to the

---

choice of term has the useful effect of signaling the uninitiated away from what is to be regarded as specialists' work, but it is interesting in another respect. Pilfered from the theological faculty, the word refers to the study of the methods of exposition of sacred texts. It is commonly distinguished from exegesis—or practical interpretation of the text. One is tempted to ask, please, for less hermeneutics, more exegesis. But religious imagery and terminology powerfully attractive to noninterpretivists, with Robert Cover, of Yale, referring to "redemptive constitutionalism" and Michael Perry, of Northwestern, advising judges to act as "prophets" of an "American Israel."

intention of the framers." Or, "the framers meant to create a democratic republic"; the purest form of democracy is one-person-one-vote, therefore imposing this rule on all governments of general jurisdiction in the United States is to be "true to the intention of the framers." Both liberty and democracy are philosophical houses of many mansions. The framers entertained certain particular notions of liberty and democracy (and of license and ochlocracy). To lunge up in abstraction from their particular conceptions to the generics "liberty" or "democracy" and then slide back down again to some currently fashionable libertarian or democratic theory is illegitimate. I suppose my favorite academic example of a broad, imputed intention used to justify a novel doctrinal suggestion is the argument by Professor Kenneth Karst of the UCLA Law School, that since the "ideal of equality runs deep in the American tradition," and "the ideal . . . was enshrined in the Declaration of Independence," all utterances (obscene, commercial, libelous, fighting words, and so on) should be regarded as equally protected speech under the First Amendment.[17] There is, of course, no such thing as a single "ideal of equality"; and the several traditional American variations on the theme of equality (discussed in chapter 6) will not help Karst much in the free speech context. Nor does he advance his case by citing in support of the "ideal of equality" John Rawls' distinctly untraditional book.[18]

THE "FUNDAMENTAL VALUES" HUSTLE

But noninterpretivism is not content with arguing from highly generalized framer intentions. Its more ambitious practitioners would free themselves from the constitutional document altogether and have judges turn to "fundamental American values" as the basis for creating new constitutional law.* Owen Fiss argues that

---

*There is a variation on "fundamental values" which speaks of "constitutional values." This sounds more respectable because it seems to steer back toward the document. Beware. Between "constitutional values" and the provisions of the Constitution a great gulf yawns. A concern for the value of privacy, for instance, might move us to initiate a protracted political process to place a prohibition on unreasonable searches of premises in our constitution. The same value—privacy—might

constitutional adjudication "is the social process by which judges give meaning to our public values," and that provisions such as the speech clause of the First Amendment and the equal protection clause of the Fourteenth "simply contain public values that must be given concrete meaning and harmonized with the general structure of the constitution." These are the same values that "give our society an identity and inner coherence—its distinctive public morality."[19] But how, pray tell, are we to know what these values are? We can learn a great deal about what particular bands of politicians intended by particular constitutional provisions (and what successive generations took them to mean), but where does one look to discover the values that give our society "identity and inner coherence?" Fiss leaves the matter ambiguous, mentioning, variously, the constitutional text itself, "history, and social ideals"; and ultimately he instructs the judge to search "for what is pure, right, or just." Other noninterpretivists have been more explicit.

Thomas C. Grey of the Stanford Law School, for instance, seeks fundamental values in a "higher" or natural law of rights and liberties which he suggests is somehow incorporated in the Constitution.[20] Unhappily, natural law adamantly refuses to reveal itself to us all in similar terms, and the evidence that open-ended provisions of natural law were incorporated into the structure of American public law is unpersuasive even to other noninterpretivists.[21] Still others, such as Dean Harry Wellington of Yale, would find fundamental American values in a kind of consensus morality which judges can discern. Thus "the Court's task is to ascertain the weight of the principle in conventional morality and convert the moral principle into a legal one by connecting it with the body of

---

suggest a number of other constitutional provisions, say, a prohibition on the use of police informers except by judicial warrant. But it was one particular manifestation of the value which was constitutionalized, not the value. The underlying value and the intention of the provision are not at all the same thing. We *might* have introduced other provisions to protect privacy, and they *might* have survived the process in whole or part, but either we didn't or they didn't. It makes all the difference. Courts properly enforce provisions, not a far more general (and indeterminant) universe of constitutional values.

constitutional law."²² But why are judges better fitted than legislators to discern the contours of a common morality? Wellington
tells us that "the environment in which legislators function makes
difficult a bias-free perspective," and that they are buffeted by
"interest groups insisting upon moral positions of their own."²³ But
is not a consensus or convention the product of the political pull
and haul of interest groups? Are not interest groups, after all, basic
mechanisms of expression in the American system?²⁴ Paul Brest, I
think, gives a franker answer. Referring to his fellow law teachers,
many of whom were "law clerks—demijudges," he lays it on the
line—"we simply do not believe that 'majorities' and legislatures
are willing or able to engage in serious, reflective moral discourse."²⁵ This void, presumably, must be filled by judges (or
"demi-judges").* Professor Ward Elliott, a political scientist, has
referred to the increasing power of the law school-judicial complex
as "the rise of guardian democracy."²⁶ Just so.

*My favorite clerk story is from an admittedly problematic source, but the
principal facts check out independently. The Mental Health Law Project is a
specialized ACLU spin-off concerned with creating new protections for the mentally ill. The intellectual touchstone for the group was Judge David Bazelon's
opinion for the District of Columbia Circuit in *Rouse* v. *Cameron*, 373 F.2d 451
(1966), in which he advanced the idea of civilly committed mental patients having
a "right to treatment" under the Constitution. Alan Dershowitz, a former Bazelon
clerk, who went on to clerk for Justice Goldberg on the Supreme Court, is an
activist professor at the Harvard Law School and has written extensively on the
need to create new rights for the mentally ill. He was an early guiding light of the
Mental Health Law Project. Joel Klein was a student of Dershowitz's at Harvard
and spent a postgraduate year as his research assistant. Klein went on to clerk for
Bazelon himself and was working for the Mental Health Law Project in Washington
when he was selected to clerk for Justice Stewart for the 1974 term. During that
term the Court accepted the case of *O'Connor* v. *Donaldson*, 422 U.S. 563 (1975).
This was a Mental Health Law Project case in which ACLU attorney Bruce J.
Ennis, Jr., and Benjamin W. Heineman, Jr., a former clerk of Justice Stewart, now
working for the Project, were arguing for damages under federal civil rights law for
a former mental patient who claimed he had been denied his constitutional right
to treatment. As Woodward and Armstrong put it in *The Brethren*, "from the day
the Court agreed to take the *Donaldson* case, . . . Joel Klein . . . was a man with
a mission." Certainly this has the ring of truth. Whether Klein later led a cabal of
clerks in subverting a draft opinion of Chief Justice Burger's (which vigorously
scouted the notion of a "right to treatment") must continue to be regarded as
speculative. Bob Woodward and Scott Armstrong, *The Brethren* (New York:
Simon and Schuster, 1979), pp. 372–83.

SOWING ILL BY DOING GOOD

The most straightforward justification of noninterpretivism is that it provides a way of seeking what is good, or objectively right. In a famous article defending judicial activism against the criticisms of Alexander Bickel and others that the Supreme Court was too often failing to ground its rulings on past compacts, federal Judge J. Skelly Wright wrote that "the ultimate test of the Justices' work, I suggest, must be goodness. . . ."[27] In the law school world, Professor Michael Perry of the Northwestern University Law School is a leading proponent of this point of view. Because he is forthright, Perry's position is a most useful example of the intellectual shortcomings of noninterpretivism.

Interpretivism, he tells us, is irrelevant because "virtually none of the important constitutional cases of the modern period—certainly in none of the controversial cases involving issues of human rights, including, for example, *Brown* v. *Board of Education*—can be explained as exercises of interpretive review."[28] This, as noted earlier, is untrue for *Brown*. As to other "human rights" cases it is sometimes true *(Roe* v. *Wade)* and sometimes not *(Katz* v. *U.S.)*. But, more importantly, Perry's premise begs the question. Even if his sweeping generalization was correct, it would as logically suggest the illegitimacy of the decisions he prizes as the irrelevance of interpretivism. It does nothing to establish the legitimacy of noninterpretivism to point out that a lot of recent decisions cannot be justified without it! It is precisely the legitimacy of these decisions that is at issue.

Having disposed of interpretivism to his satisfaction, Perry faces up to establishing the legitimacy of noninterpretive decision making. He does not understate his problem:

There is no plausible textual or historical justification for constitutional policy-making by the judiciary—no way to avoid the conclusion that noninterpretive review . . . cannot be justified by reference either to the text or to the intentions of the framers of the Constitution. The justification for the practice, if there is one, must be functional. . . ."[29]

And what is the function that will justify noninterpretive review? It allows for the Supreme Court's remedying "what would otherwise be a serious defect in American government—the absence of any policy making institution that regularly deals with fundamental political-moral problems other than by mechanical reference to established moral convictions."[30] In other words, it allows the court to impose moral judgments when the country is either divided or unconcerned. And these imposed judgments will be licit because morally right answers are discoverable; that the justices seek them in good conscience (even though they may not always find them) is enough.

This is nothing more than colossal impudence. The American nation is not an undertaking in moral perfectionism. What Perry identifies as a defect in American government is an aspect of its strength. Surely no one needs a page of footnotes attesting to the fact that the framers (1787–1791 style) did not conceive of their new national government as performing priestly or prophetic functions. It is a core theme of American thinking about government that it is a limited, procedural covenant entered into for limited purposes. As a people we seek our ultimacies in private; when we come together politically we do so in submission to pre-existing agreement on "process." What Perry does, most basically, is to attempt to uncouple legitimacy in lawmaking from agreed upon process. But it is agreement on process which is the defining American governmental agreement.* Ultimate reliance simply cannot be placed on doing "the right thing." The right thing, unprotected by the distinctive uniform of text, tradition, past majority endorsement, or close argument therefrom, has no claim to governmental legitimacy. When the right thing is challenged in the night it can identify itself (establish its binding validity) only by crying out "I am the right thing to do." The response may be "the hell you say" followed by the rattle of small arms fire. As a people we are riven

---

*This does not mean that the law may not enforce morality. Of course it may. But what it enforces is the legislatively ratified conventional morality of which Perry is so dismissive.

by divisions over the nature of the good, the fair, and the just. We disagree fundamentally about human nature, about human rights, and about how to assess human worth; we disagree over the springs of human motivation and the sources of wealth, over sexual differences and relations, and over the ways in which national security is to be pursued in an insecure world. A case can be made that these disagreements run deeper than at any period since the Civil War. To urge that new constitutional law be made on the basis of the possibility of achieving objective moral rectitude rather than reference to an existing covenant risks the legitimacy of the courts and, ultimately, of the constitutional order itself. The most elaborate and technically brilliant arguments of a Ronald Dworkin[31] or a Bruce Ackerman[32] rest on initial presumptions and intuitions which many of their fellow citizens simply do not share. John Rawls, for instance, appears to rest *A Theory of Justice* on the axiom that, as an abstract and general matter, equality must be preferred over inequality. Thus we are told that those favored by circumstances of birth or by natural talent and energy may fairly enjoy differential rewards in society only to the extent that this will "improve the situation of those who have lost out."[33] My intuition is precisely contrary, and I am therefore unimpressed by all the logical exertions which follow. I think Rawls wrongheaded (and until I lose some votes on it, I will insist a majority of my countrymen do as well). But interpreting American public law cannot turn on deciding whether Rawls is wrongheaded or I am. That must be done by reference to a discrete community decision reached by procedures which both he and I accept as binding.

In a good faith dispute over the meaning of a compact we may disagree, and the losing side can accept the loss as dictated by the rules of the game. The same is true when the loss is by vote. But there is no reason to accept a loss which rests simply on contrary moral perception. At the end of the day in America something is "right" because it was "generated in a procedurally correct manner."[34] Whatever our personal moral commitments, our dominant public philosophy (yes, I do remember John Brown) has been skeptical not millenarian.

FLUMMERY WITH FOOTNOTE FOUR

I write of this final* and most sophisticated mode of noninterpretivism with regret. Its leading exponent, Dean Ely of Stanford, has performed valuable service in exposing the weaknesses of other noninterpretivist approaches. After Ronald Dworkin published a particularly advanced essay in a left-radical bi-weekly urging that judges draw on John Rawls' theory of justice in making constitutional law,[35] Ely wrote that "The Constitution may follow the flag, but is it really supposed to keep up with the *New York Review of Books?*"[36] It's hard to quarrel with a fellow like that, but Ely, like lesser noninterpretivists, is brought low by his unwillingness to relinquish certain ill-gotten doctrinal gains of the 1960s and 1970s —most particularly that branch of equal protection analysis dealing with "suspect classifications."

By this approach the Court will require some level of extraordinary justification from government when the law or regulation in question bears on persons in one of a small number of suspect classes (the reader may be spared discussion of the efforts of the justices to explain and specify those higher levels of justification, or of "judicial scrutiny"). Now everyone is agreed that the framers of the equal protection clause were concerned to prohibit certain kinds of racial discrimination by the states, and the effect of *Brown*

---

*There are two other tricks of constitutional argumentation, used mostly by journalists, which are still worth mentioning. "The Whittling Away Winkle" involves stating some recent innovative case (say Miranda v. Arizona) to create a broader right than it did ("suspects can't be questioned without their lawyers present") and then damning some limiting application of Miranda as "whittling away" at our ancient (1966) constitutional liberties. "The Recognizing Rights Rip" seems to assume that there are all sorts of "rights" skulking around America in disguise. Thus the courts should "recognize the rights" of the handicapped, the elderly, the fetus, and so on. Legislatures can create new rights by statutes and courts can create new rights by interpretation (or noninterpretation), but "recognizing rights" suggests either appeal to natural law or an archaic (pre-legal realism) understanding by which courts "find law" which is somehow out there.

and its progeny was to round out this original intention to cover all invidious state discrimination on grounds of race. Thus race becomes the paradigmatic suspect classification. But when the Court adds aliens, illegitimate children, and women,* there are difficulties. There is no evidence that the relevant framers would have been other than astounded at the suggestion that their handiwork placed severe limitations on the states in distinguishing between men and women in their municipal law. Treating sex like (or sort-of-like) race for equal protection purposes requires a noninterpretivist approach. And while Ely has been effective in exposing the intellectual weakness of other noninterpretivist approaches, he is moved to advance his own truncated noninterpretivism for the areas of equal protection and free speech. These are held to be special as they protect participation in the political processes of election, decision, and distribution. For the sake of brevity I shall deal only with Ely's argument for the suspect classification branch of equal protection doctrine as a way of insuring fair treatment of minorities.

The point of departure for Ely's argument on minorities is the famous Footnote Four to Justice Harlan Fiske Stone's opinion in the case of *United States* v. *Carolene Products Co.* in 1938.[37] This was one of the early nails in the coffin of the old, bad judicial activism which, in a fashion we would today call noninterpretive, protected entrepreneurship against government regulation. The epitome of this old activism was *Lochner* v. *New York,* against which Oliver Wendell Holmes, Jr., so persuasively dissented. The

*Technically, sex has not been held a suspect criterion of classification; see Frontiero v. Richardson, 411 U.S. 677 (1973). But the Court has proceeded to treat sex discriminations as requiring extraordinary justification; what has been created might be called a para-suspect classification. It is worth note in passing that the Court has taken to referring to sex discrimination as "gender" discrimination, and many commentators have also slipped into this practice. Consider Fowler: "gender, n., is a grammatical term only. To talk of persons or creatures of the masculine or feminine g., meaning of the male or female sex, is either a jocularity (permissible or not according to context) or a blunder." Whatever else we may think of the justices' performance in the area of sex classifications, they were not trying to be funny. H.W. Fowler, *A Dictionary of Modern English Usage* (Oxford: Oxford University Press, 2 ed., revised by Sir Ernest Gowers, 1965), p. 221.

Corrupting Constitutional Interpretation

Court, Stone wrote, would no longer intervene aggressively against government action alleged to violate a "liberty of contract" which, though Stone did not put it so baldly, was now seen as an illegitimate outcropping in constitutional law of laissez-faire economics. In the course of this opinion came Footnote Four.[38]

Its first paragraph (apparently suggested by Chief Justice Charles Evans Hughes, in an effort at clarity) provided simply that while the Court would now defer to legislatures where the constitutionally nonexplicit liberty of contract was concerned, a similar deference was not to be expected where some explicit prohibition of the Constitution (such as a law "abridging freedom of speech") was at issue. The second and the third paragraphs, which were drafted by Stone's clerk, Louis Lusky,* and approved by Stone, suggested that the more aggressive style of judicial review might be in order as well where legislation (a) "restricts the political [electoral?] processes" or (b) where "statutes are directed at particular religions, . . . or national, . . . or racial minorities." Then the final clause of paragraph three, separated from what precedes it by a semicolon, suggests some linkage between (a) and (b): perhaps "prejudice against discrete and insular minorities . . . , which tends seriously to curtail the operation of those political processes ordinarily to be relied upon to protect minorities," may call for "a correspondingly more searching judicial inquiry."

In this space it is impossible to do justice to the elaborate argument Ely develops to justify noninterpretive review to protect minorities on the foundation of paragraphs two and three, but the foundation is inadequate to bear the weight. Consider the following:

1. To what does Stone's word "prejudice" in paragraph three refer? Does he mean *laws* that discriminate against minorities in the political process? Or does he refer to social prejudice which makes political

---

*Young Mr. Lusky, it should be noted, went on to become Professor Louis Lusky of the Columbia Law School, and in 1975 published a book questioning the constitutional legitimacy of a number of recent Superior Court decisions. See Louis Lusky, *By What Right* (Charlottesville, Va.: Michie).

success more difficult to attain? Activist commentators, including Ely, assume the latter; but, God knows, there is no textual reason to so conclude; after all, what follows a semicolon is more often an elaboration or refinement of the prior thought rather than the introduction of a new (and highly problemical) idea. Lusky assumes Stone did have social prejudice in mind, but offers no details which persuade me as to his former boss (let alone as to Hughes and the rest of the majority).[39]

2. The core concern of paragraphs two and three is for minorities within the political process—in the everyday, nonmysterious sense of voting, lobbying, organizing, running for office, and so on. Is not the least tortured interpretation of this opaque language that where discrete and insular minorities are legally protected in access to the polls and to legislatures, they can act to redress grievances? Thus, where a statute has been adopted as the result of an open political process it is hard to find authority in Footnote Four for extraordinarily close judicial scrutiny. (Unless we resort to the absurdity of saying that groups whose interests the legislature disfavors are *ipso facto* discriminated against in the political process.)

3. And remember the "discrete and insular minorities" are, according to Stone, racial, national (ethnic), and religious. Ely has to go with a "just like" argument to qualify such other groups as aliens—and women. (A discrete and insular majority?)

4. And remember, paragraphs two and three of Footnote Four themselves hang on the equal protection clause of the Fourteenth Amendment. The concern of those framers with race is clear, making it the paradigmatic suspect classification. Ethnicity fits the paradigm pretty well, but after that the exercise is increasingly procrustean. To assert that the equal protection clause constitutes a kind of roving commission to the Supreme Court to protect minorities (however these may be identified), is precisely the sort of conceit which Ely has condemned in other noninterpretivists.[40]

5. Ely argues that the "equal concern and respect principle," which he would have the Court adopt in protecting minorities, is dictated or at least implied by the system of representative democracy which is basic to the structure of the Constitution. But the representative democracy of the framers, while it relies on the forms of majoritarianism to restrain government and define winners and losers, is not result-oriented and Ely does not show us how it supports the "equal concern and respect principle." This is a principle rooted in quite recent political and social thought—not that of the founders (or the framers of the

Fourteenth Amendment, or a Lodge in 1915, or a Holmes in the 1920s, or a Corwin in the 1930s). Ely's use of "representative democracy" here is an example of a statement at a high level of abstraction which is legitimatized by reference to the "structure" the framers established, and from which a more specific principle is deduced ("equal concern and respect") which is supposed to carry the blessing with it.

6. And finally, most crudely, while remembering all about great oaks and acorns, a footnote is one hell of a way for a Court in the act of repenting one binge of noninterpretivism to lay the intellectual foundation for another.

Far from not having "been adequately elaborated,"[41] as Ely suggests, Footnote Four has been teased, massaged, and intensively fertilized. The result calls to mind David Daggett's comment on a much earlier left-perfectionist enthusiasm, "Sun-Beams May Be Extracted from Cucumbers, But the Process is Tedious."[42]

Ex Mortua Manu

A favorite slogan of those who seek to escape the discipline of interpretation is that we cannot allow ourselves to be ruled by "the dead hand of the past." Doubtless this is true if by "ruled" one means a complete denial of flexibility in the process of governing from one generation to the next. But constitutional law is not all law, or all there is to governing. Nor does interpretivism imply complete inflexibility in constitutional law. Today, however, many in the rights industry appear to live in a kind of devouring present, driven by overpowering moral imperatives which must be responded to right away. Dean Terrence Sandalow of the University of Michigan Law School writes that

Constitutional law thus emerges not as exegesis, but as a process by which each generation gives formal expression to the values it holds fundamental in the operations of government.[43]

Kenneth Karst and Harold Horowitz have given this position something like its classic statement by writing that state laws which were otherwise reasonable might be unconstitutional under the equal protection clause because they "are unacceptable in this generation's idealization of America."[44] And these commentators mean what they say. Dean Sandalow suavely observes that:

> . . . the social Darwinism of Herbert Spencer and the libertarianism of John Stuart Mill, though not in the minds of those who wrote the Constitution, have at different times each been found there by men who, no doubt sincerely, believed that the "broad, majestic language" of the Constitution was intended to guarantee that "general *sort* of relationship between the government and its citizens." Nor does it pass belief that one day soon (perhaps its dawn has already broken) the egalitarianism of John Rawls will also be found there.[45]

Perhaps so, but if large parts of constitutional law are to be no more than fashionable social theory with boots on, what happens to the core notion of *constitutionalism?* Doesn't the essence of the thing involve successive generations constructively consenting to abide by the covenants and conventions negotiated by their predecessors? Disagreeing about implications, modifying by interpretation, adding or discarding through the prescribed forms, all these are part of constitutionalism. But so is being guided, in a real sense, by the hand of the past. One does not have to be a misty-eyed Burkean to be shocked by the notion of constitutional law slipping in and out of ideological outfits as fashions change and the decades roll by.

But won't changes in the national intellectual climate and culture inevitably be registered in constitutional law? (We do not, after all, expect the justices to write sham-Augustan prose.) Certainly, but the matter, as always, is one of degree; new knowledge, even new sensibilities, can discover new applications for existing provisions. The reason the Supreme Court cannot find capital punishment cruel and unusual under the Eighth Amendment, is that it is not massively so regarded in the country—if and when it is, the Court can. But it must be the country which broadly changes, not just Judge Bork's gentry.* And discovering whole new "liberties" where none were understood before is out. Either Justice Holmes was right in his *Lochner* dissent or he was not, and to rely on one generation's idealization of America (as generations briskly succeed one another through time) is to move beyond the borders of anything that could be called constitutionalism and to debauch into a howling wilderness of subjectivity.

But what of the "heuristic" role of the Court, about which many in the right industry rhapsodize? May not the justices, although initially speaking for an enlightened minority, lead the country into a new consensus? After all, should such a consensus not form— should real resistance develop which indicates the Court is attempting to take the country in a direction where a majority will not follow—the Court can always be reversed.

But how is this to be accomplished? The amending process, as a practical political matter (and good thing it is), requires not an ordinary majority in the country but a wide, deep, stable consensus. What can result from an ill-considered judicial activism is the agony of a *Roe* v. *Wade* situation. The decision cannot win wide,

---

*It may be objected that by this time there will be little for the Court to do but restrain the occasional maverick legislature. This is not so much an objection as it is a description (if only partial) of the proper role of the Court in the American system. The alternative is to rely on elite views. The desire to do this now appears strongly on the political left, but it was not always so. In the early decades of this century people we now call conservatives (they called themselves "liberals," and with better intellectual warrant than many who rejoice in that description today) held the prominent professorships and pulpits; they set the tone of publishing and public discourse and the flower of the bar drew on their wisdom to protect corporate clients. The result was the fabled judicial activism on behalf of "liberty of contract" (understood as a sweeping prohibition on government regulation of entrepreneurship) which culminated in Lochner v. New York. It is ironic that some contemporary conservatives (for which that honorable appellation seems to mean little more than a callow libertarianism in economics) want to have it both ways. That is, they excoriate recent activism but defend it in the past. When their cherished ideas were elevated to constitutional doctrine by way of judicial prepossession it was OK, because the framers had "really" intended such outcomes, or at least favored them "in spirit," even though they never quite got around to saying so.

general approval and its opponents cannot marshall sufficient support to amend it away. The only other way of "overruling" the Court is for Congress to exercise its power under Article III to make exceptions to the Court's appellate jurisdiction—to exclude it from consideration of certain kinds of statutory or even constitutional issues. Most constitutional lawyers recoil from such a prospect, seeing in it a fundamental threat to the independence of the judiciary. This includes most of the rights professionals. Thus we are entitled to be skeptical when Michael Perry, in urging a prophetic style on the justices, argues that "the legislative power of Congress . . . to define, and therefore to limit, the appellate jurisdiction of the Supreme Court" is an adequate and practical "political control" over the institution.[46] As one reviewer put it:

Whenever a bill to withdraw jurisdiction seems to have even a remote chance of passage, however, the organized bar and the academic establishment descend on Washington (I believe Harvard and Yale must charter buses) to pronounce constitutional anathemas. . . . Many members of Congress who strongly and genuinely oppose some Court decisions nevertheless oppose jurisdiction-withdrawing legislation because they have been convinced of its unconstitutionality. Other legislators use the perception of unconstitutionality as a shield against constituent pressure to do something about anti-majoritarian court decisions.[47]

It simply won't do. Perry's noninterpretivist fellows would be first to the barricades, and most of the rest of us, however regretfully, would join them! The fact cannot be blinked that majorities in America are evanescent things. They come together for a brief season, something is established in their name, and they dissolve into the political mists. But what they leave behind is to be respected, interpreted, applied, and maintained until another majority forms to sweep the compact away or change it substantially.

What we have witnessed often in recent decades is a rights industry, armed with an impressive constitutional rhetoric, operating through courts and administrative agencies to create rules and regulations in the empty policy space between majorities, and then saying, in effect, to Congress and country, "come get me if you can." But that a majority may not exist for the legal equivalent of a punitive expedition cannot be taken as *post hoc* consent or democratic justification. Nor can it seriously be argued that because majorities are difficult to create, it is acceptable for an enlightened minority to "resolve ambiguity" in its chosen ways. As Laurence H. Silberman puts it:

> A lack of congressional action usually means a strong public consensus has not formed—which, in democratic theory, normally means that until it does, the government should not act, no matter how offensive the state of affairs to those who are "certain" of the need for a governmental response. It does not follow that the political system is not working merely because debate on an issue does not lead to a [decision].[48]

To try to integrate noninterpretivism into democratic theory by variations on the notion that "they can change it" is futile.* Certainly the American version of democracy provides for the protection of minorities, but it is well to remember that the framers saw minorities principally in regional terms, and saw significant protection arising from the structure of government. Other protections, which involve overriding the will of a majority must rest upon some reasonably tight inference from previous organic agreement (by a previous majority) to limit future majorities. And here we are back at square one.

*While the subject of this chapter is constitutional interpretation, arguments that "they can always change it," or "they haven't changed it and that makes it OK" occur even more frequently as a way of defending adventurous statutory interpretations by courts and executive agencies. But given the nature of legislative assemblies (and especially Congress) this is either naive or disingenuous. The same set of interest groups that are insufficient to persuade Congress to adopt a policy in the first place, may be quite sufficient, if the policy can be put in place judicially or bureaucratically, to keep the legislature from disestablishing it. In assemblies it takes a good, healthy, stable majority to act and properly so; but a skilled minority can stop action. What purports to be legislative policy must be able to point to the day it commanded a majority; pointing to the day it was defended successfully against opponents who failed at being a majority is not good enough.

Yes, Virginia,

There is a Constitution—and an accessible constitutional history and tradition. These are far from providing all the answers or relieving judges of the task of interpretation, but they are equally far from being unknowable, or hopelessly ambiguous, or so various as to be irrelevant. And when these materials do not furnish guidance to the constitutional decision maker, that's guidance too. Within the rights industry, however, a kind of expeditious agnosticism prevails with respect to the American past. The reason for this, I have suggested, is not that political ideas and legal intentions of various framing generations or legislative coalitions are somehow unrecoverable, it is that, from the perspective of many professional rights makers, these ideas and intentions are an encumbrance. The past is not a trust, but a threat. If one takes the trouble to expose oneself intellectually to the constitutionally relevant aspects of the past, one might come to feel some obligation toward it. Far better to protect oneself with clichés about the past being visible only through the lens of one's present politics (which implies that all views of the past are equally valid since we are all entitled to the lens of our choice); or that there are so many co-equal strands of American thought bearing constitutional issues that none can be regarded as canonical for purposes of interpretation.* (This latter tactic usually involves moving some fringe figures or movements in toward the axis of American intellectual history—thus a Paine equals an Adams, a Garrison equals a Lincoln or late nineteenth-century communitarian thought—Robert Owen, John Humphrey Noyes, and such like—trotted out as an "alternative" to the individuality and contractarian core of our political tradition.

*It is true that we view the past through our own intellectual lenses, and always with some distortion. But some lenses are relatively sharp, and produce relatively less distortion, while others appear to have the optical properties of Coke bottle bottoms. See Robert M. Cover, "*Nomos* and *Narrative,*" 97 *Harvard Law Review* 4 (1983).

Another problem our constitutionally relevant past poses for today's rights makers is that (once the dusts of progressive historiography have been swept away) it is seen to speak largely in formal terms—of how policy is to be made rather than the content of policy. That we are a culturally and ideologically diverse people (precluding policy making based on "the right thing") does not mean we are simply a collection of ethnics huddled around a standard of living. But what unites us (or should) is a rich intellectual inheritance concerning the ways we agree to make common decisions and on the limits of our communality. In a recent short article Harvey Mansfield stressed the centrality of form in a democracy and noted the threat to it from a new populism (with an obsessive concern for results) which was born in the New Left "Movement" of the 1960s and survives powerfully among so many middle-aged university educated Americans:

. . . the power of government is to be exercised against, not through, its formal institutions, and whatever agency is available will be used to effect the people's will (as discerned or presumed by the populists), regardless of the formal character of the agency. Judicial activism was one obvious result; though "elitist" in a superficial sense, it is in a deeper sense quite populist.[49]

To the extent that we are a people, a nation in the sense of possessing a common, inherited political culture, we are a people of forms. As Mansfield puts it "overflowing informality is a source of tyranny and rebellion."[50]

Finally, there is a central truth about those original framers from which our activists must be at extraordinary pains to shield themselves. As Martin Diamond put it:

. . . for the founding generation it was liberty that was the comprehensive good, the end against which political things had to be measured; and democracy was only a form of government which, like any other form of government, had to prove itself adequately instrumental to the security of liberty.[51]

While a general proposition does not, in and of itself, answer any particular interpretive question, it casts a revealing light on the more specific materials relevant to the interpretation of particular constitutional provisions. And it explains why our canonical covenants are formal and positivistic rather than redemptive or prophetic.

The typical response to this by the egalitarians of the rights industry, stripped of the legalistic and academic niceties, is that a social contract resting on a preoccupation with liberty and form does not respond to the "needs of our time." And that, in fact, a new contract has emerged by fits and starts over the past few decades—a contract based on the primacy of "equal personhood" which accepts the role of the courts as expositors of a national morality. In a sense, this is correct; I do not sense much concern for the primacy of liberty in the professional circles within which I move. But what does this mean for those of us (and our number quickly increases as one moves from campus walk onto Main or Market Street) whose consent to the governmental order is defined in more pristine terms? Is it enough for rights makers of the dominant persuasion to say "you lose?" Constitutional traditionalists are certainly in the process of losing, but why such losses need be regarded as legitimate is not clear. The best way of escaping the question is to stop losing. And to stop losing the single most useful intellectual tactic is to ask insistently of the rights professionals "who are these people?"

CHAPTER 8

What Is To Be Done?

THE QUESTION "who are these people" is simply another way of asking "what are the politics of these people?" To answer this and suggest further steps necessary to stop losing, it remains to do two things: first, to grapple with the question of why so many professional civil libertarians are caught up in thoughtless enthusiasm for evermore ambitious rights creating, and second, to suggest what critics of this intellectual tendency (presently a minority among practitioners and students of constitutional politics) should do if they want to improve things.

The Politics of Disaffection

What accounts for the careless behavior of many in the rights industry toward American society? What prompts intelligent lawyers to develop strained, fiercely abstract, and verbally clotted arguments to urge on judges. What prompts literate publicists to ignore, distort, or "remanufacture" the American past to justify some novel policy in the present?

There are several rather obvious partial answers. The first involves the need to achieve the immediate heart's desire of one's own interest group. Who cares if substantive due process is a discredited concept; if it is the only possible axis of constitutional attack on state abortion laws, take it! A second partial answer involves reflexive sympathy for the underdog. This is often described as a distinctive American cultural trait, and so it is. But for many professional rights makers it would appear that the country is largely populated by victims of one sort or another. The rights makers elevate compassion to the level of a mystique; but still there is the question why?

At a fundamental level I think the answer is that the engorged capacity for empathy displayed by so many who people these pages can be indulged because so little value is placed on the society that must, in various forms, bear the costs of creating new rights. Now sympathy for this underdog is an admirable characteristic, but only when coupled with a discriminating sense which allows one to distinguish between vicious curs and whipped puppies, and with a sense of balance which seriously calculates the costs of creating rights—costs in dollars, costs in foregone opportunities for excellence, costs in pain to unconsenting innocents, costs in subversion of majority preferences. Bluntly, the not-so-obvious-explanation of the social carelessness of many rights professionals is that they are profoundly disaffected from American culture and society. And because of their disaffection they feel free to lumber that society with new and expensive rights.

Howls of denial will rise to the heavens at this charge. In response, it must be stressed that I am talking about disaffection toward the real American society—the one we have now, which our forebearers experienced and contributed to in essentially the same form. This is a crucial point because of the characteristic form of denial of the charge of disaffection. "I'm not indifferent (or hostile) to America; I love her as she ought to be"; or "I am the truest sort of patriot because I demand America live up to its ideals"; or "A person's first loyalty must be to justice, fairness, and freedom. America must be judged against these ideals and accorded the respect it deserves"; or "I want to be proud of our institutions" (with the unspoken implication that it is impossible to be proud of the present towns, the existing churches, this university, or these state legislatures).

Far from rebutting the charge of disaffection, such protests are telltale evidence of its advanced state. Intellectual and emotional commitment to an idealization of a society is no substitute for some serious attachment to the actual one. Certainly it is necessary to criticize imperfect institutions in order to improve them, but when one's primary psychological investment is in the ideals, not the existing institutions, one becomes unhinged. No longer restrained by the intellectual balancing required of the serious legal reformer, the liberated idealist is free to act as an unrestrained crusader for the underdog of the hour.

But aren't ideals important? Of course. Ideals are as important as they are dangerous. Like the sun they should never be contemplated directly. Healthy change in human institutions is usually incremental and usually slow, and always involves compromise and tradeoffs between competing, legitimate values—there really is no such thing as a free lunch or a "good solution." Only through the protective lens of this abiding truth can ideals be contemplated with safety. As long as one realizes that ideals are not of this world —that at best they can only occasionally be approximated—can ideals inspire and revivify the world weary. But too often ideals are approached incautiously; then their awful symmetry and soaring simplicity dazzle the beholder. Idealists in this sense are always fundamentally alienated from the societies in which they find themselves. They may make good saints or martyrs but very poor constitutional lawyers and judges.

Is it not true that the disaffected idealist makes a contribution to society by his moral witness and by posing radical alternatives? Of course. But who wants a homeopath attempting brain surgery? My purpose is not to persuade radical idealists that they ought to like America more. Perhaps they are right not to. What I do argue is that prescriptions for constitutional and other legal adjustment of the present order (to which the vast majority of Americans are positively committed) written by people who are indifferent toward it, or who actively despise it, should be received with suspicion.

There is a further point to be made about the first-loyalty-to-ideals approach, suggested by the use of the term "radical" above. While one finds "ideals junkies" on both the political right and left (remember Ayn Rand's puerile dismissal of claims by the collectivity on the heroic individual), the rights industry is composed of overwhelmingly disaffected idealists of the left. Not only are they dazzled, but often the ideals on which they fixate are not ones with deep rooting in American history and tradition (for example, equality of results). This has the effect of increasing the disaffection. ("Oh, there's a lot in the American experience I can identify with.") Sure there is: some snippets from Tom Paine, a little out-of-context Jefferson, Nat Turner, Mary Ellen Lease, jazz, the New Deal, the Institute for Policy Studies, and Michael Doonesbury.

Here, based on long observation, are ten political tenets broadly shared by rights industry activists:

1. The nation-state is becoming less important, and properly so. Our security and future well being are not so much dependent on the strength and prosperity of a specific set of political, economic and social institutions called America as they are on the emergence of new global understandings and arrangements which will de-emphasize the individual national units, promote greater equality among populations, and minimize aggression by reducing national competition.
2. Military force is of declining importance to the future well-being of Americans. "Force never solves anything."
3. Police, prosecutors, courts, and prisons cannot really have any effect on crime. Only greater economic and social equality will do that.
4. The major institutions of American society (firm, school, family) are washed up in their present form. They must mutate into very new

forms so there is no sense in being too solicitous of their present welfare.

5. There is little of value in the political, economic and social traditions of the American past (private ownership, federalism, voluntarism, individualism, local control, and so on). In a very real sense America only began to become admirable after 1933.

6. Institutional efficiency and the pursuit of excellence for its own sake have been overvalued in the past and can safely be discounted. Besides, the pursuit of efficiency and excellence was often an excuse, or camouflage for, racial, ethnic, and sex discrimination.

7. Extreme skepticism is the proper approach to all forms of authority. One must have faith in the potential of human beings to cooperate within the framework of a universally accepted secular rationality. (This is coupled with a neo-Rousseauian conception of human nature, buttressed by some dubious "social science.") Leaders are to be restricted, hierarchies subverted.

8. The state is to be preferred over private agencies in the delivery of social services. This involves especial hostility toward nonpublic schools and private charities. (N.B. There is an element of paradox here. While desiring state agencies to do more and more, rights professionals continue cheerfully disabling these very institutions—more and more elaborate hearings, lawyers popping out of the woodwork to undermine the authority of administrators, and new "causes of action" to employ the surplus of bright young law school graduates. This paradox is well noted in the literature.[1]

9. The traditional American conceptions of equality as "equality before the law" and "equality of opportunity" must be replaced or substantially supplemented by an insistence on equality of results. Actual differences in human intelligence, creativity, character, energy, and achievement are not sufficiently significant to justify the differentials of reward and status which characterize America today.

10. The traditional "bourgeois morality" of America with its emphasis on conforming to rules of behavior must be replaced by a "new morality" which will be "truly person-oriented" and accepting of "alternative" life and sexual styles.

These propositions may or may not constitute enlightened political theory, but whatever else they are, I suggest, they are in conflict with the attitudes of the majority of Americans. At the simplest level the ten propositions just outlined constitute a constellation of opinion far on the left of the contemporary political firmament. It corresponds roughly to Harvey Mansfield's "new populism." It is an ideological outlook frequently encountered on university faculties, among media elites, and within certain specialized elements of the legal profession, but in a national context it is idiosyncratic. The extent to which the political world view of the rights industry diverges from the American mainstream is underlined by recent survey research.

Most relevant are data reported by S. Robert Lichter and Stanley Rothman from a survey of 157 "leaders and top staffers" of what the investigators call "public interest" groups.[2] This category overlaps substantially with what I have been calling the rights industry; among the groups included were the ACLU, the Center for Law and Social Policy, the Children's Defense Fund, and the Women's Legal Defense Fund. (Groups from "the civil rights community" such as the NAACP and Lawyers Committee for Civil Rights were not included, but it is doubtful that this omission affects the results significantly.) Lichter and Rothman conclude that:

> The liberalism of public interest leaders shades into profound dissatisfaction with the American social and economic order, a feeling not shared by the public. In fact, their alienation was one of our most striking findings. Forty-eight percent agree that our institutions should be completely overhauled, and a majority (51 percent) believe that the country would be better off if we moved toward socialism.[3]

This public interest elite supports "a new morality," endorses alternative life styles, "is critical of the United States and its international role . . . [and] reluctant to support military spending." It is the "profound dissatisfaction with the system" of the interest group leaders which "makes them staunch supporters of affirmative action. . . ." These public interest (including rights industry) cadres "would decrease the influence of traditional elites like business, religion, and the military" and place new groups, themselves, "at the very top rung."

What Is To Be Done?

To repeat, I am concerned here neither to convert the disaffected nor condemn their alienating left-radical ideology—only to illuminate it. Political, social, and cultural subversion are protected by the First Amendment. But as an intellectual matter we need not passively accept lawmaking, and especially constitutional law making, as a form of subversive activity.

Crucial to an understanding of the rights industry is the fact that it derives its principal supply and support from the talkers. That is, from members of a class of people that earns its living by manipulating words and symbols rather than by making things or purposefully directing the energies of others toward achieving specific, tangible goals. Talkers, typically, have some university level education and hold service jobs ranging from journalist to school teacher to marriage counselor. They are essentially the same group which Daniel Bell describes as constituting an "adversary culture." According to Bell's analyses:

> . . . the present size is large enough for these individuals no longer to be outcasts, or a bohemian enclave, in the society. They function institutionally as a group, bound by a consciousness of kind. [And] while minority life-styles and cultures have often conflicted with those of the majority, what is striking today is that that protagonists of the adversary culture, despite their sincere and avowed subversive intentions, do substantially influence, if not dominate, the cultural establishments today—the publishing houses, museums, galleries, the theatre, film, and the universities.
>
> Today, each new generation, starting off at the benchmarks attained by the adversary culture of their cultural parents, declares in sweeping fashion that the status quo represents a state of absolute repression, so that, in a widening gyre, new and fresh assaults on the social structure are mounted. This, I believe, has been happening in the last two decades.[4]

In a very real sense this apostate culture constitutes an internal defection, and the rights industry, which it nourishes, is its instrument of legal infiltration and sabotage directed against the existing order. Nor is Bell alone in emphasizing the gap between elite and majority loyalties. The division is a central theme of Aaron Wildavsky:

The conflict between the radical elite and the conservative mass is rooted in deep subcultural differences in American society. The conflict has emerged with additional force and clarity because the pool from which the elite is drawn—the upper middle class and upper class—has expanded markedly.[5]

And approaching on a somewhat different tack, Peter Berger has written of the almost universal rejection by the *illuminati* of their country's foreign policy and its use of power in the world arena. Berger concludes that "most American intellectuals have since Vietnam come to believe that the exercise of American power is immoral."[6]

The combination of the postwar baby boom, unprecedented affluence, and rapid expansion (and degradation) of university education has created a very large vocational cohort devoted primarily to verbal activity. It is perhaps best described not as the intellectual class or as a "new" class, but as—"the talking class."* Its income and rewards tend to come from service institutions (government, universities, foundations, church bureaucracies, the communications industry, and so on) which are only indirectly linked to the economy. The life style of the talking class ranges from middle to upper middle income. While this provides comfortable insulation from the competitive vicissitudes of the marketplace and the anxieties of working-class life, it still leaves most members of the talking class with less money, less immediate power, and less prestige than

*Perhaps "verbal class" would be more accurate, but the commitment within this group to the discipline of the written word is quite uneven. Whereas meetings, conferences, panels, "presentations"—all principally oral forms of communication —are pandemic.

typically enjoyed by successful men of action—investment bankers, corporate executives, highway contractors, generals, brain surgeons, and so on.

This breeds both envy and contempt among the talkers. They are, by definition, skilled at intellectualizing—verbalizing, and manipulating verbal abstractions of reality. They also tend to identify intellectual ability with intelligence (a very grave error), and accord it pride of place among human abilities. This means that the men of action are both less able and less deserving because they are less smart. Inferior people are seen as controlling major institutions and being rewarded more lavishly than the more able talkers. What can the talking class do about this? It can use its verbal skills to delegitimatize nonintellectual elites; and it can seek to extend its imperium by insisting on evermore intellectualized decision making in all spheres of activity. To the extent this strategy succeeds it will have the secular effect of shifting power and, eventually, money and prestige in the direction of those who will police the verbal manipulating. And as important as its roots in the talking class, is the fact that in its branch and flower the rights industry is mostly composed of lawyers. These very specialized verbal manipulators exemplify strikingly the general tendencies of the talkers.

The most sinister thing about this is the pretense that it is not going on. The manifest objectives are always "fairness" and "rationality." The latent, but equally significant objective is to shift the focus of those decisions that bestow money, power, and prestige into the arena in which your own resources are more relevant, and the other fellow's (whether it be experience, or capital, or interpersonal skills) are rendered less relevant. This does not mean that rights professionals and their backers are not intensely sincere in their desire to create new rights and limit the authority and discretion of traditional institutional leaderships. It does mean that their intensity has something to do with the fact that their ideals and self-interest are congruent.

Rules of Engagement

Those committed to protection and responsible improvement of American institutions must do a more effective job of opposing the dominant forces within the rights industry. There must be a fiercer effort at the level of constitutional argument; but more important, a sustained attack must be mounted on the political and social assumptions on the basis of which so many rights professionals operate. Their radicalism must not be allowed to remain a privileged sanctuary while the battle rages over the original understanding of the equal protection clause or whether it is permissible to ignore the letter of the Civil Rights Act of 1964 and to further a broad imputed purpose. Furthermore, there should be an end to reticence with respect to the anti-Americanism which prevails in much of the rights industry. It deprives no one of his political freedom, nor is it in any way uncivil to attack an argument for some legal or constitutional innovation by pointing out that it rests on an implicit indifference or hostility to the actual institutions involved. Here are a few key propositions concerning rights and liberties which can no longer be allowed to pass unchallenged. To the limits of good manners they should be scouted whenever they are advanced. These are the dirty half-dozen.

1. *Judges must step in to create new rights because legislators and executives fail to act.*

An hyperactive judiciary should not be further excited or encouraged. On 10 January 1983, as the result of a squalid dispute between George Steinbrenner, owner of the New York Yankees baseball club, and the Parks Department of the City of New York, the caretaker of Yankee Stadium, over a proposal of Steinbrenner's to play the first three games of the 1983 season in Denver's Mile High Stadium, Acting Justice Richard S. Lane of the State Supreme Court in Manhattan (New York, perversely, calls its county courts State Supreme Courts) ordered the Yankees to open in the Bronx. Justice Lane wrote

What Is To Be Done?

The Yankee pin stripes belong to New York like Central Park, like the Statue of Liberty, like the Metropolitan Museum of Art, like the Metropolitan Opera, like the Stock Exchange, like the Lights of Broadway, etc. Collectively they are "the Big Apple". Any loss represents diminution of the quality of life here, a blow to the city's standing at the top, however narcissistic that perception may be.[7]

What is going on here? Such an effusion might be expected from a second rate press agent but surely not from a responsible judge. Yet can Justice Lane really be blamed? When the best and the brightest of the law schools, the universities, and the media have been urging the judiciary for decades to be "realistic" and to think in terms of desirable results, and when one considers the example that has been set by the William O. Douglases and Minor Wisdoms of the last three decades, Justice Lane's judicial style becomes understandable if not forgivable.

Consider the words of Professor Arthur Selwyn Miller, Professor emeritus of the George Washington University Law School:

In a rapidly changing society, the pressing need is to get judges to do more. Indeed, as the "public interest" movement in law indicates, that is what many Americans want. . . . People do not believe they can move unresponsive state legislatures or Congress, so the judiciary becomes an object of pressure group tactics. The feet of government officers are held to the flame of enduring constitutional values. That is the essence of democracy, not its antithesis (as critics charge).

One reason for increased resort to the courts is that the political system of pluralism is not working properly. Too many people believe they are outside the system, without muscle adequate to move it.

What remains in the constitutional system is the judiciary; and of it, mainly the Supreme Court. . . . Americans have no spokesman for national values other than the Supreme Court. . . .[8]

That the "public interest" sector of the legal profession might be quite unrepresentative of public opinion (cf., Lichter and Rothman) does not seem to have occurred to Professor Miller. And that those "unresponsive state legislatures" are made up of people who happen to have been elected appears a detail of little consequence.

It must also be recalled in connection with this "someone-has-to-do-it" rationale for activism that the past two decades have seen a significant relaxation of traditional requirements of standing to maintain a law suit. This has enabled almost anybody to get into court to complain about almost any act or omission of government. Certainly it is the glory of judicial review that it provides for suspending the majoritarian dispensation, which is the organizing principle of the system, to protect individuals, but only in exceptional situations when certain fairly familiar and well understandable rights are violated. Otherwise the exception eats up the rule. For the ordinary run of public business the answer to Professor Miller must be that governmental failure to act is just what it looks like—a decision by an imperfectly democratic but altogether legitimate community which is to be respected no matter how badly it goes down at the faculty club.

2. *"We are under the Constitution, but the Constitution is what the judges say it is."*[9]

Surely this uncharacteristic quip of Charles Evans Hughes must rank among the most mischievous lines in our constitutional literature. One does not have to believe that constitutional law is brought by the stork (or that the judge just lays "the article of the Constitution which is invoked beside the statute which is challenged" and decides "whether the latter squares with the former")[10] to find Hughes' proposition unacceptable. Of course judges make law, but not out of whole cloth. If they do, they betray the underlying morality of constitutionalism. Ours is a constitutional polity; that illusive "consent" of which political philosophers earnestly write depends precisely on our being able to recognize in new law the lineaments of the doctrine of government agreed upon and venerated by our forefathers. Certainly this doctrine has and must evolve. But that is not the same thing as saying that there is no core to the doctrine to which the political preferences and social consciences of judges must submit. Certain major political choices have been made for America (allocative choices vested in the legislature, primacy of private sector, equality defined as equality before the law) and these are knowable and relatively unambiguous. There is a Constitution and a constitutional tradition, and it is now necessary, once again in our history, to insist on the distinction between the Constitution and what the Supreme Court says about the Constitution. This is not a call to disobedience; the system requires that we accept the Court's decisions as law. But decisions can be undone and there are limits to what we need regard as legitimate. It is allowed to hope for better times when the idiom of constitutional law will not be tinged with cynicism; when a crack like George Will's ("The Supreme Court has adjourned and the Constitution is safe until October") might seem impudent rather than devastating.

3. *We must progress from a "negative" to a "positive" conception of constitutional rights.*

Properly understood, rights and liberties in America involve not having certain things done to you by government. Government cannot pull you down from the soap box except under very special conditions, government cannot turn you away from the polls because of race, government cannot force its way into your home in search of contraband except under very special circumstances.

But in recent years the most advanced and sensitive souls within the rights industry have set their hearts on a new goal—establishing legally enforceable rights to have government provide social services. "Adequate" welfare payments, day care facilities, medical care, and alike would become personal, judicially enforceable rights. An expanding welfare state would be constitutionally guaranteed—the master fantasy of the left come true! The "right to treatment" of mental patients is illustrative of the problems here. Despite the fact that there is little medical agreement about what constitutes effective treatment of many varieties of mental disorders (or even what the varieties are), some judges have not hesitated to hold that whatever it is, government must provide it.[11]

The argumentative innovations relied on to support new "positive" rights are manifold—constitutional arguments are based on the due process clauses, the equal protection clause, or the prohibition of cruel and unusual punishments; statutory arguments often involve strained interpretations of the organic legislation creating state systems of prisons and mental hospitals. And for judges to set standards of care or condition is to mandate allocations of the scarce resources of the community. Often one finds that the "minimally acceptable" standards the judge is insisting on have been generated by the guild of professionals who manage the system involved. Associations of penologists develop standards for prisons, mental health professionals develop standards for their institutions (or for deinstitutionalization), and "special education" professionals develop standards for teaching the handicapped. These standards are then endorsed by sympathetic rights industry activists as the minimum acceptable to a civilized society and owed victim populations as matters of legal right.

The institutions disabled here are the legislatures (to the extent they are impeded in responding to the desires of their constituents) and the "loser sectors" (the judicially desired dollars have to be taken from somewhere, and this is an especial problem in a period of tax rate constriction—Proposition 13, Two-and-a-Half, and so on). One frustrated observer (Nathan Glazer) recently wondered aloud how long it would be before one of the "new breed" of federal judges nerved himself up to the ultimate activism, ordering a state or municipality to raise taxes in order to upgrade some public facility or other to the level regarded by the Court as "minimally acceptable." But the business won't go that far. The shrewd activist judge will realize that such adventurism might expose the judiciary to political retaliation of the sort bruted from time to time in Congress. Far better to proceed by threatening closure of facilities which are not brought up to the standard. This will almost always have the desired effect of moving a grudging legislature to reallocate resources away from the pattern endorsed by local political structure.

4. *Organizations such as the American Civil Liberties Union may be guilty of occasional excesses of enthusiasm, but they perform a valuable service because they assert a "pure civil liberties position."*

What Is To Be Done?

At least for the ACLU this is untrue; and given the semiofficial status which that organization has come to enjoy in recent years, it is important to be clear about the matter.* The ACLU was, in its inception, concerned with advancing radical change in America well beyond the areas of free speech, procedural due process, voting, and such like. Roger Baldwin, the founding father of ACLU, was a Boston Unitarian who went from social work, through anarchism (Emma Goldman style), to pacifism during World War I, to Marxism in the 1920s and 1930s. It is important to remember that the ACLU's first incarnation was as the "American Union Against Militarism." And while it is beyond the scope of this book to catalogue the variety of heady doctrines which in our century have marched under the banner of "antimilitarism," suffice it that the term has always implied an extensive left-looking agenda—much more than simple pacifism or concern that the social customs of nineteenth-century Prussia might take root in America. The issue was never the rise of *junkerism* in the middle west or of dueling societies in the universities, and the keynote was relentless opposition to all existing social and economic hierarchies and disciplines in name of a utopian future in which human conflict would be abated and order would exist without the necessity of external restraint.

To his credit, Roger Baldwin recoiled from Stalinism after the Nazi-Soviet Pact and led the charge which expelled the communists from the leadership of the union in 1940.[12] During the 1950s the organizational leadership was broadened by including more conservatives and political moderates such as Whitney North Seymour, a former president of the American Bar Association. And under the executive directorship of John de J. Pemberton in the late 1950s and early 1960s, while still markedly left of center, the union

---

*In Washington today, union staffers are built into the policy-making process on a wide range of issues. For instance, in the 1983 struggle over amendments to the Freedom of Information Act to protect sensitive CIA files from disclosure, it was reported that the agency had "cut a deal" with the ACLU to move the legislative process forward. This was denied by union officials but in a most self-satisfied fashion. See the exchange in the *Nation,* 24 September 1983.

was close as ever it came to being a "pure civil liberties" group—one made up of persons of diverse political persuasions come together to debate positions on a crucial but limited range of public policy issues concerning the relationship between the individual and the state. But the Vietnam War and the boiling enthusiasm of the radical "Movement" of the late 1960s changed all that. The old impulses of "antimilitarism" surged through the organization, and by 1970 its political character and style came again to resemble the Baldwin persuasion of the 1920s, with the core doctrine no longer described as Marxist, but as "radical-humanist."[13] In recent years the politics of the union has been an almost uninterrupted passage into leftist sectarianism.

The point is twofold. First, given the pervasive political radicalism of the ACLU (and especially the state and local affiliates), one must continually be alert to the extent that the civil liberties arguments advanced by union activists are driven by disaffection. Second, and more serious, it must be borne in mind that the Union's concern for civil liberties is selective, extending typically to those rights and liberties that are instrumental to social and political change (speech, due process, equal protection) and ignoring those the protection of which might perpetuate the *status quo* (property, private association, and the state action doctrine which protects against massive government preemption of private choice). I do not mean to suggest intellectual dishonesty here. The ACLU has exerted itself over the years on behalf of persons of whom it heartily disapproved when the issue involved was one which it recognized as a civil liberties matter. Thus ACLU spokesmen have defended the speech rights of Nazis and Klansmen. It is not that the union is biased as regards persons, but as regards issues. Hamilton's observation from *Federalist 78* that "a power over a man's substance amounts to a power over his will" is an important part of the American tradition of civil liberty, but it has never produced sympathetic echoes at the ACLU. And that most basic of all civil rights, the right to govern ourselves and our communities by majoritarian processes, has received decidedly short shrift.

What Is To Be Done?

One of the most successful rhetorical tricks of rights industry professionals is to stigmatize those who disagree with them over whether some new right should be created as "anti-civil liberties." To be "committed" to civil liberties is to oppose those restrictions on individual liberty which the professionals tend to oppose (for example, conscription for military service) and favor the restrictions they tend to favor (for example, the imposition of affirmative action "goals"). In fact, there is both more and less to "civil liberty," property defined, than is reflected in the contemporary concerns of the ACLU. Concern for civil liberties is not the sole property of the left, however insistently it is made out to be. And it is fully time to reclaim the rhetoric of rights from those who have so often employed it selectively in a spirit of hostility to much of America's past and present.

5. *There are technical, lawyerly matters which only the initiates really understand.*

This putdown comes with exceeding ill grace from lawyers who take the gospel of "legal realism" for granted; who have been taught and now teach the desirability and, indeed, inevitability of result-oriented jurisprudence. But come it does. An example involves Gary McDowell's 1982 book, *Equity and the Constitution.* [14] This is a sophisticated argument that part of the mischief of recent judicial activism results from a misuse by courts of the concept of equity—the capacity of judges to order remedies not provided for by explicit provisions of statutory law. As every schoolboy knows, courts of equity evolved to achieve fair resolution of disputes by remedies (for example, injunctions) not provided for in what had become a rigidified and highly formalistic body of common law. And as the same schoolboy knows, courts of equity themselves built up bodies of law (precedent) and progressively formalized their rules so that the distinctions of style between the two systems became blurred and a single body of civil law emerged. Therefore, for a contemporary court to exercise equity jurisdiction is not to have the judge operate as platonic guardian to order "the right thing" for society. The judge in equity is bound to be guided by precedent and tradition just as in law—albeit by a difficult body of rules and traditions. But McDowell contends that the Supreme Court, in particular,

> . . . in using its "historic equitable remedial powers" to impose its politics on society, is often forced to ignore or deny the great tradition of equitable principle and precedents, which had always been viewed as the inherent source of restraint in equitable dispensations.[15]

The bulk of the book is a careful historical tracing of equitable principle and precedents leading to the conclusion that these will not support such sweeping equitable remedies as racial balance orders.

The attack on McDowell's book was quick in coming in the *Harvard Law Review*. In an unsigned note, the intellectual youthful offenders at Gannett House (the campus home of the *Review*) charged that McDowell ignored "crucial aspects of evolution and expansion of the concept" of equity.[16] And McDowell's careful argument against "sociological equity" was dismissed by the future judicial clerks with the usual canard that sweeping judicially crafted remedies (applying to whole classes of persons rather than to the specific situations of individual litigants) are "mandated" by the equal protection clause. The note ends by suggesting darkly that McDowell's proposals with respect to equity are "motivated by . . . a fundamental disagreement with some aspect of the Supreme Court's interpretation of the Constitution," and that "the appropriateness of remedies cannot be separated from judgment on the validity of substantive law." The note is legalistic chaff blown in order to evade an incoming argument that the activism of today's judges has much to do with the sorts of broad (as opposed to individualized) remedial orders they are persuaded to issue and that such orders represent a recent and sinister departure from the Anglo-American tradition in the matter of equitable relief.*

*The essential novelty of the new modes of equitable relief could hardly be denied by the editors since it has been regularly celebrated in their pages. Most notoriously by Abraham Chayes, "The Role of the Judge in Public Law Litigation," 89 *Harvard Law Review* 1280 (1976).

What Is To Be Done?

6. *Open and systematic decision making according to published rules and written criteria is always to be preferred.*

It marks the success of the rights industry in our time that many will ask "What's wrong with that?" Especially those of us who ear ː our livings at intellectual work are conditioned to identify rationalized, highly articulated decision making as good and nonverbalized, more intuitive decision making as bad—that's where "prejudice" slips in! In fact, what mostly "slips into" such decisions are situationally relevant factors and dimensions too subtle to be captured and provided for in a necessarily crude, abstract set of rules or criteria. Thomas Sowell, among others, has pointed out how the process of articulation often results in the loss of information:

> The definition or articulation of product characteristics by third parties [a neutral rule maker or rule adjudicator] seldom covers as many dimensions as are unconsciously coordinated in unarticulated market processes. . . . The characteristics of even relatively simple things like an apartment or a can of peas cannot be exhaustively articulated, or even articulated enough in most cases to match the systemic control of characteristics through voluntary transactions.[17]

Employment decisions are paradigmatic in this respect. It is quite absurd to suppose that the dimensions of any but the simplest, most menial of jobs can be fully and systematically articulated. Only someone intimately involved in sustaining or directing a purposeful enterprise will have knowledge of what kind of human addition is actually required to advance it. This knowledge will be of the sort Michael Oakeshott describes as "practical knowledge." Practical knowledge is altogether rational; it simply cannot be fitted into the verbal containers required by the systematic-rationalistic model of decision-making. " 'Rational' conduct," Oakeshott writes,

> is acting in such a way that the coherence of the idiom of activity to which the conduct belongs is preserved and possibly enhanced. This, of course, is something different from faithfulness to principles or rules or

stated purposes (if any have been discovered) of the activity; principles, values and purposes are mere abridgements of the coherence of the activity, and we may easily be faithful to them while losing touch with the activity itself.[18]

Usually only the crudest (and less important) requirements of a job can be spelled out in a job description or a list of "desired qualities" or "criteria for employment" (Ph.D. completed, good physical health, fluent French, and so on). For persons outside an enterprise to attempt to specify what characteristics of applicants are, or are not, "job related" is folly. This does not mean that we should leave employment decisions, or other decisions that have significant externalities, to the unresisted discretion of institutional leaders. It does mean that we must resist the impulse to reflexively legalize that decision making. If we do not resist, we shall, in the cause of even further narrowing the possibilities of racial, sexual, or other prejudice, be hustled into incurring enormous costs in efficiency and creativity.

The "Meanness" Issue

It is only very recently that the adversary culture in America has been subjected to serious intellectual challenge. A characteristic response to the unfamiliar sting of criticism has been to charge the critics with "meanness." This charge is most often lodged with respect to differences over economic policy, but it has been found serviceable as well in the area of rights policy. The dominant radicals within the rights industry manifest "compassion," their critics a resurgent meanness of spirit which, alas, has not quite been exorcised from the American character. The usual counter to the charge of meanness is to point out the radical conception of compassion is often marred by a sentimental slack-mindedness. (Who was it who defined sentimentality as "unearned emotion?") It can hardly be overstressed these days that promiscuous compassion is less than ennobling.

Before me as I write is a small sheaf of newspaper clippings which record the affair of Jack Henry Abbott—a fable for our time. Having spent most of his adult life in prison for violent crimes, Abbott was serving time in a federal prison in Utah when he was discovered by novelist Norman Mailer, who was writing about the executed Utah murderer, Gary Gilmore, and had become interested in the problems of long-term prisoners. Mailer arranged for Abbott's crude but passionate letters about prison life to be published under the arresting title *In the Belly of the Beast*.[19] Even more important, Mailer arranged for Abbott to be paroled to a "halfway house" in New York City so that he could serve as the novelist's research assistant. *In the Belly of the Beast* was widely praised in the prestige media. Terrence DesPres, in the *New York Times Book Review* called it "fiercely visionary," and delivered himself of the astonishing opinion that those who "romanticize" prison life are "less moral" than the prisoners.[20] It was Mr. DesPres' bad luck to have his silly puff appear the day after the convict-author stabbed a waiter to death outside a Greenwich Village restaurant in a dispute over a locked toilet.

Norman Mailer is not a rights professional, nor were most of the reviewers who praised Abbott's book and celebrated the release into society of "a new writer of the largest stature." But the undiscriminating compassion which is the common property of the American left, rights professionals, and *literati* alike, was very much on display in the Abbott case. It overrode not only common sense but common decency.

However, it is not an adequate response to the charge of meanness simply to impeach the fashionable notion of compassion. There must be a positive dimension to the response as well. For what is so frequently denominated "meanness" is, in fact, that modicum of mental toughness needed to maintain social institutions and improve them in orderly ways.

This issue has been most elegantly addressed by John Sparrow, late Warden of All Souls, Oxford, in a small but important book titled *Too Much of a Good Thing*.[21] Sparrow, a lawyer, argues that certain undeniably good tendencies at work in the contemporary West can be overvalued. This, in turn, can end up making the world a worse place. One of these is a tendency toward increased humanity, by which Sparrow means the disposition to be kind and gentle to others and to shrink from imposing our will by force upon our fellow men or inflicting pain or injury upon them. And one good thing may be overvalued at the expense of others:

> It is a bad thing to be hard: but it does not follow that it is a good thing to be soft. . . . There are two reasons why our tenderheartedness needs to be supplemented by toughness. First, because someone who can't face the fact of suffering cannot adequately meet the responsibilities that fall his lot as a member of society. Second because . . . the refusal to countenance the deliberate imposition of force and the deliberate infliction of pain may prove to be self-defeating: it may well produce a greater volume of suffering in the long run than it saves in the short run,. . . .[22]

An example of the first need for toughness might involve one's making a professional decision (concerning a promotion, a research grant, a new command) which will necessarily hurt a friend. An example of the second need might involve a society imposing upon itself the pain of military conscription in the present to lessen the likelihood of war in the future. The responsible conduct of our common and our private affairs—the pursuit of virtue—sometimes requires us to treat other people as means to some important end, rather than as ends in themselves (at least in a particular decision-making context). Always treating people as ends in themselves may be an acceptable principle for a commune, but it is moral lunacy for an advanced society made up of complicated, interlocking, purposeful institutions which require for their working (not to mention efficiency) degrees of hierarchical direction and achievement-oriented impersonality. To exalt an inflated concept of "personhood," according to which the subjective feelings of individuals are reflexively preferred over broader social values such as order and efficiency is to shrink from the necessary moral calculus of social life into a moralistic escapism.

Au fond, we must recognize that there are claims being made for protection of persons which are simply too trivial, precious, or bizarre to be accorded great weight as against broader social values. Are Jehovah's Witnesses really impaired in any serious way in the free exercise of religion by an ordinance that evenhandedly forbids the nuisance of door-to-door solicitation? Are hardened political activists (of the left or right) "chilled" in their political speaking by the fact that government may be noting and filing summaries of what they say and do in public forums? Is a healthy child of atheist parents really brutalized by witnessing a short prayer recited at school? Is the sidewalk demonstrator really deprived of any significant part of his capacity for political communication by a law forbidding his use of racial epithets and the earthier Anglo-Saxon expletives? And finally, will the self-expression of Hugh Heffner and Larry Flint really be cruelly suppressed if local communities are able to decide for themselves whether the spread-eagled pictorial wares produced by these gentry should be displayed for sale within their borders?

There may be good public policy arguments against nonsolicitation ordinances, school prayer, government surveillance of political demonstrations, group libel laws, and banning *Hustler.* But they must rest on something more than naked assertion of individual interest; they must be based on objective determinations of serious injury or deprivation. That is not being mean, just balanced.

Of course we must guard against overreaction, even while smiting rights professionals hip and thigh. There have been serious abuses of public and private power in America, and the rights industry has an honorable history of opposing and curbing these abuses. Many of us are old enough to remember state-imposed racial discrimination, governmental overreaction to domestic communism, and the routine use of real "third-degree" techniques by police. There have been dragons abroad in the land and if some of

the knights who girded themselves to kill dragons now seem to
have run amok and be skewering our milch cows, we must not
forget that dragons can always come back again. And abuses of
power continue today. They may not be dragons, but they aren't
milch cows either (the recent disclosures of third-degree techniques
employed by the New Orleans police is an example), and a society
without a rights industry is just as uncomfortable to contemplate
as a society without policemen. Ultimately our criticism should be
animated by a concern for the rights industry as well as a concern
for institutional excellence and public decency. The rights industry
needs to shrink, moderate, and ideologically detoxify itself in order
to serve effectively as guardian of the open society rather than its
traducer. But this is no excuse for forgetting that there is much that
is admirable about the people and groups we are criticizing.

NOTES

Chapter 1

1. *New York Times,* 28 December 1983.
2. See Raoul Berger, *Death Penalties: The Supreme Court's Obstacle Course* (Cambridge: Harvard University Press, 1982).
3. See Richard E. Morgan, *Domestic Intelligence: Monitoring Dissent in America* (Austin: University of Texas Press, 1980).
4. As early as the Ford administration, George Gilder was writing that: "A new alliance between Pentagon personnel administrators and policy makers and the women's liberation movement has emerged, pushing the United States military into a position where women will be so fully and flexibly involved in our armed-services organizational structure that, in a war emergency, it will be difficult (if not impossible) to separate them out." From "The Case Against Women in Combat," *New York Times Sunday Magazine,* (January 1979). Eliot Cohen, assistant professor of government at Harvard, has also written eloquently of this problem; see "Why We Need A Draft," *Commentary,* (April 1982). See also Seth Cropsey, "Women in Combat," *The Public Interest* (Fall 1980).
5. Henry Wadsworth Longfellow, *The Song of Hiawatha* (New York: Bounty Books edition, 1968), p. 1.
6. Horace Flack, *The Adoption of the Fourteenth Amendment* (Baltimore: Johns Hopkins University Press, 1908).
7. See Charles Fairman, "Does the Fourteenth Amendment Incorporate the Bill of Rights?" 2 *Stanford Law Review* 5 (1949). See also Stanley Morrison, "Does the Fourteenth Amendment Incorporate the Bill of Rights?", 2 *Stanford Law Review* 140 (1949). See also the chapter on "The Civil Rights Act Reconsidered, and the Fourteenth Amendment," in Charles Fairman, *Reconstruction and Reunion, 1864–88* (New York: Macmillan, 1971), pp. 1207–1300.
8. J. B. James, *The Framing of the Fourteenth Amendment* (Urbana: University of Illinois Press, 1956). And more modestly, Jacobus ten Broek, *The Antislavery Origins of the Fourteenth Amendment* (Berkeley: University of California Press, 1951). But consider, *per contra,* Raoul Berger, *Government by Judiciary: The Transformation of the Fourteenth Amendment* (Cambridge: Harvard University Press, 1977). While Berger's historical rendition is persuasive, it is not completely so.

Representative Bingham and Senator Howard really did want to overrule Barron v. Baltimore, F Pet. 243 (1833), even if no one else really did. My own position, by way of comparison, is as follows: I agree with Raoul Berger that the absence of a convincing case *for* total incorporation concludes the matter negatively. I am not persuaded, however, that the intentions of the framers of the Fourteenth Amendment were quite as narrowly circumscribed as Berger makes out—that they intended nothing more than to settle the question of citizenship, apply Fifth Amendment due process, and constitutionalize the Civil Rights Act of 1866. Reading and rereading the materials, on a clear day with fair wind, I can see arguable intentions to provide a federal protection of free speech and of the fundamental principles of fairness inhering in the Anglo-American tradition of criminal justice, even if these were beyond what was then generally understood to be comprehended by Fifth Amendment due process. Thus I can sail as far as Gitlow v. New York, 268 U.S. 652 (1925)—although I would have spoken less casually and more guardedly than Justice Sanford. And I can make it to Cardoza's opinion in Palko v. Connecticut, 302 U.S. 319 (1937), without cheating. Beyond that, I suggest, interpretation must give way to something else (unless you can believe in the historical bullet). On the incorporation of the religion clauses of the First Amendment, see Philip Kurland, "The Irrelevance of the Constitution: The Religion Clauses of the First Amendment and the Supreme Court," 24 *Villanova Law Review* 3 (1978–79).

Chapter 2

1. Robert L. Cord, *Separation of Church and State: Historical Fact and Current Fiction* (New York: Lameth Press, 1982).

2. Michael J. Malbin, "The Supreme Court and the Definition of Religion," (Ph.D diss., Cornell, 1973). An abbreviated version of the relevant chapters is Malbin, *Religion and Politics: The Intentions of the Authors of the First Amendment* (Washington, D.C.: American Enterprise Institute, 1978). Paul J. Webber "James Madison and Religious Equality," *The Review of Politics* (April 1982). Louis Luskey, *By What Right? A Commentary on the Supreme Court's Power to Revise the Constitution* (Charlottesville, Va.: Michie, 1975), pp. 167–78. Even earlier, see Edward S. Corwin, "The Supreme Court as National School Board," 14 *Law and Contemporary Problems* 3 (1949); and J.M. O'Neill, *Religion and Education Under the Constitution* (New York: Harper Brothers, 1949).

3. Daniel Patrick Moynihan, "What Do You Do When the Supreme Court Is Wrong?" *The Public Interest* (Fall 1979).

4. Nathan Glazer, "Toward A New Concordat?" *This World,* Summer 1982.

5. Everson v. Board of Education, 333 U.S. 1 (1947).

6. ———, 330 U.S. 1, 15–16.

7. ———, 330 U.S. 1, 19.

8. The following year, in McCollum v. Board of Education, Justice Reed dissented. In doing so, he paid lip service to the theory of separation enunciated by Black in *Everson,* but indicated in several statements that his own views were, perhaps, more tentative. "The phrase 'an establishment of religion' may have been intended by Congress to be aimed only at a state church." 333 U.S. 203, 244. And

Notes

". . . the 'wall of separation between church and State' that Mr. Jefferson built at the University [of Virginia] which he founded did not exclude religious education from the school." 333 U.S. 203, 247. Further indication that Reed could not have been altogether happy with Black's historical case for strict separation is found in his (Reed's) dissent in Murdock v. Pennsylvania, in 1944. See 319 U.S. 105, 125.

9. McCollum v. Board of Education, 333 U.S. 203 (1948).

10. McCollum v. Board of Education, 333 U.S. 203, 210.

11. Zorach v. Clauson, 343 U.S. 306 (1952).

12. Zorach v. Clauson, 343 U.S. 306, 312–314.

13. The New York "Regent's Prayer Case" was Engle v. Vitale, 370 U.S. 421 (1962); both the Pennsylvania Bible-reading and the Maryland Lord's Prayer cases were reported Sub. Nom. School District of Abington Township v. Schempp, 374 U.S. 203 (1963).

14. Engle v. Vitale, 370 U.S. 421, 441.

15. Engle v. Vitale, 370 U.S. 421, 445.

16. See Stewart's concurrence in Sherbert v. Verner, 374 U.S. 413–418.

17. Board of Education v. Allen, 392 U.S. 236 (1968).

18. Lemon v. Kurtzman, 403 U.S. 602 (1971).

19. Committee for Public Education v. Nyquist, 413 U.S. 756 (1973).

20. The original formulation was by Justice Clark in Schempp, 374 U.S. 203, 222 (1963). In the years between Schempp and Nyquist it was possible to believe that a secondary or indirect positive impact on a church-related institution might not, even by radical separationist canon, require a conclusion of unconstitutionality. Justice Powell's broadening of "primary effect" in to "effect of advancing" foreclosed on any such good sense.

21. Meek v. Pettinger, 421 U.S. 349 (1975).

22. Wolman v. Walter, 433 U.S. 229 (1977).

23. Committee v. Regan, 444 U.S. 646 (1980).

24. Levitt v. Committee, 431 U.S. 472 (1973).

25. Committee v. Regan, 444 U.S. 646, 671.

26. Mark DeWolfe Howe, *The Garden and the Wilderness: Religion and Government in American Constitutional History* (Chicago: University of Chicago Press, 1965), p. 4.

27. 1 *Annals of Congress* 434 (emphasis added).

28. Michael J. Malbin, *The Supreme Court and the Definition of Religion* (Ph.D. diss., Cornell University, 1973), pp. 70–95. The standard history, Robert A. Rutland, *The Birth of the Bill of Rights, 1776–1791* (Chapel Hill: University of North Carolina Press, 1955), is singularly unhelpful on this point. For one thing, Rutland is relentlessly concerned to enlist the framers in support of the contemporary "liberal" orthodoxy, and has little effort to spare to figure out what *they* might have meant by the word they used.

29. 1 *Annals of Congress* 731 (emphasis added).

30. 1 *Annals of Congress* 731.

31. 3 *Elliot's Debates* (2d ed. 1836) 330.

32. Cord, *Separation of Church and State*, pp. 29–36.

33. Malbin, *The Supreme Court and the Definition of Religion*, pp. 103–105.

34. Cord, *Separation of Church and State*, p. 45.

35. Ibid., p. 38.

36. The letter is reproduced in Anson Phelps Stokes and Leo Pfeffer, *Church and State in the United States* (New York: Harper & Row, 1964), p. 88.

37. Abington School District v. Schempp, 374 U.S. 203, 235 (1963).

38. Joseph Story, *Commentaries on the Constitution of the United States*, 2nd ed., vol. II (Boston: Little, Brown, 1851), p. 591.

39. Thomas M. Cooley, *Constitutional Limitations* (Boston: Little, Brown, 1868), pp. 470–71.

40. Thomas M. Cooley, *The General Principles of Constitutional Law in the United States of America* (Boston: Little, Brown, 1880), p. 207.

41. Philip Schaff, *Church and State in the United States* (New York: Charles Scribner's Sons, 1888), p. 69. See also Isaac A. Cornelison, *The Relation of Religion to Civil Government in the United States of America* (New York: G.P. Putnam's Sons, 1895).

42. Ray Allen Billington, *The Protestant Crusade, 1800–1860* (Chicago: Quadrangle Books, 1964); John Higham, *Strangers in the Land* (New Brunswick, N.J.: Rutgers University Press, 1955).

43. Higham, *Strangers*, p. 28. See also Donald L. Kinzer, *An Episode in Anti-Catholicism: The American Protective Association* (Seattle: University of Washington Press, 1964).

44. Quoted in Anson Phelps Stokes, *Church and State in the United States*, vol. II (New York: Harper and Bros., 1950), p. 722.

45. Ibid., p. 723.

46. These matters are covered in greater detail in Richard E. Morgan, "Backs to the Wall: A Study in the Contemporary Politics of Church and State" (Ph.D. diss., Columbia University, 1967), pp. 7–54.

47. On the extent to which the strict separationist campaign in the courts was an interest group effort, see Frank J. Sorauf, *The Wall of Separation: The Constitutional Politics of Church and State* (Princeton: Princeton University Press, 1976).

48. Alvin W. Johnson, *The Legal Status of Church-State Relationships in the United States* (Minneapolis: University of Minnesota Press, 1934), p. 196.

49. Smith v. Donahue, 202 App. Div. 656, 195 N.Y.S. 715 (1922).

50. Donahoe v. Richards, 38 Me. 376 (1854).

51. Alvin W. Johnson and Frank H. Yost, *Separation of Church and State* (Minneapolis: University of Minnesota Press, 1948).

52. Irving Brant, *James Madison: The Nationalist, 1780–1787* (Indianapolis: Bobbs-Merrill, 1948).

53. In 1943, for instance, between volumes one and two of the Madison biography, Brant published a little book looking forward to the end of World War II titled *Road to Peace and Freedom* (Indianapolis: Bobbs-Merrill). He concluded, inter alia, that "conditions in Russia point to the spread of democracy." (p. 197).

54. Brant, *James Madison*, p. 355.

55. Ibid., p. 351 (emphasis added).

56. Irving Brant, *James Madison: Father of the Constitution, 1787–1800* (Indianapolis: Bobbs-Merrill, 1950), p. 272.

57. See, for example, Loren P. Beth, *The American Theory of Church and State* (Gainesville: University of Florida Press, 1958), pp. 69–71. Or consider Milton R.

Notes

Konvitz, a usually careful and lawyerly commentator in "Whittling Away Religious Freedom," *Commentary* (June 1946). "For the last hundred years . . . the sharp separation of church and state was considered an inviolable principle of American democracy." By whom? On what evidence? With respect to what kinds of issues? Konvitz gave no answers. He seemed to assume that this was just something everyone knew.

58. Paul Blanshard, *American Freedom and Catholic Power* (Boston: Beacon Press, 1949).

59. Joseph L. Blau, *Cornerstones of Religious Freedom in America* (Boston: Beacon Press, 1949).

60. In Vidal v. Girard's Executors, 2 Howard 61 (1844), Webster made his famous argument that a will containing an anti-Christian provision could not be probated because Christianity was part of the common law of the state in question (Pennsylvania) and the probate would thus be contrary to public policy. Justice Story agreed with the incorporation argument, but, held it to be condition by the free exercise provision of the Pennsylvania Constitution.

61. R. Freeman Butts, *The American Tradition in Religion and Education* (Boston: Beacon Press, 1950).

62. V.T. Thayer, *The Attack Upon the American Secular School* (Boston: Beacon Press, 1951).

63. Conrad Henry Moehlman, *The Wall of Separation Between Church and State* (Boston: Beacon Press, 1951).

64. Leo Pfeffer, *Church, State, and Freedom* (Boston: Beacon Press, 1953).

65. Ibid., p. 108.

66. Cord, *Separation of Church and State*, p. 62.

67. Anson Phelps Stokes, *Church and State in the United States,* vol III (New York: Harper Brothers, 1950), p. 165.

68. Anson Phelps Stokes (1874–1958) and Leo Pfeffer, *Church and State in the United States,* revised one-volume edition (New York: Harper & Row, 1964), p. 579.

69. Vernon L. Parrington, *The Colonial Mind, 1620–1800* (New York: Harcourt Brace, 1927).

70. Charles A. Beard, *The Republic: Conversations on Fundamentalists* (New York: Viking Press, 1943). Cast in the form of a dialogue with a (hopefully fictitious) local doctor and his wife, Beard reassures his skeptical questioners that the American constitutional government is sufficiently democratic and "progressive" to warrant their continuing support.

71. Ibid., p. 165.

72. Peter L. Berger and Richard John Neuhaus, *To Empower People* (Washington, D.C.: American Enterprise Institute, 1977), p. 28.

73. Donald A. Erickson, "The School as a Mediating Structure: Some Concerns About Subversion and Co-optation," in Jay Mechling, ed., *Church, State, and Public Policy: The New Shape of the Church-State Debate* (Washington, D.C.: American Enterprise Institute, 1978), p. 73.

74. James S. Coleman, Thomas Hoffer, and Sally Kilgore, *High School Achievement: Public, Catholic, and Private Schools Compared* (New York: Basic Books, 1982), p. 187.

75. Robert L. Cord, "Separation of Church and State: Crisis in the American

Constitutional System," Robert D. Klein Lecture, (Northeastern University, 28 May 1981), pp. 9–10.

76. See Alexander M. Bickel, *The Supreme Court and the Idea of Progress* (New York: Harper & Row, 1970), pp. 148–49.

Chapter 3

1. See Robert W. Kagan, "A Relic of the New Age: The National Education Association," *The American Spectator* (February 1982). See also Chester E. Finn, Jr., "Teacher Politics," *Commentary,* (February 1983).

2. Robert Michels, *Political Parties* (New York: Collier Books edition, 1962).

3. Mancur Olsen, *The Logic of Collective Action* (Cambridge: Harvard University Press, 1965).

4. Plessey v. Ferguson, 163 U.S. 537 (1896).

5. Brown v. Board of Education, 347 U.S. 483 (1954).

6. Brown II, 349 U.S. 294 (1955).

7. For criticism of the clarity and coherence of Chief Justice Warren's Brown opinion from different points of view, see Edmond Cahn, "Jurisprudence," 30 *New York University Law Review* 150 (1955); and Herbert Wechsler, "Toward Neutral Principles of Constitutional Law," 73 *Harvard Law Review* 1 (1959). In fact, Warren's opinion was so loosely jointed that it was possible for Owen Fiss, now of the Yale Law School to argue a decade later, that it *really* rested on an "equal-educational-opportunity principle" which might be interpreted to require the schools be racially balanced! See Fiss, "Racial Imbalance in the Public Schools: The Constitutional Concepts," 78 *Harvard Law Review* 594 (1965). But remembering the amount of intra-Court jockeying and intentional obfuscation necessary to gain unanimous agreement to the "stop segregating schools" judgment of Brown, Fiss' effort is far-fetched. See Dennis J. Hutchinson, "Unanimity and Desegregation," 68 *Georgetown Law Journal* 1 (1979).

8. Cooper v. Aaron, 358 U.S. 1 (1958).

9. Griffin v. Prince Edward County School Board, 377 U.S. 218 (1964).

10. An excellent review of the evolution in the understanding of "desegregation" by the federal judiciary is Fred T. Read "Judicial Evolution of the Law of School Integration Since Brown v. Board of Education," 39 *Law and Contemporary Problems* 7 (1975). Read sees three distinct phases of this evolution: the "Muted Response"—1955–1983, the "Search for Standards"—1963–1967, and "Massive Integration"—1968–1972.

11. Green v. Board of Education, 391 U.S. 430 (1968).

12. Swann v. Charotte Macklenberg Board of Education, 402 U.S. 1 (1971).

13. Keyes v. School District No. 1, Denver, Colo., 413 U.S. 189 (1973).

14. Lino A. Graglia, *Disaster By Decree: The Supreme Court Decisions on Race and the Schools* (Ithaca: Cornell University Press, 1976), p. 35.

15. Briggs v. Elliott, 132 F. Supp. 776, 777 (1955).

16. Bell v. School City of Gary, Indiana, 324 F.2d 209 (1963).

17. Quoted in Graglia, *Disaster By Decree,* p. 48.

18. Graglia, *Disaster By Decree,* p. 48.

19. 110 *Congressional Record* 12715.

20. Ibid., pp. 12716–12717.

Notes

21. Graglia, *Disaster By Decree,* p. 53.
22. Nathan Glazer, "Is Busing Necessary," *Commentary,* (March 1972).
23. Graglia, *Disaster By Decree,* p. 54.
24. U.S. Commission on Civil Rights, *Survey of School Desegregation in the Southern and Border States, 1965–66* (Washington, D.C.: Government Printing Office, 1966), pp. 53–54.
25. Graglia, *Disaster By Decree,* p. 55.
26. 45 *Code of Federal Regulations,* sect. 181 (1967).
27. United States v. Jefferson County Board of Education, 372 F.2d 836 (1966).
28. Graglia, *Disaster By Decree,* p. 58.
29. Owen M. Fiss, "The Jurisprudence of Busing," 39 *Law and Contemporary Problems* 194, 210 (1975).
30. Ronald Dworkin, "Social Sciences and Constitutional Rights—The Consequences of Uncertainty," 6 *Journal of Law and Education* 3 (1977).
31. David L. Kirp, "Legalism and Politics in School Desegregation," 1981 *Wisconsin Law Review* 924, 969.
32. James S. Coleman, Sara D. Kelley, and John H. Moore, *Trends in School Segregation* (Washington, D.C.: Urban Institute, 1975).
33. David J. Armor, "The Evidence on Busing," *The Public Interest,* (Summer 1972). See also "The Double Standard: A Reply," *The Public Interest* (Winter 1973).
34. Nancy St. John, *School Desegregation: Outcomes for Children* (New York: Wiley, 1975). See also "The Effects of School Desegregation on Children: A Re-Review of Research Evidence," paper presented to the American Academy of Arts and Sciences Study Group on Urban School Desegregation, (October 1977).
35. The most thorough and careful pro-busing response is Gary Orfield, *Must We Bus?* (Washington, D.C.: Brookings Institution, 1978). I will not characterize this volume, but leave it to the judgment of anyone up to Orfield's 450 pages to judge how well his arguments stand up six years later.
36. Milliken v. Bradley, 418 U.S. 717 (1974).
37. Diane Ratvich, "The White Flight Controversy," *The Public Interest,* (Spring 1978).
38. *New York Times,* 4 January 1983.
39. *New York Times,* 8 January 1983.
40. Theodore M. Black, *Straight Talk About American Education* (New York: Harcourt Brace Jovanovich, 1982), p. 123.
41. In re fault, 387 U.S. 1.
42. In re Winship, 394 U.S. 358.
43. American Civil Liberties Union, *Academic Freedom in the Secondary Schools* (New York: American Civil Liberties Union, 1968).
44. Gerald Grant, "Children's Rights and Adult Confusions," *The Public Interest* (Fall 1982): 91.
45. Tinker v. Des Moines, 393 U.S. 503.
46. Note, "Individual Rights Within the Public School System," 74 *Michigan Law Review* 1420, 1460 (1976).
47. Goss v. Lopez, 419 U.S. 565. Among the *amicus curiae* briefs supporting the punch spikers were submissions from the ACLU, the NAACP, and the Children's Defense Fund.
48. Wood v. Strickland, 420 U.S. 308 (1975).
49. Smith v. Wade, 51 *Law Week* 4407.

50. *New York Times,* 11 November 1982. Three months earlier the *Times* had reported the happy news that serious student crimes against teachers were down 22 percent from the year before—from 3,534 to 2,730. This followed a year in which the Board of Education spent $24 million security and Chancellor Frank J. Macchiarola had instituted a policy of immediate suspension of any student caught bringing a weapon into a school building. Albert Shanker, president of the United Federation of Teachers, concluded that ". . . this should tell the public that most New York City schools are pretty safe places. . . ." A less sanguine observer might conclude that the situation still left much to be desired.

51. Grant, "Children's Rights," pp. 92–93.

52. National Institute of Education, *Violent Schools—Safe Schools* (Washington, D.C.: Government Printing Office, 1978).

53. Jackson Toby, "Crime in American Public Schools," *The Public Interest* (Winter 1980): 29–30.

54. U.S. Senate, Preliminary Report Subcommittee to Investigate Juvenile Delinquency, *Our Nations Schools—A Report Card* (Washington, D.C.: Government Printing Office, 1975), p. 10.

55. Illustrative of this elite preoccupation with democracy in the schools was the work of the short-lived Center for Research and Education in American Liberties of Columbia University and Teachers College. Funded principally by the Ford Foundation and the U.S. Office of Education (in its period of enthusiasm for "change agents"), that center was directed by Professor Alan F. Westin, who went on to edit the ACLU's ill-fated bimonthly *The Civil Liberties Review* and has been one of the principle theoreticians of privacy rights—a major area of growth in public law in the 1970s. I have long repented my youthful involvement in this enterprise.

56. The litany of names bring a flood of memories—none very pleasant: Charles E. Silberman, *Crisis in the Classroom;* Jonathan Kozol, *Death at an Early Age* and *Free Schools;* Paul Goodman, *Growing Up Absurd;* Edgar Z. Friedenberg, *Coming of Age in America;* and so on.

57. Note, "Due Process, Due Politics and Due Respect: The Models of Legitimate School Governance," 94 *Harvard Law Review* 1106, 1109–1110 (1981).

58. Mark G. Yudof, "Legalization of Dispute Resolution, Distrust of Authority, and Organizational Theory: Implementing Due Process for Students in the Public Schools," 1981 *Wisconsin Law Review* 891, 893.

59. Edward A. Wynne, "What the Courts Are Doing to Our Children," *The Public Interest* (Summer 1981): 15.

60. See especially Barbara Lerner, "American Education: How Are We Doing," *The Public Interest,* (Fall 1982). See also the "Goodlad Study," *New York Times,* 19 July 1983, and the "Open Letter to the American People" of the National Commission on Excellence in Education," *New York Times,* 23 April 1983. And we have already noted James S. Coleman, Thomas Hoffer, and Sally Kilgore, *High School Achievement* (New York: Basic Books, 1982).

61. *New York Times,* 3 May 1982.

Chapter 4

1. For instance, Ted Robert Gurr, *Rogues, Rebels, and Reformers: A Political History of Urban Crime and Conflict* (Beverly Hills, Cal.: Sage, 1976). See also Ted

Notes

Robert Gurr, Peter N. Grabosk, and Richard C. Hula, *The Politics of Crime and Conflict* (Beverly Hills, Cal.: Sage, 1977).

2. See Sir Leon Radzinowicz and Joan King, *The Growth of Crime* (New York: Basic Books, 1977), pp. 74–84.

3. On this point there is no better set of responses to the "institutional nihilists" than that developed by James Q. Wilson. See especially "Crime and American Culture," *The Public Interest* (Winter 1983).

4. See especially Lloyd L. Weinreb, *Denial of Justice* (New York: The Free Press, 1977). While Weinreb would emphatically disagree with much of my analysis of *why* law enforcement is working so poorly (and I disagree with his prescriptions), his portrayal of disarray is telling.

5. John H. Langbein, "Torture and Plea Bargaining," *The Public Interest,* (Winter 1980). See also Macklin Fleming, *The Price of Perfect Justice* (New York: Basic Books, 1974).

6. For instance, the student Note, "Restructuring the Plea Bargain," 82 *Yale Law Journal* 286 (1972). See especially Arnold Enker, *Perspectives on Plea Bargaining*, in President's Commission on Law Enforcement and the Administration of Justice, Task Force Report: The Courts (Washington, D.C.: Government Printing Office, 1975). For an empirical study of the ways in which prosecutors, attorneys, and judges adapt to a system of disposition at variance with their expectations, see Milton Heumon, *Plea Bargaining* (Chicago: University of Chicago Press, 1977).

7. Franklin E. Zimring and Richard S. Fraise, *The Criminal Justice System: Materials on the Administration and Reform of the Criminal Law* (Boston: Little, Brown, 1980).

8. Ibid., pp. 560–61.

9. Ibid., p. 497.

10. Ibid.

11. Criminal Law Revision Committee, *Eleventh Report, Evidence (General),* (London: Her Majesty's Stationary Office, 1972), p. 9.

12. William Blackstone, *Commentaries on the Laws of England* (Oxford: Clarendon Press, 4 vols., 1765–69), Vol. III, pp. 349–385 and Vol. IV, pp. 350–353.

13. John Henry Wigmore, *On Evidence* 10 vols., 3rd ed. (Boston: Little, Brown, 1940), see vol. VIII, sec. 2183, at 4-3. See also Wigmore's distinguished predecessor Simon Greenleaf, *A Treatise on the Law of Evidence* (Boston: Little, Brown, 16th ed., 1899), vol. I, pp. 353–55.

14. Twining v. New Jersey, 211 U.S. 78.

15. Barron v. Baltimore, 7 Pet. 243.

16. Brown v. Mississippi, 297 U.S. 278, 285 (1936).

17. Ibid.

18. Rogers v. Richmond, 365 U.S. 534 (1961).

19. Spano v. New York, 360 U.S. 315 (1959).

20. Chambers v. Florida, 309 U.S. 227 (1940).

21. Ashcraft v. Tennessee, 322 U.S. 143 (1944).

22. Lisemba v. California, 314 U.S. 219 (1941). Raymond Lisemba, the "Rattlesnake Murderer" was questioned, on and off, without sleep for over thirty-six hours, but the majority found that the man who had heavily insured and brutally murdered two wives, and finally been caught up for incest, had "exhibited a self-possession, a coolness, and an acumen throughout his questioning . . . which negates the view that he had lost his freedom of action. . . ."

23. Watts v. Indiana, 338 U.S. 49.

24. Miranda v. Arizona, 384 U.S. 439.

25. Malloy v. Hogan, 378 U.S. 1.

26. Samuel Dash, "Forward" to Richard J. Medalie, *From Escobedo to Miranda: The Anatomy of a Supreme Court Decision* (Washington, D.C.: Lerner, 1966), p. xvii.

27. Yale Kamisar, *Police Interrogation and Confessions: Essays in Law and Policy* (Ann Arbor: University of Michigan Press, 1980), pp. 107–110.

28. Ibid., p. xii.

29. State v. Biron, 266 Minn. 272 (1963).

30. Kamisar, *Police Interrogation*, p. xiii.

31. Kamisar, *Politic Interrogation*, p. xiii.

32. Malloy v. Hagan, 378 U.S. 1.

33. Kamisar, *Police Interrogation*, p. 48.

34. See Leonard W. Levy, *Origins of the Fifth Amendment: The Right Against Self-Incrimination* (New York: Oxford University Press, 1968).

35. Kamisar, *Police Interrogation*, p. 36.

36. Ibid., p. 44.

37. Paul G. Kauper, "Judicial Examination of the Accused—A Remedy for the Third Degree," 30 *Michigan Law Review* 1224 (1932).

38. Edmund M. Morgan, "The Privilege Against Self-Incrimination," 34 *Minnesota Law Review* 1 (1949).

39. Ibid., p. 27.

40. See E.F. Bleiler's introduction to *Richmond: Scenes in the Life of a Bow Street Runner* (New York: Dover Books, 1976). See also J.J. Tobias, "Police and Public in the United Kingdom," in George L. Moose, *Police Forces in History* (Beverly Hills, Cal.: Sage, 1975).

41. Indeed, Kauper gives an example of this process without realizing its significance: ". . . there were in American history forces inimical to the exercise of police functions by a magistrate. In a frontier country the prosecuting attorney, and even the sheriff, eclipsed the justice of the peace as investigators of crime." "Judicial Examination," p. 1236.

42. Kamisar, Police Interrogation, p. 43.

43. Ibid., p. 44.

44. Davis v. North Carolina, 384 U.S. 737 (1966).

45. This particular formulation is from the chapter on police interrogation in Kamisar, et. al., *Basic Criminal Procedure* (St. Paul, Minn.: West, 1980), p. 557.

46. Culombe v. Connecticut, 367 U.S. 568, 571 (1961).

47. Kamisar, *Police Interrogations*, p. 102.

48. See Geoffrey R. Stone, "The Miranda Doctrine and the Burger Court," 1977 *Supreme Court Review* 99.

49. United States v. Garson, 291 F. 646, 649 (1923).

50. Abraham S. Goldstein, "The State and the Accused: Balance of Advantage in Criminal Procedure," 69 *Yale Law Journal* 1149, 1152 (1960).

51. Abraham S. Goldstein, "Defining the Role of the Victim in Criminal Prosecution," 52 *Mississippi Law Journal* 515 (1982).

52. Radzinowicz and King, *Growth of Crime*, pp. 31–54.

53. John T. McNaughton, "The Privilege Against Self-Incrimination: Its Constitutional Affectation, Raison d'Etre and Miscellaneous Implications," in Claude R. Sowle, ed., *Police Power and Individual Freedom* (Chicago: Aldine, 1962), pp. 227, 236.

Notes

54. Walter V. Schaffer, "Federalism and State Criminal Procedure," 70 *Harvard Law Review* 26 (1956).

55. Sir Basil Thompson, *The Criminal* (London: Hodder and Stoughton, 1925), pp. 217–19.

Chapter 5

1. Roger Starr, "Officers of the Law," *Commentary* (October 1973).

2. The relationship between police in the streets patrolling aggressively and the control of crime was once a commonplace. It was deemphasized by the enthusiasm for technology as a why of compensating for personnel cuts, and because of heightened levels of concern about white, Anglo cops creating "community relations" problems on patrol in black and hispanic neighborhoods.

3. James Q. Wilson, "The Urban Unease: Community vs. City," *The Public Interest,* (Summer 1968).

4. Nathan Glazer, "On Subway Graffiti in New York," *The Public Interest* (Winter 1979): 4.

5. James Q. Wilson and George L. Kelling, "Broken Windows," *The Atlantic Monthly,* (March 1982).

6. See, for instance, Herbert Jacob, *Crime and Justice in Urban America* (Englewood Cliffs, N.J.: Prentice-Hall, 1980), pp. 24–25.

7. James Q. Wilson and Barbara Boland, "The Effect of the Police on Crime," 12 *Law and Society Review* 367, 370 (1978).

8. For the actual San Diego data see John E. Boydstun, *San Diego Field Interrogation: Final Report* (Washington, D.C.: The Police Foundation, 1977).

9. Wilson and Boland, "Effect of the Police," p. 370.

10. For other work suggesting the importance of an aggressive style of police patrol, particularly response rates and times, see Calvin Clawson and Samson Chang, "The Relationship of Response Delays and Arrest Rates," 5 *Journal of Police Science and Administration* 53 (1977); and Herbert Isaacs, "A Study of Communications, Crimes and Arrests in a Metropolitan Police Department," in President's Commission on Law Enforcement and Administration of Justice, *Task Force Report: Science and Technology* (Washington, D.C.: Government Printing Office, 1967).

11. Kolender v. Lawson, 51 *Law Week* 4532.

12. Note, "The Vagrancy Concept Reconsidered: Problems and Abuses of Status Criminality", 37 *New York University Law Review* 102 (1962). See especially Thompson v. Louisville, 362 U.S. 199 (1960); Shuttlesworth v. Birmingham, 382 U.S. 87 (1965); and U.S. v. Mazurie, 419 U.S. 544, 550 (1975).

13. Papachristo v. City of Jacksonville, 405 U.S. 156.

14. Anthony Amsterdam, "Federal Constitutional Restrictions on the Punishment of Crimes of Status, Crimes of General Obnoxiousness, Crimes of Displeasing Police Officers, and the Like," 3 *Criminal Law Bulletin* 205, 226 (1967). Quoted at 405 U.S. 156, 170–171.

15. Terry v. Ohio, 392 U.S. 1 (1968).

16. People v. Salomon, 33 Cal. App. 3d 429 (1973).

17. Gooding v. Wilson, 405 U.S. 518 (1972).

18. Chaplinsky v. New Hampshire, 315 U.S. 568 (1942).

19. U.S. v. Delaware and Hudson Co., 231 U.S. 366, 407 (1909); see also Justice Brandeis' concurring opinion in Ashwander v. TVA, 297 U.S. 288, 346–348 (1936) —a text once considered canonical but now largely forgotten.

20. It should be noted here that there is a disagreement in the technical literature over precisely how this exception to the general duty of the Court to preserve statutes by narrowing interpretation should be understood. Some commentators, such as Professor Tribe of Harvard see this as a form of third-party standing, that is an exception to the general rule of standing that holds that one may not raise anyone's constitutional rights but one's own. By this understanding the defendant in Gooding v. Wilson was actually raising the constitutional rights of some theoretical third party whose future choice of language might be chilled by the statute. (See *American Constitutional Law,* Mineola, N.Y.: Foundation Press, 1978, pp. 720–722.) On the other hand, Henry Moynihan, of Boston University insists that overbreadth inseparability is not a facet of standing doctrine at all but rather a matter of the substantive First Amendment constitutional law—that individuals have a substantive right not to be called to account before a law which is constitutionally imperfect as to possible others even if their own conduct is unprotected. The matter, however, is an embroidery on error.

21. Elmore v. State, 15 Ga. App. 461, 463 (1914).

22. Rosenfeld v. New Jersey, 408 U.S. 901 (1972).

23. Brown v. Oklahoma, 408 U.S. 914 (1972).

24. Lewis v. New Orleans, 408 U.S. 193 (1972).

25. Laurence H. Tribe, *American Constitutional Law* (Mineola, N.Y.: Foundation Press, 1978), pp. 889.

26. Ibid., p. 578.

27. Ibid.

28. Ibid., p. 715.

29. John Stuart Mill, *On Liberty and Considerations on Representative Government,* R.B. McCallum, ed., (Oxford: Blackwell, 1948), p. 8.

30. Thomas Grey, *The Legal Enforcement of Morality* (Chicago: American Bar Association, 1980), p. 1.

31. Lochner v. New York, 198 U.S. 45 (1905).

32. Ibid., p. 75.

33. James Fitzjames Stephen, *Liberty, Equality, Fraternity* (Cambridge: Cambridge University Press, 1967), p. 83.

34. Gertrude Himmelfarb, *On Liberty and Liberalism: The Case of John Stuart Mill* (New York: Knopf, 1974).

35. Ibid., pp. 336–38.

36. Patrick Devlin, *The Enforcement of Morals* (London: Oxford University Press, 1965), pp. 124–39.

37. Ibid., p. 67.

38. Peter Shaw, "John Hinckley—A Face in the Crowd," *Commentary* (September 1981).

39. Ibid., p. 67.

40. Sir Robert Peel, to the Duke of Wellington, 5 November 1829, in C.S. Parker, ed., *Sir Robert Peel From His Private Papers* (London: Greeman, 1899), vol. II, p. 115.

41. Lloyd L. Weinreb, *Denial of Justice* (New York: The Free Press, 1977), p. viii.

Notes

42. Aquilar v. Texas, 378 U.S. 108 (1964); Spinelli v. U.S., 393 U.S. 410 (1969); and the leading Maine case, State v. Hawkins, 261 A. 2d 255 (1970).

43. Office of the Attorney General, State of Maine, *Law Enforcement Officer's Manual* (Augusta, Me.: Maine Criminal Justice Academy, 1983), p. 1–A35.

44. Carroll v. U.S., 267 U.S. 132 (1925).

45. Illinois v. Gates, 51 *Law Week* 4709.

Chapter 6

1. Herbert J. Storing, "The Constitution and the Bill of Rights," in Mont Judd Harmon, ed., *Essays on the Constitution of the United States* (Port Washington, N.Y.: Kennikat Press, 1978).

2. See Herbert J. Storing, *What the Anti-Federalist Were For: The Political Thought of the Opponents of the Constitution* (Chicago: University of Chicago Press, 1981).

3. Storing, "The Constitution and the Bill of Rights," p. 41.

4. Ibid., p. 40.

5. Especially good on this point is John H. Schaar, "Some Ways of Thinking About Equality," 26 *Journal of Politics* 867 (1964).

6. Of course thoughtful Americans of the formative period were aware that for the state to treat rich and poor men in the same way would sometimes result in advantages for the rich man. This was not thought an argument against identical treatment. That the rich man could more effectively defend himself against a criminal charge was regarded as just another advantage of being rich—not unlike being able to afford a better dinner or a faster horse. The notion that the state must afford *differential* treatment to the rich and poor in order to equalize the likelihood of favorable outcomes is a recent development. This is not to suggest that more recent conceptions of "equality of result" must always give way to a pure "equality before the law" approach, but only that the framers would have tended to decide that way. And their "identical public treatment" conception is far from contemptible. Anyone who seriously contemplates a legal order scrambling to arrange outcomes "fairly" for different "ranks" of subjects will see Anatole France's famous putdown of neutrality ("the law, in its majesty, permits both the rich and the poor to sleep under the bridges of Paris") for the silliness it is. Representative of modern, more grandiose conceptions of equality is John Rawls, "Justice as Fairness" in Peter Laslett and W.G. Runciman, eds., *Philosophy, Politics and Society,* 2d series, (New York: Barnes and Noble, 1962); and *A Theory of Justice* (Cambridge: Harvard University Press, 1971).

7. The classic expression of this position is contained in Max Weber's essay on "Politics as a Vocation" in H.H. Gerth and C. Wright Mills, eds., *From Max Weber: Essays in Sociology* (New York: Oxford University Press, 1946).

8. Michael Novak, "The Danger of Egalityranny," *The American Spectator* (August 1982).

9. Walter Berns, "Does the Constitution 'Secure These Rights'?," in Robert A. Goldwin and William A. Schambra, eds., *How Democratic is the Constitution?* (Washington, D.C.: American Enterprise Institute, 1980), p. 76.

10. Paul Johnson, *Modern Times: The World From the Twenties to the Eighties* (New York: Harper & Row, 1983), p. 729.

11. Frances E. Olsen, "The Family and the Market: A Study of Ideology and Legal Reform," 96 *Harvard Law Review* 1497, 1559 (1983).

12. See, for instance, John Silard, "A Constitutional Forecast: Demise of the 'State Action' Limit on the Equal Protection Guarantee," 66 *Columbia Law Review* 855 (1966); and Jerre S. Williams, "The Twilight of State Action," 41 *Texas Law Review* 347 (1963). The obituaries happily, were, premature.

13. Heart of Atlanta Motel v. United States, 379 U.S. 241 (1964).

14. See Amalgamated Food Employers Union v. Local Valley Plaza, 391 U.S. 328 (1968). This decision was limited to its facts by Lloyd Corp. v. Tanner, 407 U.S. 551 (1972), and announced to have been overruled in Hudgens v. NLRB, 424 U.S. 507 (1976).

15. Jones v. Alfred H. Mayer Co., 392 U.S. 409 (1968); and Runyon v. McCray, 427 U.S. 160 (1976). Of the sitting justices, White, Rehnquist, Powell, and Stevens have doubted the correctness of this as a matter of statutory interpretation, but there it is.

16. See Peter H. Schuck, "The Graying of Civil Rights Law: The Age Discrimination Act of 1975," 89 *Yale Law Journal* 27 (1979).

17. Plessy v. Ferguson, 163 U.S. 537 (1896).

18. For a thorough review of the mischief which began here, see Andree Kahn Blumstein, "Doing Good the Wrong Way: The Case for Delimiting Presidential Power Under Executive Order No. 11246," 33 *Vanderbilt Law Review* 921 (1980).

19. This order was issued in 1970. (Emphasis added.) By 1971 "under utilization" had come to be defined as "fewer minorities and women in a particular job classification than would be expected by their availability. . . ." In such a situation the burden of proof would be on the employer to show he was not discriminating.

20. *New York Times,* 6 June 1981.

21. See particularly Kenneth Karst and Harold Horowitz, "Affirmative Action and Equal Protection," 60 *Virginia Law Review* 47 (1974).

22. University of California Regents v. Bakke, 438 U.S. 265 (1978).

23. United Steele Workers v. Webber, 443 U.S. 193 (1979).

24. 110 *Congressional Record* 7213.

25. Fullilove v. Klutznick, 448 U.S. 448 (1980).

26. There is no need to turn a footnote into an honor roll but among the most effective have been Thomas Sowell, "*Weber* and *Bakke,* and the Presuppositions of 'Affirmative Action'," in W.E. Block and M.A. Walker, *Discrimination, Affirmative Action, and Equal Employment* (Vancouver, B.C.: The Fraser Institute, 1982); Walter Berns "Let Me Call You Quota, Sweetheart," *Commentary,* (May 1981); and, of course, Nathan Glazer, *Ethnic Dilemmas* (Cambridge: Harvard University Press, 1983). See also Terry Eastland and William J. Gennett, *Counting By Race: Equality From the Founding Fathers to Bakke and Weber* (New York: Basic Books, 1980).

27. Edward Hoagland, *The Tugman's Passage* (New York: Random House, 1981), p. 147. It is the more regrettable that Hoagland compounds his error with urban provincialism, adding that only in "backwoods America" would the truth of his observations be denied.

28. Carl Hoffmann and John Shelton Reed, "Sex Discrimination?: The XYZ Affair," *The Public Interest* (Winter 1981): 33–34.

29. Thomas Sowell, "Are Quotas Good for Blacks?" *Commentary* (June 1978).

Notes

30. See Rachel Flick, "The New Feminism and the World of Work," *The Public Interest* (Spring 1983): 44.

31. For the consequences of the decline in testing see Barbara Lerner, "Employment Discrimination: Adverse Impact, Validity, and Equality," 1979 *Supreme Court Review* 17, 49.

32. Senator George J. Mitchell, "Reports to Women," (July 1982).

33. John Sparrow, *Too Much Good Thing* (Chicago: University of Chicago Press, 1977), p. 91.

34. Antonin Scalia, "The Disease as Cure," *Washington Law Quarterly* 147, 149 (1979).

35. Ralph K. Winter, "Improving the Economic Status of Negroes Through Laws Against Discrimination: A Reply to Professor Sovern," 34 *University of Chicago Law Review* 817 (1967).

36. Perhaps the single most poignant case of egalitarian excess I have run across is the ACLU assult on Long Island's volunteer fire companies for sex discrimination. See *New York Times,* 5 August 1983.

37. Paul Seabury, "HEW and the Universities," *Commentary* (February 1972).

38. Thomas A. Kearns, "On De-Moralizing Due Process," in J. Roland Pennock and John W. Chapman eds., *Nomos XVII—Due Process* (New York: New York University Press, 1977).

39. Silard, "Constitutional Forecast," p. 871.

40. Daniel Patrick Moynihan, "State vs. Academe," *Harper's,* (December 1980), p. 40.

41. Alexis de Tocqueville, *Democracy in America* (New York: Oxford University Press, 1977), p. 490.

42. Quoted by Robert Blake in *Disraeli* (London: Macmillan, 1966), pp. 358–59.

Chapter 7

1. In the beginning was Marbury v. Madison, 1 Cranch 137 (1803).

2. An excellent review of this development is Jerome R. Corsi, *Judicial Politics* (Englewood Cliffs, N.J.: Prentice-Hall, 1984), pp. 6–44.

3. Henry Cabot Lodge, *The Democracy of the Constitution* (New York: Scribner's, 1915).

4. John W. Burgess, *Political Science and Comparative Constitutional Law,* 2 vols., (Boston: Ginn and Co., 1890).

5. George Bancroft, *History of the Formation of the Constitution of the United States of America* (New York: Appleton, 1884); and *A Plea for the Constitution of the U.S. of America Wounded in the House of its Guardians* (New York: Harper and Brothers, 1886).

6. While Haines' comprehensive work, *The Role of the Supreme Court in American Government and Politics* appeared in 1944 (the volume 1789–1835) and 1957 (the volume 1835–1864, with Robert H. Sherwood), both from the University of California Press, he had contributed frequently and substantially from the publication of his doctoral dissertation in 1909, *The Conflict Over Judicial Powers* (New York: Columbia University Press). Especially interesting is *The Revival of Natural Law Concepts* (Cambridge: Harvard University Press, 1930).

7. Albert J. Beveridge, *The Life of John Marshall,* 4 vols (Boston: Houghton Mifflin, 1916–1919).

8. John Hart Ely, *Democracy and Distrust: A Theory of Judicial Review* (Cambridge: Harvard University Press, 1980), pp. 1–2.

9. Thus the doctrine of Olmstead v. United States, 277 U.S. 438 (1928) was properly superseded by the doctrine of Katz v. United States, 389 U.S. 347 (1967) —see especially the concurring opinion by Justice Harlan.

10. Legal realism is one of those terms which it is easier to bandy than to define. Suffice it for our purpose that it applies to that revisionist legal scholarship of the 1930s and 1940s which made it clear that law was not just "found" by judges— that judges actually made law by their interpretation of constitutions and statutes. However, the more racial expressions of the realist impulse suggested that perhaps the policy preferences of the judge was all there was (or need be) to judge-made laws. We are dealing with the mischievous emanations of this today. See Hans Linde, "Judges, Critics, and the Realist Tradition," 82 *Yale Law Journal* 227 (1972).

11. Harry H. Wellington, "History and Morals in Constitutional Adjudication," review of Michael J. Perry's *The Constitution, the Courts, and Human Rights,* 97 *Harvard Law Review* 326 (1983).

12. Robert Bork, "The Struggle Over the Role of the Court," *National Review,* 17 September 1982, p. 1138. The best statement of Bork's own views is contained in "Neutral Principles and Some First Amendment Problems," 47 *Indiana Law Journal* 1 (1971).

13. William H. Rehnquist, "The Notion of a Living Constitution," 54 *Texas Law Review* 693 (1976).

14. See Wellington, "History and Morals," p. 328, suggesting that all non-single-author documents are open textured, and judges therefore must operate as something like full policy-making partners or co-authors in applying such legislated language to reality.

15. For example, W.W. Crossky, *Politics and the Constitution in the History of the United States* (Chicago: University of Chicago Press, 1953). For the consensus view with adequate citations see Henry J. Abraham, *The Judicial Process* (New York: Oxford University Press, 1980), pp. 322–23. "The records of the Constitutional Convention," Abraham writes, "prove conclusively that the idea of judicial review was widely recognized and accepted."

16. Paul Brest, "The Misconceived Quest for the Original Understanding," 60 *Boston University Law Review* 204, 226 (1980).

17. Kenneth L. Karst, "Equality as a Central Principle in the First Amendment," 43 *University of Chicago Law Review* 20 (1975).

18. John Rawls, *A Theory of Justice* (Cambridge: Harvard University Press, 1971).

19. Owen M. Fiss, "The Forms of Justice," 93 *Harvard Law Review* 1, 2, 11 (1979).

20. Thomas C. Grey, "Do We Have An Unwritten Constitution?," 27 *Stanford Law Review* 703 (1975).

21. See John Hart Ely, "On Discovering Fundamental Values," 92 *Harvard Law Review* 5, 22–32 (1978).

22. Harry H. Wellington, "Common Law Rules and Constitutional Double Standards: Some Notes on Adjudication," 83 *Yale Law Journal* 221, 284 (1973).

23. Ibid., p. 249.

Notes

24. So viewed in classics of our political literature from Madison's *Federalist No. 10* to David B. Truman's *The Governmental Process* (New York: Knopf, 1952).

25. Paul Brest, "The Fundamental Rights Controversy: The Essential Contradictions of Normative Constitutional Scholarship," 90 *Yale Law Journal* 1063, 1106 (1981).

26. Ward E.Y. Elliott, *The Rise of Guardian Democracy: The Supreme Court's Role in Voting Rights Disputes, 1845–1969* (Cambridge: Harvard University Press, 1974).

27. J. Skelly Wright, "Professor Bickel, The Scholarly Tradition, and the Supreme Court," 84 *Harvard Law Review* 769 (1971).

28. Michael J. Perry, *The Constitution, the Courts, and Human Rights* (New Haven: Yale University Press, 1982), p. 19.

29. Ibid., p. 24.

30. Ibid., p. 101.

31. Ronald Dworkin, *Taking Rights Seriously* (London: Duckworth, 1977).

32. Bruce A. Ackerman, *Private Property and the Constitution* (New Haven: Yale University Press, 1977).

33. Rawls, *Theory of Justice*, p. 101. The intuition of Mallock strikes me as surer. See William Hurrell Mallock, *Social Equality* (New York: G.P. Putnam's Sons, 1882).

34. Perry, *The Constitution*, p. 104. Elsewhere Perry has written "the skeptical view that the process of policy making is a higher value than the content of policy making is a difficult position to defend in this post-Holocaustal age." See "The Abortion Funding Cases: A Comment on the Supreme Court's Role in American Government," 66 *Georgetown Law Review* 1191, 1216 (1978). Is this to suggest that the Holocaust might have been avoided by a prophetic rather than a procedurally majoritarian decisional process? Or is it to suggest that the kinds of "wrongs" confronted by the contemporary Supreme Court are of the same magnitude and moral clarity as (real) genocide? Either way the meaning is vague and vaguely offensive.

35. Ronald Dworkin, "The Jurisprudence of Richard Nixon," *New York Review of Books*, 4 May 1972.

36. Ely, "Fundamental Values," p. 37.

37. United States v. Carolene Products Co., 304 U.S. 144 (1938).

38. The standard account of the authorship of the note is Alpheus T. Mason, *Harlan Fiske Stone, Pillar of the Law* (New York: Viking, 1956), pp. 513–15. See also Louis Lusky, "Footnote Redux: A Carolene Products Reminiscence," 82 *Columbia Law Review* 1093 (1982).
The relevant text of Footnote Four is as follows:

There may be narrower scope for operation of the presumption of constitutionality when legislation appears on its face to be within a specific prohibition of the Constitution, such as those of the first ten Amendments,. . . .

It is unnecessary to consider now whether legislation which restricts those political processes which can ordinarily be expected to bring about repeal of undesirable legislation, is to be subjected to more exacting judicial scrutiny under the general prohibitions of the Fourteenth Amendment than are most other types of legislation. . . .

Nor need we enquire whether similar considerations enter into the review of statutes directed at particular religious, or national, or racial minorities; whether prejudice against discrete and insular minorities may be a special condition, which tends seriously to curtail the operation of those political processes ordinarily to be relied upon to protect minorities, and which may call for a correspondingly more searching judicial inquiry. . . .

39. Louis Lusky, *By What Right* (Charlottesville, Va.: Michie, 1975), pp. 109–110.

40. Ely, "Fundamental Values," pp. 23–24. This scouts the suggestion that the Constitution somehow adopted natural law.

41. Ely, *Democracy and Distrust,* p. 76.

42. In Gordon S. Wood, ed., *The Rising Glory of America, 1760–1820* (New York: Braziller, 1971), p. 176.

43. Terrance Sandalow, "Constitutional Interpretation," 79 *Michigan Law Review* 1033, 1068 (1981).

44. Kenneth Karst and Harold Horowitz, "Reitman v. Mulkey: A Teleophase of Substantive Equal Protection," 1967 *Supreme Court Review* 39.

45. Sandalow, "Constitutional Interpretation," pp. 1038–39.

46. Perry, *The Constitution,* p. 128.

47. Grover Rees, III, "Prophets Without Portfolio," *National Review,* 2 September 1983.

48. Laurence H. Silberman, "Will Lawyering Strangle Democratic Capitalism?" *Regulation* (March/April, 1978).

49. Harvey C. Mansfield, Jr., "The Forms and Formalities of Liberty," *The Public Interest* (Winter, 1983): 125.

50. Ibid., p. 123.

51. Martin Diamond, "The Declaration and the Constitution: Liberty, Democracy, and the Founders," in Nathan Glazer, ed., *The American Commonwealth,* 1976 (New York: Harper Colophon Books, 1976), p. 47.

Chapter 8

1. Even Professor Tribe has been troubled by the prospect of over legalization. See Laurence H. Tribe, "Too Much Law, Too Little Justice," *The Atlantic,* July 1979. A sharper edge is Laurence H. Silberman, *Will Lawyering Strangle Capitalism* (Washington, D.C.: Ethics and Public Policy Center, 1978).

2. S. Robert Lichter and Stanley Rothman, "What Interests the Public and What Interests the Public Interests," *Public Opinion,* (April/May 1983). Other work demonstrates the gap between mass opinion and that of what are often identified,

Notes

misleadingly, as "liberal" elites. Especially intriguing is study of the work by Everett Carll Ladd and G. Donald Ferree, Jr., on the attitudes of teachers in religious seminaries and how these contrast to those of the general population. See "The Politics of American Theological Faculty," *This World,* (Summer 1982). Also on point is Everett Carll Ladd, "The Lines are Drawn," *Public Opinion* (July/August, 1978).

3. Lichter and Rothman, "What Interests," p. 46.

4. Daniel Bell has developed this analysis at length in *The Cultural Contradictions of Capitalism* (New York: Basic Books, 1975). The quotation here is from Bell's article of the same title in *The Public Interest* (Fall, 1970): 23.

5. Aaron Wildavsky, *The Revolt Against the Masses* (New York: Basic Books, 1971), p. 31.

6. Peter L. Berger, "The Greening of American Foreign Policy," *Commentary,* (March 1970), p. 24.

7. *New York Times,* 11 January 1983.

8. Arthur Selwyn Miller, *Toward Increased Judicial Activism* (Westport, Conn.: Greenwood Press, 1982), pp. 316–17.

9. Charles Evans Hughes, *Addresses* (New York: Harper's, 1916), p. 185.

10. Justice Owen J. Robert's formulation from United States v. Butler, 297 U.S. 1, 62 (1936).

11. See then Chief Judge David L. Bazelon's opinion for Court of Appeals of the District of Columbia in Rouse v. Cameron, 373 F.2d 451 (1966); see also Bazelon's article defending this opinion "Implementing the Right to Treatment," 36 *University of Chicago Law Review* 742 (1969).

12. Baldwin's obituary in the *New York Times,* 27 August 1981 noted that in the 1920s and 1930s he was widely regarded as "a dangerous eccentric"—with the clear implication that this judgment was mistaken. But the balance of the piece makes clear that with the exception of renouncing united front tactics in 1940, Baldwin's "holy discontent" with America changed very little over the years. One of Baldwin's last pictures shows him embraced by Gloria Steinem—no doubt celebrating Miss Steinem's conclusion that "feminism is an essential element of socialism."

13. An objective, analytical history of the ACLU has yet to be written. What has appeared thus far are reminiscences and acts of literary piety by the faithful. See Charles Lam Markmann, *The Noblest Cry* (New York: St. Martin's, 1965); and Alan Reitman, ed., *The Pulse of Freedom* (New York: W.W. Norton, 1975).

14. Gary L. McDowell, *Equity and the Constitution: The Supreme Court, Equitable Relief, and Public Policy* (Chicago: University of Chicago Press, 1982).

15. Ibid., p. 4.

16. "Book Note," 96 *Harvard Law Review* 555 (1982). The only significant specific offered in support of this charge was McDowell's failure to recognize that the class action had deep roots in the equity tradition. But this quite misses McDowell's point, that what is novel is not the class action but the substitution of broad demographic or sociological conceptions of "class" for the traditional equity conception of a "class" as a group of persons who are "similarly situated" to the plaintiffs in the sense of having suffered identical, specific injury, capable of individual location in time and space.

17. Thomas Sowell, *Knowledge and Decisions* (New York: Basic Books, 1980), p. 335.

18. Michael Oakeshott, *Rationalism in Politics* (London: Methuen, 1962), p. 101.

19. Jack Henry Abbott, *In the Belly of the Beast: Letters from Prison* (New York: Random House, 1980).

20. *New York Times Book Review,* 19 July 1981.

21. John Sparrow, *Too Much of a Good Thing* (Chicago: University of Chicago Press, 1977).

22. Ibid., p. 25.

INDEX OF CASES

235

INDEX

Index

Index

Index

112; patrolling activities of, 107–108, 110–118, 119, 138; racial balance on forces, 147; racism and, 124n, restrictions on, 130–133; see also Crime, Evidence, Exclusionary Rule

Police Foundation, The, 110

Political Science and Constitutional Law (Burgess), 164

Pottinger, J. Stanley, 146–147

Poverty, 108

Powell, Lewis: on race cases, 49–50, 148–149, 151; on religion cases, 20, 21, 217n20

Protestants and Other Americans United for Separation of Church and State (Americans United), 14, 33, 35, 37–39

Public Works Employment Act of 1977, 151

Quotas, 140, 145, 147

Rand, Ayn, 194

Ravitch, Diane, 61

Rawls, John, 173, 178, 179, 184

Reagan, Ronald, 55; assassination attempt, 129

Reed, John Shelton, 153

Reed, Stanley, 16, 216n8

Reeve, Tapping, 163

Rehnquist, William H., 19, 170; on "law and order" cases, 117; on race cases, 148, 151; on religion cases, 21, 44n, 122n

Reich, Charles, 114n

Republic, The (Beard), 41

Right to Counsel, 87

Right to Remain Silent, 87

Rights Industry, 3, 46, 68, 71, 107, 153;

components of, 45; indifference to past of, 188–190; libertarianism of, 124–130; motives of, 191–194, 198–199; views of, 194–196

Rogers, Will, 153

Roman Catholic Archdiocese of New York, 14

Rothman, Stanley, 196, 201, 232n5

Rutland, Robert A., 217n28

Rutledge, Wiley, 16, 39; on religion cases, 15, 36; sources for arguments by, 26

"Safe and Clean Neighborhoods Program" (New Jersey), 110–111

St. John, Nancy, 60

Sandalow, Terrence, 183, 184

Scalia, Antonin, 156

Schaff, Philip, 30

Schaffer, Walter V., 105

Schools, Catholic parochial: achievement in, 42–43; economic pressures on, 18; transportation to, 14

Schools, private: hostility toward, 46; state aid to, 14–16, 18–22, 37

Schools, public: attendance districts within, 59; and children's rights, 63, 65–73; costs of integration, 60; decline of, 73; and discipline, 63–71; local control of, 43; and neighborhoods, 50; and opposition to aid for private schools, 33; prayer in, 17, 203; racial balance in, 8, 47–62, 143, 144; reading Bible in, 17, 28–29; and released time for religious instruction, 16; rural, 69; as socializing institutions, 43–44, 46; in South, 49, 50; suburban, 60–61, 69; transportation to, 14; urban, 46, 59–60, 69

Schulz, Charles, 106

Schumpeter, Joseph, 160

Seabury, Paul, 157–158

Index